THE LOCH NESS MYSTERY RELOADED

Ronald Binns

Zoilus Press

A Zoilus Press paperback
First published in Great Britain by Zoilus Press in 2017

ISBN 978-1-9997359-0-6

Typeset by Electrograd
Cover design by The Ever Shifting Subject.
Cover photograph © Ronald Binns

Contents

Plates

1. Covers of the 1983 first edition of *The Loch Ness Mystery Solved* (Open Books) and the 1984 U.K. paperback (Star Books).
2. A momentary encounter with a deer on the shoreline of Loch Ness.
3. Outside Alex Campbell's cottage.
4. The 'Perrier' Monster.
5. A 'monstrous' boat's wake at Loch Ness.
6. A sign of the times, Drumnadrochit.

All photographs © Ronald Binns

Preface

My book *The Loch Ness Mystery Solved*, written in collaboration with Rod Bell, was published in May 1983, to mark the fiftieth anniversary of the birth of the Loch Ness Monster. Over those five decades since Alex Campbell's anonymous news report in the *Inverness Courier* (May 2, 1933) the idea that a large unknown animal or animals lived in the loch had become globally famous. There were photographs and film and hundreds of eye-witness reports to lend credibility to the creature affectionately known as Nessie. There were also books, deadly serious in their commitment to the monster's reality. Rupert Gould produced the pioneering classic text in 1934 and in 1957 Constance Whyte revived what was by then a dormant mystery. Tim Dinsdale soon followed with the personal account of a monster-hunter who had actually succeeded in filming the legendary creature. Fishing writer F. W. Holiday identified the fossil from which the monster had evolved and argued that global dragon legends were rooted in a zoological reality. All of these authors pleaded for the monster to be taken seriously. They were echoed by other active monster-hunters who contributed books on the subject, including Nicholas Witchell and Roy Mackal.

The only significant dissenting voice in this broad culture of belief was that of naturalist Maurice Burton. His 1961 book, aptly titled *The Elusive Monster*, challenged monster lore which had become iconic. Horned monsters, he suggested, were simply deer swimming in the loch. Massive turbulence at the surface indicated something other than an aquatic animal. Dinsdale, he believed, had filmed not a monster but merely a distant dinghy containing fishermen. But although *The Elusive Monster* is often identified by careless commentators as the first sceptical book about Nessie, this is not the case. Burton still believed there was a large unidentified animal at the loch. Some sightings simply could not be explained away. One possible solution, he suggested, was a previously unknown species of giant otter. *The Elusive Monster* offered a radical reappraisal and slimming down of the legend but it failed to make any impression with its revisionist angle. For a variety of reasons, including an over-reliance on an unconvincing gas-propelled vegetable mat theory, Burton became a discredited figure.

On Nessie's fiftieth anniversary the orthodox narrative continued to dominate understanding of the monster. Then, suddenly and unexpectedly, *The Loch Ness Mystery Solved* exploded out of nowhere to shatter the culture of the monster faithful. *The Loch Ness Mystery Solved* benefited from being the work of two individuals who had each been involved with the Loch Ness Phenomena Investigation Bureau. We knew the loch and some of its leading personalities, as well as the literature. Going into many areas left unexplored by Burton, including the misty origins of the supposed mystery, the book was a work of apostasy. It asserted unequivocally that there were no monsters in Loch Ness and there never had been.

Since 1983 books have continued to appear on the subject but the only ones of genuine interest are those which have authoritatively refined knowledge of classic monster lore or which have attempted to open up new areas of knowledge. In the former category are those which offered innovative critical analysis of the JARIC report, uncovered the convoluted story which lay behind the Surgeon's photograph, and provided insights from the archive of Sir Peter Scott's correspondence. In the latter category are revived efforts to reconstruct a monster tradition with reference to the water kelpie legend.

This book is not so much a sequel to *The Loch Ness Mystery Solved* as an appendix to it. My view of the monster has not changed since 1983. *The Loch Ness Mystery Reloaded* takes a fresh look at some of the classic material in the light of new information and debate but it does not purport to offer a comprehensive examination of the entire body of evidence which has accumulated since 1933. It is not concerned with the Loch Ness story, which has been told many times before. Nor does it describe the background to the writing of *The Loch Ness Mystery Solved* or its critical reception upon publication. These last two aspects comprise another story altogether.

1

The Never Ending Story

Shall I at least set my lands in order?
  T. S. Eliot

Looking back on *The Loch Ness Mystery Solved* thirty-four years after it was first published is to see how influential it was. Today, scepticism reigns supreme and the book's pioneering analysis and conclusions have been endorsed, refined and sometimes plagiarised by a wide variety of later writers and investigators. On Nessie's fiftieth birthday *The Loch Ness Mystery Solved* drew a line under the whole affair. The mystery was over. The Loch Ness Monster did not exist. There were no large unknown animals in Loch Ness and there never had been. Since then nothing has happened to disturb that uncompromising conclusion.

The book's analysis has stood the test of time. Writing in the American *National Post* in 2012, Josh Bazell recorded:

The first person to definitively lay bare the Loch Ness monster hoax was Ronald Binns, in *The Loch Ness Mystery: Solved* (Open Books, 1983). Additional particulars and confessions have come out since, but none that contradict Binns'[s] research or surmises.

In the years since my book first appeared I've noticed that North American writers have been far more generous in assessing the book's merits and in acknowledging its influence than British ones. In *Lake Monster Mysteries: Investigating The World's Most Elusive Creatures*

(2006) Benjamin Radford and Joe Nickell describe it as the 'definitive, skeptical book on the subject'.

It is worth remembering what the situation was in May 1983 when *The Loch Ness Mystery Solved* was published. It was still very much the world according to Tim Dinsdale and Constance Whyte. The Loch Ness Monster definitely existed. Alex Campbell was treated with enormous respect as the pre-eminent monster guru. The classic photographs were regarded with great seriousness. The April 1960 Dinsdale film continued to be regarded reverentially as extraordinary proof of the reality of the monster (Dick Raynor continued to believe in it to the end of Dinsdale's life). No one had publicly challenged its credibility since Maurice Burton in 1961. Rupert Gould, Constance Whyte, Roy Mackal and other propagandists for Nessie were, like Tim Dinsdale, viewed as impressive authorities. At Loch Ness one or two people knew that the circumstances surrounding the taking of the Academy of Applied Science's underwater photographs were very different to the Academy's claims, but they held their tongues. Adrian Shine was still in thrall to the magnetic power of eye-witness evidence and was keen to promote the notion that there was a mystery to be solved, and he was the man to crack it by using sonar. Six years after my book appeared Nicholas Witchell simply blanked its existence, and brought out a new edition of *The Loch Ness Story* which reproduced the conventional narrative, in complete denial of all its contradictions and inconsistencies. But as more and more of the classic evidence collapsed even Witchell eventually performed a spectacular and astonishing somersault, though he did so in silence, without a word of explanation.

Maurice Burton had been right all along in arguing in *The Elusive Monster* that Dinsdale had filmed a boat and that witnesses such as Greta Finlay had mistaken known animals for monsters, but as Ted Holiday triumphantly crowed, 'This book…failed to achieve its aims.' Burton's critique of some evidence did not dent belief in the monster and failed to address the rich variety of inconsistencies in the conventional Loch Ness story. This was perhaps unsurprising since his long engagement with the monster involved spectacular switches of interpretation and theory. *The Elusive Monster* was further distorted by Burton's off-stage feud with Dinsdale and by the zoologist's lingering belief in a mysterious unknown animal at Loch Ness.

Maurice Burton had targeted the heart of the mystery when he noticed 'one of the greatest difficulties' in understanding the mystery lay in 'accounting for the many shapes and guises in which the monster appears'. Instead of concluding that different witnesses were seeing different things and that *all* were mistaken, not just Finlay and Dinsdale, he capitulated to their sheer quantity. His silver bullet 'vegetable mat theory' explained all those sightings involving variable humps, shape-changing, surface turbulence and vertical descents. Pleasingly, there was some impressive evidence which clinched the theory: G. E. Taylor's 1938 film of an enigmatic humped object which constantly changed its shape (possibly only a sheet of sacking containing trapped air but in principle the same as a vegetable mat). There was furthermore a truly remarkable photograph of vegetable matter exploding at the surface of Loch Lochy with a distinctly reptilian appearance. Burton also received an anecdote dating back to the 1880s which confirmed the existence of gas-propelled vegetable mats at Loch Ness.

But none of this explained the sightings of people like Norah Atkinson, who encountered at close range a monster with a long swan-like neck and a small head. Burton concluded that witnesses like her really *had* encountered a large unknown animal. He suggested that perhaps an unknown species of giant otter accounted for such experiences. But substituting an entirely new species of otter which lurked in the land around the loch for a plesiosaur which swam below the surface devalued his other, saner, natural history explanations. *The Elusive Monster* was also too narrow in its focus, completely ignoring the origins of the monster in the mass media of 1933. The book is the work of someone who was only half-disenchanted and who remained in thrall to a residue of eye-witness testimony.

Ironically, Ted Holiday, that pugnacious critic of Burton, eventually arrived at similar conclusions, albeit by a very different route. Burton's shift from believer to a mid-way position between scepticism and continuing faith had apparently been triggered by his friendship with Tim Dinsdale and his response to the latter's film and the personality change which went with it. By contrast Ted Holiday's retreat from a biological monster began with his perplexity at the failure to produce results by the organised mass surveillance of the Loch Ness Investigation. The monster only ever seemed to appear out of camera range, which could not be explained simply by bad luck, and which suggested that the monster *knew* it was being hunted. Holiday's research activities at small Irish loughs which contained monsters established that the animals did not, after all, live off fish. Indeed, they didn't seem to require food at all. Everything pointed to monsters being some type of psychic phenomenon, not a zoological one.

Burton and Holiday were both intelligent men who separately arrived at conclusions which invited the awesome possibility that the monster simply did not exist in the form in which it had conventionally been understood. But both shied away from pursuing their understanding to its dreadful and inevitable conclusion: *the Loch Ness Monster did not exist and never had.* Both men evaded facing up to the possibility that a photograph such as Lachlan Stuart's was simply a fake. Burton wrote that 'there could be no doubt the photograph was genuine'. Holiday, who plainly would have had difficulty getting the image to conform to his 'great orm' hypothesis, simply ignored it altogether. Holiday drifted off into the paranormal and found comfort in metaphysics. Burton eventually went over completely to the dark side but his credibility as a sceptic was damaged both by his long history of contradictory opinions and by his occasionally dogmatic, haughty manner.

The Loch Ness Mystery Solved was prepared to go where no monster book had gone before. It adopted a holistic approach. It ripped apart fifty years of monster lore, from every possible angle. It was a combative book because it was single-handedly overturning fifty years of tradition and accumulated wisdom. But it was also partly a comical book, full of gentle wit. Believers have never seen it like that, of course. Fundamentalists are rarely known for their sense of humour.

Crucially, this deconstruction of Nessie was performed from within the monster movement. It was an iconoclastic book which moved around the great temple of belief, bringing down everything that was sacred. It was a work of apostasy. This was a book written by someone who knew Loch Ness and who had participated in the great monster hunt. Its comprehensive demolition work was assisted by two other old LNI hands, Rod Bell and Ian Johnson. The support these two figures gave me was of great significance. Rod was then a professional zookeeper and an ornithologist with a passion for wild life and mysteries. Ian was a scientist. The three of us had come monster-hunting from very different backgrounds, with two of us fervent believers and one sympathetic to the possibility of unknown animals. In time we each arrived at the same conclusion: the monster was a myth, not a reality.

A simple study of the files of the *Inverness Courier* for 1933 – something no one had bothered to do in half a century of writings about the monster – revealed a very different narrative to the one told and retold in monster books. It exposed the hitherto unscrutinised role of

Alex Campbell as both journalist and star witness. In 1933-4 Campbell, hidden by a shield of anonymity, had energetically promoted the monster from every conceivable angle. Later he had emerged into the limelight as a man whose sightings established him in later years as the guru of a monster-hunting generation. In the Walt Disney documentary *Man, Monsters and Mysteries* (1973) he described how he had seen the monster on eighteen separate occasions. No one ever asked him why he never seemed to have a camera with him. There isn't even a record of the details of these eighteen sightings (dates, locations, descriptions).

Just a few minutes' scrutiny of the pages of the newspaper for 1933 quickly established that there had always been a local sceptical counter-narrative and that a fellow journalist on the *Courier* regarded Campbell as a bit of a joke, even going to the trouble of satirising him for his monster mania. Another of my great discoveries was Captain John Macdonald, who informed the paper that he had been sailing on Loch Ness for fifty years and had never heard of this so-called monster, let alone seen it. Later, other local people stepped forward with sceptical, naturalistic explanations for the 'monster' which others reported seeing.

The mythology of the Loch Ness Monster collapsed at the first sceptical scrutiny. There was no sightings record dating back centuries. The notion that Loch Ness was a lonely, unvisited place before 1933 was a delusion rooted in Constance Whyte and Tim Dinsdale's gross ignorance of Scottish social history. The 'new' road along the north shore merely improved a carriageway which had existed since the end of the eighteenth century and which motorists had been using since the invention of the automobile. In reality, the Great Glen had always been a major communications route across the Highlands and metropolitan Englishmen had been arriving at Loch Ness since the seventeenth century. It beggared belief that, over the course of three centuries, no one had ever once made reference to a strange, unidentifiable animal in the loch. If there really was a herd of large unknown aquatic animals living there, their presence would have been noted and recorded long before 1933.

Furthermore, *The Loch Ness Mystery Solved* argued, the classic 'hard' evidence for the monster was devoid of value. The photographs were either fakes (Gray, Wilson, Stuart, O'Connor) or explicable phenomena (Macnab and Cockrell). As for the 1972 and 1975 underwater photographs, my book observed that, although the 'Academy of Applied Science' sounded impressive, it was a private body made up of businessmen, not scientists. Its leader, Robert Rines, basked in the title 'Dr', but the qualification had been awarded by a South Korean institution and did not appear to have required the years of hard work and rigour associated with better-known universities. The underwater photographs proved nothing and may have involved fraud (a suggestion which would later turn out to be entirely accurate).

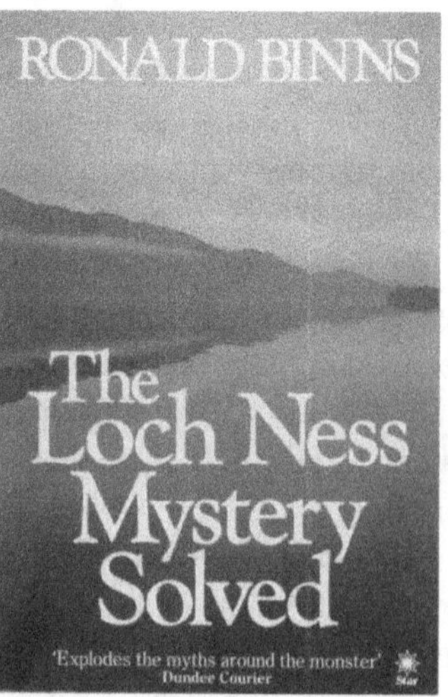

1. The 1983 first edition (Open Books) and the 1984 U.K. paperback
(Star Books)

As for the Dinsdale film, his own account of the circumstances in which he took his film could be reconstructed to show that his was an acute case of what Rupert Gould described as 'expectant attention'. My revival of Maurice Burton's original argument that Tim Dinsdale's film showed not a monster but a distant boat threw a small depth charge into the Loch Ness world of 1983, prompting a thorough reconsideration of the legendary and massively influential Dinsdale film. Three years later Steuart Campbell would administer the *coup de grâce* with his devastating technical analysis.

The Loch Ness Investigation had demonstrated that the more you looked for the monster, the less you saw it. The biggest and longest-running organised hunt for the monster, running from 1962-1972, failed to shoot any film of a large unknown animal at the surface. This was simply because there was nothing there to film. *The Loch Ness Mystery Solved* concluded that monster-sightings involved not one phenomenon but a wide variety, especially boats' wakes, birds and otters. It asserted that 'No single phenomenon can possibly account for the totality of fifty years of widely differing eye-witness reports from Loch Ness.'

The book focused on the issue at the very heart of the Loch Ness story:

> The case for the Loch Ness monster rests overwhelmingly on eye-witness evidence, and this is just where the difficulty lies. No one has been able to film what eye-witnesses claim they see. This paradox lies at the heart of the Loch Ness mystery.

Chapter Nine of *The Loch Ness Mystery Solved* addressed this difficulty, explaining the limitations of individual testimony and offering explanations for what the witnesses claimed to see. It also demonstrated how the classic monster authors had cherry-picked the evidence and manipulated it to make it conform to their own preferred breed of monster. In his own way, Tim Dinsdale was just as guilty as Robert Rines of manipulating images to make them appear more plausibly monstrous. His re-sketched versions of the Alex Campbell and Greta Finlay sightings are exaggerated and re-shaped in order to armour-plate them against sceptical interpretation. This kind of dishonesty rather undermined his reiterated pious insistence on his commitment to 'the Truth' (with a capital T).

Finally, *The Loch Ness Mystery Solved* addressed the wider cultural context of human fascination with monsters and the role played by nineteenth century palaeontology, dinosaur fossils and the great Victorian sea-serpent craze, which was later channelled through popular fiction and works like *The Lost World* and then reproduced through the medium of cinema. The book noted that the birth of the Loch Ness Monster coincided with the release of *King Kong*. It predicted that people would go on seeing monsters at Loch Ness, not because it contains them but because its diversity of phenomena is rich enough to feed and shape the expectations and perceptions of observers.

The *Loch Ness Mystery Solved* had an impact which would in time extend as far as Hollywood (that very well informed romantic drama *Loch Ness* (1996) contains a number of in-jokes, including a character called 'Dr Binns'). The book also transformed conventional belief in monsters into widespread scepticism. Whereas once TV documentaries took the position that all the evidence pointed to something odd and unusual in the loch, henceforth there was a slew of programmes devoted to debunking Nessie. In the short term it exploded beneath the complacent certainties of Loch Ness Monster orthodoxy with all the force of a small nuclear detonation.

One by one, fervent believers in Nessie revised their assumptions and went over to the dark side. Tony Harmsworth jeered that my book was 'rather prematurely titled' but said nothing about how it had criticised him in his earlier role as fervent believer, let alone how it transformed understanding of the mystery and created a generation of sceptics, which now included himself. Adrian Shine, who in 1983 still believed in the monster, would later become Nessie's most prominent sceptic in the mass media. Dick Raynor, admired for his intriguing 1967 film of a mysterious wake, and a firm believer in the Dinsdale film, would later join the ranks of the heretics, echoing the conclusions of *The Loch Ness Mystery Solved* to assert that Tim Dinsdale filmed a boat, that classic photographs such as those of Lachlan Stuart and Peter O'Connor were fraudulent, and that legendary episodes such as the land sighting of Torquil Macleod involved gross exaggeration.

Perhaps most astonishingly of all, Nicholas Witchell, one of the most high-profile and successful Nessie authors of the previous decade, would later become an apostate and accept that the Loch Ness Monster did not exist. This was a remarkable *volte-face* from someone who, six years after publication of *The Loch Ness Mystery Solved*, was still loudly insisting that the conventional narrative was the only true one. But back then even Witchell was grudgingly forced to concede that although sightings continued, 'there do seem to be rather fewer of them these days'. Even affable and energetic Ivor Newby, who had followed the monster trail from Ness to Morar and as far as the west coast of Ireland, eventually went over to the dark side.

The impact at Loch Ness itself was noticeable. Tony Harmsworth, designer and curator of the exhibition which opened in 1980 in the Drumnadrochit Hotel, describes how it promoted a belief in monsters and was 'biased towards the plesiosaur theory as that seemed to be the general consensus'. After publication of *The Loch Ness Mystery Solved* there was a remarkable shift in emphasis. Harsmworth describes how 'it became important to try to introduce a healthy scepticism into the presentation of the exhibits. This began in 1984…' Quite.

Since the publication of *The Loch Ness Mystery Solved* there have been no sensational close-up photographs of the monster, no footage to match the Dinsdale film, and physical evidence remains as absent today as it has always been. Faith in Nessie has collapsed. Today, monster-hunting is a niche activity. The fraternity of enthusiastic believers in the Monster has shrunk to a tiny minority.

The story has continued but the song remains the same. At heart the Loch Ness monster is a sociological, not a zoological, phenomenon. Others have reiterated and refined my case against the monster, but the reality was that after 1983 the search for a Loch Ness Monster was finished. Continuing the great Nessie hunt was an exercise in futility. There is no species of large unknown animal in the loch but the possibility that there just *might be* continues to enthral a small number for whom eye-witness evidence outweighs all other considerations.

Since *The Loch Ness Mystery Solved* first appeared in May 1983, many prominent figures in the Loch Ness story have died – Alex Campbell, Tim Dinsdale, Peter Baker, David James, Frank Searle, Peter Scott, Maurice Burton, Roy Mackal and Robert Rines. This has allowed a fuller, more critical assessment of their role than was possible when they were alive. In addition, where the classic evidence is concerned, new material has occasionally emerged, reinforcing the sceptical position.

New information has come to light since 1983 in other areas, reinforcing the book's analysis and conclusions. *The Loch Ness Mystery Solved* made only passing reference to seals and my own knowledge of these animals at that time was based on sightings of gregarious, sociable seals along the Scottish coast. Rupert Gould had acknowledged that the theory that the monster might be a seal represented 'the most plausible theory of all' but then asserted that the largest type, the grey seal, had 'never been seen, hitherto, in Loch Ness'. He then imposed his standard false logic by applying the seal theory to *all* the eyewitness and photographic evidence, to assert that seals could not be responsible for sightings of a line of humps or head and neck sightings or monsters with tails or violent commotion at the surface or the object in the Surgeon's photograph. The accepted wisdom continued that no seal had ever been sighted in Loch Ness, but the year after my book's publication a seal was observed in the loch, and remained there for seven months until it was shot in June 1985. Since writing my book I have had much more experience of the behaviour of solitary seals, and it now seems to me highly likely that there was a seal at Loch Ness during the period 1933-1934, helping to add to the misperceptions of impressionable and inexperienced eye-witnesses.

The single most spectacular new revelation of the past three decades has been the comprehensive exposure of the iconic Surgeon's Photograph as a hoax, thanks to the pioneering detective work of David Martin and Alastair Boyd. Other surprises have included the belated revelation that Rupert Gould had long ago privately disavowed the Spicer land sighting.

My examination of the inconsistencies of Alex Campbell's record as an eye-witness and his crucial role as midwife to the monster through his behind-the-scenes media manipulations of the early 1930s has now become embedded as a key aspect of the Loch Ness story. Campbell died within weeks of publication of *The Loch Ness Mystery Solved* but, disappointingly, later writers have added nothing of any substance regarding his life since that date. He is central to the Loch Ness story but the man himself remains an enigma.

The Loch Ness Mystery Solved cracked open the legend. There are no giant unknown animals in Loch Ness and the entire edifice of eye-witness sightings and 'hard' evidence – photographs, motion film, sonar traces – is explicable. But the Loch Ness story never ends. The 'classic' evidence of the first half century is subject to unending refinement, as shown by the revelations regarding the Surgeon's photograph and the Spicer sighting. Much of the human side remains undocumented and unexplored.

The Loch Ness Mystery Solved hinted that Robert Rines and his underwater photographs were dodgy but was suitably circumspect about what it said about a lawyer. That incompetence, dogmatic and wildly inaccurate interpretation of sonar readings and even fraud formed a fundamental aspect of Robert Rines's Nessie enthusiasms and research did not become obvious until a much later date.

The story ran on after 1983 with new sightings, new photographs and new books on the subject. But various things became obvious after 1983. The number of reported sightings began to dwindle and still no one managed to come up with any persuasive movie film. The dream of capturing close-up images or film of the Loch Ness Monster remained (and still remains) as distant and elusive as ever.

Today, the Monster is embedded as part of the Loch Ness tourist experience, with 'lifesize' models at the roadside, two competing exhibitions and a thriving cruise industry, offering such delights as 'Finding Nessie', a 'Monster Blast' and the 'Urquhart Castle Experience'. But the hunt for Nessie has collapsed. Nowadays it remains the preserve of solitary enthusiasts or the occasional academic or business 'research project' which promises an exciting new angle, the results of which never quite manage to equal all the publicity.

Meanwhile Alex Campbell, the man who first publicised the existence of a Loch Ness Monster, lies in a quiet grave in Strathoich Cemetery outside Fort Augustus. Far from the tourist hubbub, he is forgotten by everyone except a few elderly local residents and hard core devotees of the Monster. When I last visited the grave it had a neglected appearance. A solitary mourner at a distant, flower-stacked grave came over to find out what I was up to, as I took photographs. He turned out to be a local man who'd known Campbell. I learned from him that Campbell had two brothers and that his wife Mary had been the local registrar of births, marriages and deaths. His parting words to me were, 'If half the lies Campbell told were true, the world would be a wonderful place.'

There has been one major cultural change affecting the evolving Loch Ness story which did not exist when *The Loch Ness Mystery Solved* was published thirty-four years ago. At the time that I wrote my book, research involved trips to libraries to look at old newspapers and rare books. Publication involved submitting a manuscript to a publisher and hoping to find a company that was interested.

All this changed with the advent of the internet and the home computer. Now, in the digital age, information is available at the touch of a keyboard and anyone can publish their opinions online using personal websites, Facebook, Twitter and numerous other outlets. Companies like Amazon enable anyone to self-publish a monster book. This innovation has been a double-edged thing. On the one hand, interesting new material has appeared online, but on the other the internet is awash with Nessie fakes, misinformation and lazy, ill-informed opinions expressed in intemperate language.

Roland Watson's blog *Loch Ness Monster* ('Reclaiming the Loch Ness Monster from the current tide of debunking and scepticism') epitomises both the best and the worst of the digital age. His website is a valuable resource which no one interested in the subject can ignore. By going back to basics, Watson has uncovered interesting new material, including a hitherto unpublished photograph by H. L. Cockrell, a contemporary sketch of Alex Campbell's first monster sighting, and a plausible new theory about precisely where Margaret Munro saw her monster on land. He has also questioned in some detail the plausibility of Richard Frere's account of Lachlan Stuart's supposed 'confession'.

Unfortunately the considerable merits of Roland Watson's blog are marred by his belligerent tone towards those who disagree with him. He has described sceptics as 'jackboot fascists' and his blog hosts unpleasant and infantile invective against named individuals. As Daniel Loxton remarked, responding to Watson's 2013 review of *Abominable Science!* :

Hostility toward critics does nothing to advance the case for cryptozoology, but it does cast cryptozoology in an ugly, pseudoscientific light. Cryptozoologists need not do themselves this disservice.

Three years later Darren Naish published *Hunting Monsters: Cryptozoology and the Reality Behind the Myths*, which also dared to suggest that the Loch Ness Monster had no tangible existence as a giant unknown animal but was more to do with 'how people imagine the world'. It produced yet another furious reaction from Watson, who wildly suggested that Naish was being manipulated by another prominent Nessie sceptic. Bizarrely, Watson claimed that 'the question of succession seems to be a serious question for Loch Ness sceptics'. Naish's assertion that Watson inhabits 'an idiosyncratic intellectual landscape' was a generous and measured response.

Ironically, in an arena of debate where some believers hurl abuse and invective, sceptics who dare to suggest that certain classic photographs were faked or that individuals who enjoy multiple sightings of Nessie ought to be regarded as dubious witnesses, are then immediately accused of 'character assassination'. But then, on the internet, all opinions are equal – along with facts, falsehoods, fabrications, fantasies and flimflam.

The World Wide Web is also a medium which can be far less tangible than hard copy. For example, in the final decade of the twentieth century there was an extraordinary and detailed sighting of the Loch Ness Monster by two passing tourists who witnessed a huge, humped animal at least twenty feet in length very close to the south shore. It occurred in an area associated with a number of classic Monster encounters, and the experience was so terrifying that the two witnesses preferred to avoid all publicity. It was only some twenty-six years later that they consented to allow their sighting to be revealed to the wider world, exclusively through the medium of Roland Watson's Loch Ness Monster blog.

But when I came to consult this remarkable sighting during the course of writing this book I made a curious discovery. Watson had deleted all trace of it. Perhaps he subsequently had reason to doubt the veracity of this sensational story. Whatever the reason, it has vanished.

What interests me is that this extraordinary eye-witness sighting has been erased from the record by Watson *without acknowledgement or comment*. It's another reminder that the Loch Ness story involves a continual process of revisionism and air-brushing which would have been very familiar to Winston Smith in his cubicle at the Records Department of the Ministry of Truth.

2

Brief Encounters

A developing thing may expand in any given way or form.
  Bram Stoker, *The Lair of the White Worm* (1911)

After my book had gone to print in 1983 the *Daily Mail* tracked down Donaldina ('Aldie') Mackay, whose sighting famously put the monster on the map. The newspaper obtained the first interview she'd given on the subject of her sighting since talking to Rupert Gould fifty years earlier. She described the experience to *Mail* journalist Clive Limpkin:

> 'It was March, 1933, and we were hurrying back from a house sale in Inverness. Suddenly at the seven-mile stone ... you couldn't believe what you were seeing, never having seen such an enormous thing ...'
> 'What, there was a neck and – ?'
> 'No, no, just an enormous black body up and down.' Her hands made a switch-back motion. 'You could not put a name to it. It could have been an elephant or a whale ...'

But when Tony Harmsworth and Nicholas Witchell went to question her three years later, she gave the size of her monster as being 'At least six feet, maybe nine.' In a televised interview she now recalled that upon sighting a disturbance in the water she cried out to her husband, 'Stop! The beast!'

If this belated recollection is at all accurate it indicates an awareness of a monster tradition at the loch, which would further suggest that this seminal sighting was a classic case of expectant attention rather than a wholly unexpected event. Rupert Gould brilliantly defined what 'expectant attention' amounts to:

> Broadly speaking, it is undoubtedly true that, if you are consciously or unconsciously expecting to see something, and are sufficiently favoured by circumstances, the chances are that you will ultimately come to imagine that you see it. This result may come about as a pure effort of imagination; but, more probably, you will graft on to some object which you really see the qualities and appearance of a thing which you are expecting to see.

If Donaldina Mackay's sighting did involve expectant attention, the source of her monster awareness seems most likely to have been her brother-in-law, Kenneth Mackay. He was the man who in 1933 told Gould that, some fifteen to twenty years earlier, the head keeper of the Balmacaan estate had been fishing in Loch Ness when an 'enormous animal' had surfaced close to his boat. It had evidently been a shocking and unnerving experience. The story could not be verified because the man, James Cameron, was now dead. Cameron had also refused to enlarge upon his experience, so the shape and appearance of this 'enormous animal' were unknown. Donaldina Mackay's sighting replicated Cameron's in so far as it involved 'something large' (the visible portions of which, she told Gould, stretched to twenty feet in length). However, if Kenneth Mackay did share his private knowledge of a strange 'enormous animal' in the loch, it is hard to understand his claim that as news of the monster began to spread in the summer of 1933 he 'remained entirely sceptical' until 'one day' he suddenly remembered James Cameron's experience. One wonders how many accounts of the monster he had to read before that moment of revelation occurred.

What Mrs Mackay saw cannot ever be known and her sighting remains hotly contested. My own view is that her sighting of humps which 'rose and sank in an undulating manner' is a classic instance of someone mistaking a boat's wake for a living animal. 'Monsters' with two or more humps can almost always be confidently identified as wake effects, no matter how lifelike they might appear to an inexperienced observer. The 1914 report of 'Porpoises in Loch Ness', which involved 'wet dark bodies…eight or nine of them', sounds like a possible case of mistaken identity (although some reports indicate that porpoises really did enter the loch). The longevity of boats' wakes in Loch Ness is notorious, as is their deceptive appearance. What one observer possibly misinterpreted as porpoises, the arguably monster-primed Mrs Mackay perceived as a large unknown animal.

A Nessie believer will insist that Mrs Mackay *did* see the monster, because the phenomenon she witnessed did not behave like a boat's wake. The humps moved towards Aldourie Pier, then turned sharply to the left and 'after describing a half-circle, sank suddenly with considerable commotion'. But the Mackay sighting is a classic in a way which has not previously been noted. In retrospect, what is striking about some of the primary Nessie eyewitness evidence is *how often it depends on sightings from a moving vehicle or vessel.* Tim Dinsdale never once saw the monster when he positioned himself on land, stationary beside a tripod, waiting for the creature to surface. To see monsters required him being in motion, the first time inside a car, the second and third times on a boat.

What is never discussed is the length of time of the Mackay sighting. It lasted approximately one minute. Her husband braked, stopped the car – and saw nothing, apart from waves reaching the shore. Mrs Mackay, a witness in a moving vehicle, caught a glimpse of a disturbance at the surface. She described it as 'a violent commotion in the water near-by, about 100 yards from shore. She thought at first it was caused by two ducks fighting; but on reflection it seemed far too extensive to be caused in this way.' From her description this sounds very much like one arm of a boat's wake, left by a vessel which had by now vanished from sight. Quite possibly the vessel in question was the *Scot II*, a notorious source of monster sightings in later years. This converted ice-breaker tug was present at Loch Ness from 1931 and remained in use for another sixty years.

Her two humps were simply a feature of the matching wake. The Mackays were driving south-west, towards Drumnadrochit. The two humps were moving in the opposite direction. The loch was flat calm, magnifying the impact which the wake made on the witness.

As an observer in a moving vehicle, Mrs Mackay was in a poor position to make an authoritative judgement of the size and direction of the phenomenon she was momentarily witnessing, yet, as always happens with eye-witness accounts, her description has been treated as a kind of verbal photograph, exact in all its particulars.

The Spicer Sighting

The same objection can be levelled against the second legendary sighting of 1933 – the Spicer land sighting. This is problematic in all kinds of ways. As in the case of Donaldina Mackay, the observers were in a moving vehicle, from which they briefly glimpsed something in motion. Their view of the object(s) was restricted, as the phenomenon lay just beyond the brow of a hill.

Mr and Mrs Spicer's experience was a momentary one. It was an absurdly short, inconclusive encounter, yet it has become enshrined as a classic. It also, of course, supplied the foundation of the belief that Loch Ness not only contained a species of huge unknown animal, but that this creature was both long-necked and amphibious, sometimes emerging on to the surrounding land. Despite the brevity of the experience and his restricted view of the phenomenon, George Spicer confidently identified it as resembling 'a dragon or prehistoric animal'.

Spicer claimed never to have heard of the Loch Ness Monster before his sighting, but this is very hard to believe. This surely was another case of expectant attention, in which awareness of the loch's mystery creature, presumably derived from reading the *Inverness Courier*, was further shaped by the powerful influence of *King Kong*, either at the time of the sighting or, later, in Spicer's memory of it. Today, the original *King Kong* movie seems jerky and crude in its special effects, not a patch on *Jurassic Park* and all the other modern wonders of CGI. But in 1933 it was sensational: both terrifying and convincingly realistic. Daniel Loxton has argued that the description which the Spicers gave to Rupert Gould reproduces in a startlingly detailed way the scene involving a Diplodocus-like sauropod in *King Kong*.

The Spicer narrative was popularised for the great monster-hunting generation of the 1960s and 1970s by Constance Whyte, who smoothed out the contradictions and inconsistencies in George Spicer's account. This was duly echoed by later writers like Dinsdale and Witchell. She reported the 'annoyance' of the couple that reports were circulated that they had seen the monster with a lamb in its mouth, characterising it as typical of 'distorted or incomplete accounts' which were common in the media at that time. But as I discovered when I went back to look at the files of the *Inverness Courier* for 1933, this aspect of the story originated with none other than George Spicer himself. When Rupert Gould wrote that 'the incident originally found its way into print in a rather incorrect form, and with one or two misleading details', the reader might well deduce that this is a reference to sloppy, careless journalism. Gould failed to make it clear that he was referring to *George Spicer changing his mind* about his earliest version of the sighting.

In place of a dragon/prehistoric animal carrying a lamb, Spicer substituted 'something "flopping up and down" which, on reflection, he thought might have been the end of a long tail swung round to the far side of the body'. When Spicer originally wrote that something resembling 'a dragon or prehistoric animal' had crossed the road 'and appeared to be carrying a small lamb or animal of some kind' it bore the clear implication that the lamb was in the animal's *mouth*. Now Spicer suggested that the lamb had been carried on the animal's *back* – and was not a lamb but part of a tail. It is far from clear whether this was the clarification of an original unintended ambiguity or an imaginative man reshaping his brief encounter in order to make it seem more plausible.

Acknowledging this rewriting of the original version, Gould gnomically explained that the sight of the monster carrying a small animal such as a lamb 'was based upon an appearance for which there is another – and, to my mind, a much more probable – explanation'. What that explanation was Gould, bizarrely, did not trouble to inform his readers. Perhaps he had in mind the creature's tail or a flipper.

Gould's sketch portrayed the new version of the sighting – a creature with an improbably twisting, serpentine neck attached to a large half-moon torso from which protrudes a small club-shaped object. This image was then utterly transformed by Constance Whyte, who re-created it to show a plesiosaur-like creature with a long tail. Whyte's sketch is a travesty of Gould's, smoothing out the curves of that improbable neck and transforming the club-like object into a long, thick tail.

Her account of the Spicer sighting is equally problematic. She presents one which is set apart from the main text of her chapter, as though it were a witness statement. In fact it is given in the third person, not the first – i.e. it is a version shaped by Whyte herself, though it purports to be 'as far as possible, in Mr and Mrs Spicer's own words as recorded soon after the event'. Mrs Whyte had evidently been in correspondence with Spicer but she fails to cite anything from this communication or to supply dates.

Tim Dinsdale then weighed in with his own version of Gould's sketch. This is not such an exaggerated distortion as Whyte's but it is nevertheless not an exact reproduction. Dinsdale smoothes out the twisting neck, albeit not so radically as Whyte, and relocates the mysterious club-shaped lump of flesh to beyond the torso, so that the ostensible tail is on the far side, not the near side.

Underlining the distorting strategies of the classic monster authors, Ted Holiday supplied yet another pictorial version. Fixated on his 'Great Orm' theory, Holiday exaggerated the bulk of Spicer's 'monster' and transformed the 'flopping' tail into what he grandly identified as 'the anterior lateral organ of the Orm'. This analysis furthered his case for Nessie being a gigantic evolved form of *Tullimonstrum gregarium* – a fossilized invertebrate found only in the neighbourhood of Chicago, the longest known specimen being some fourteen inches in length. Holiday fleshed out the prospective 'tail' and then reversed the image to establish its amazing similarity to the object in the Hugh Gray photograph. Holiday's version of what the Gray picture shows is, to put it mildly, somewhat subjective.

The manipulations of the evidence did not stop there. None of the classic authors quoted George Spicer's original rambling letter to the *Courier*, simply because they had never bothered to examine its files for 1933. Instead they drew on Rupert Gould, who had done his best to make sense of this bizarre and improbable incident, incorporating changes by the witnesses which made the observed phenomenon bigger and even more abominably monstrous. In the revised version it resembled 'a huge snail with a long neck'. Spicer's original letter to the *Courier* is an eccentric document, which reveals a willingness to speculate wildly about something which was glimpsed only partially and very briefly: 'if there were any feet they must have been of the web kind'. *Must?* Why?

In an impressive example of monster fever, the young Ted Holiday wrote a letter to George Spicer enquiring about his sensational sighting. This was some three and a half years after the event. Spicer graciously replied to the enthusiastic teenager. His response sheds yet more light on his fundamental unreliability as a witness and on the way primary material is tampered with by monster authors in order to persuade the reader.

In the original published account Spicer described how the animal was crossing the road 'about fifty yards ahead'. He described it as 'Length from six feet to eight feet and very ugly.' In conclusion, he wrote, 'It is difficult to give you a better description, as it moved so swiftly, and the whole thing was so sudden. There is no doubt it exists.'

By the time Rupert Gould tracked the couple down and interviewed them, the episode had become more detailed in its particulars and George Spicer was now certain that the creature 'must have been at least 25 feet in length'. By December 1933 Spicer was confident it had been 'about 30 feet long'.

The length of the monster was not the only thing which grew and grew. Ted Holiday quotes from the letter which George Spicer sent his adolescent self. In it Spicer wrote that the monster was 'about 200 yards away' – four times his original estimate. He also informed the youthful monster fan, 'I got out of the car and could see traces of where it had gone through the bracken.' But three years earlier the Spicers informed Rupert Gould that 'They did not stop'. Spicer also informed Holiday that 'Apparently, it could not move fast', yet in his original *Courier* letter he described how the animal 'moved so swiftly, and the whole thing was so sudden'.

But not only was George Spicer's narrative one which kept changing. So, too, was the transmission of this narrative in monster books. Ted Holiday had shared his letter from Spicer with Tim Dinsdale, who quoted from it in *The Leviathans*, published two years earlier than *The Great Orm of Loch Ness*. But no one seems ever to have noticed the difference between the two versions. Dinsdale was plainly citing the original, which he identifies as being dated December 16, 1936. He quotes large chunks of the letter, using ellipses to indicate those sections which he chooses to omit. Holiday, by contrast, supplies an account which purports to be a complete text. Comparing the two it becomes obvious that Holiday had edited the letter, cutting and re-arranging its contents. In the original text, Spicer gendered the monster: 'he came down from the hillside... He was elephantine in colour... before we reached him he had disappeared into the loch.' In each instance Holiday replaced 'he' with 'it'.

Holiday's silent editorial changes transformed the original text, making it appear more structured and less odd. Dinsdale, by contrast, simply witheld material which he presumably felt was unsuitable. Dinsdale abruptly cuts off the sentence beginning, 'We did not see any feet...'. Holiday cites it in full: 'We did not see any feet and I think its tail was curved round the other side from our view for convenience of going along the ground.' Dinsdale then quotes six (possibly seven) more sentences, with five sections omitted and replaced by ellipses. Holiday, without ever acknowledging his editorial changes, compresses this closing part of the letter into two short sentences. The result is that we can never know what Spicer actually said in those sections blanked out by both Dinsdale and Holiday. It is obvious that both authors were endeavouring to make Spicer's account seem more plausible, more persuasive, and less colourful than it was in the original.

Problematically, the two texts do not always match in other ways. The disparities can be troubling. Dinsdale quotes Spicer writing, 'when he was broadside on he took up all the road; which I have measured, and it is 20 feet wide'. Holiday, by contrast, has: 'When it was broadside on it took up all the road. This I have measured and it is twelve feet wide.' Dinsdale never changed the figure in the two later, revised editions of the book, although the figure cited by Holiday parallels Rupert Gould's estimate of the road's width along this section of highway. Holiday also quotes from a source undiscovered by any other writer on the Monster – 'an account given to a reporter shortly after the incident took place'. This supplied another version of the Spicer narrative and it was one which emphasized just how repulsive the animal was: 'It was horrible – an abomination... a loathsome sight... It was terrible... It looked like a huge snail with a long neck.' But Holiday declined to name the reporter, or the publication in which the interview had appeared, or the date, so it is impossible to tell how accurate his reproduction of the article is.

It is obvious that whatever George Spicer saw that day had a powerful effect on him. As he revealed in his December 1936 letter, he had 'been to the spot many times since' (although Rupert Gould wrote that he personally had 'not succeeded in determining the exact spot' despite assistance from Spicer and the local road contractor). But it is equally obvious that the Spicers' sighting was riddled with contradictions and inconsistencies. The briefest of experiences was imaginatively reconstructed, becoming more and more luridly detailed. Something possibly only six feet long, glimpsed momentarily on the road ahead, was imaginatively transformed into a massive 'trunk-like thing' which emerged from bracken on the hillside. Some 25-30 feet long, it jerked across the road and into the loch. It was like a dragon, a prehistoric animal and a gigantic snail. Although it was a loathsome abomination, terrible in appearance and big enough to have tipped over the Spicers' Austin motor car, Spicer went back to the scene of his awesome sighting 'many times' but had 'never been fortunate enough to see him again'.

This house of cards came tumbling down in 2006 when Jonathan Betts's biography of Rupert Gould, *Time Restored*, was published.

Betts had access to a copy of The *Loch Ness Monster and Others* which Gould had annotated. It was revealed that at the foot of page 43 the author had written:

> Were I re-writing the book, I should have omitted this case. I think the Spicers saw a huddle of deer crossing the road.

This was an astonishing *volte-face*, bearing in mind that Gould had personally interviewed both husband and wife about their sighting. Betts comments that he is left 'rather perplexed' at Gould's somersault, bearing in mind that the author had devoted three and a half pages in discussing 'what, on the face of it, seems a highly implausible account' and that after hearing the couple's story from their own lips he became and remained convinced 'that it was entirely *bona fide*'.

But this last formulation can be misleading, since no one has ever doubted that the couple genuinely believed they had experienced something unusual. The sincerity of eye-witnesses is very rarely in doubt. Gould himself was impressed by the impact which the encounter had made upon the couple, who had evidently 'undergone a most unusual experience which had left a lasting and rather unpleasant impression'. In his original *Courier* letter Spicer wrote, 'I think it should be destroyed'. But the reaction of George Spicer to this apparently unnerving and repellent experience was a little odd, in so far as he subsequently returned to Loch Ness on a number of occasions, hoping for another sighting at the same location.

There can be little doubt that a living animal or animals occupied the carriageway which the Spicers were travelling on. The real issue concerns identification and how the phenomenon was processed analytically, not whether it occurred. The second question is why Gould changed his mind after the 1934 publication of his book. This aspect remains unclear. Gould may just conceivably have met up with Spicer again when he returned to Loch Ness in 1934 or he may have become aware of Spicer's continuing fascination with the Monster and seen something he had written. Spicer wrote letters to the press which have escaped the attention of writers on the monster (for example, his letter to the *Inverness Courier* of October 3, 1933 urging that 'some authority ought to take steps in the matter'). Probably we will never know why Gould changed his mind, though perhaps the answer lies in the account published in his book.

At first sight the explanation that the Spicers saw a huddle of deer is hard to square with the eye-witness descriptions. In any case, what *is* a *huddle* of deer? Presumably Gould meant a closely-packed group of three or more deer. The clue to his change of heart, I think, lies near the end of his account. In London, Gould interviewed both witnesses separately. Mr Spicer had previously written that the animal was fifty yards ahead of the car. In Mrs Spicer's version it was four times as far away (which makes Gould's sketch deeply misleading in so far as it indicates the proximity of the phenomenon). She told him that 'On the upper side of the body, at the point where the neck began, she saw something which she took to be the head and neck of some smaller animal – for example, a young deer'.

2. A momentary encounter with a nervous, fleeing deer on the shoreline of Loch Ness

One plausible interpretation of this sighting is that the main torso of the Monster was simply the back of a deer, with a young deer alongside it. That improbably convoluted neck was merely the back of two or three other deer. Spicer's suggestion of a giant snail was the memory of a pair of antlers (or, even more likely bearing mind that this was a July sighting, a deer in velvet). The jerky movement of the monster was simply the deer springing after one another, disturbed by the approaching vehicle. The entire experience was over in seconds and the Spicers' vision was restricted by the brow of the hill. It was a classic case of expectant attention involving an impressionable individual (the husband). The location was in a wooded part of the lochside where deer existed and still exist in substantial numbers. Groups of deer can be encountered on both the north and south shores of the loch in the daytime, though they are secretive and shy creatures and do indeed run off when disturbed.

The notion that a large creature of the depths had amphibious tendencies at a location like this is inherently absurd. Between the road and the loch is a sloping landscape which today is unlikely to have been significantly different to what it was in 1933, in so far as it is steep, wooded and filled with obstructions for a legless amphibian, in the shape of fallen trees, bracken and a rough, uneven beach full of rocks. This is not difficult terrain for deer, but not even a seal would wish to slither here, let alone a huge, smooth-stomached monster propelled, at best, by flippers. Every aspect of the Spicer sighting falls apart when examined critically, with a full knowledge of the loch's habitat.

In the end Mr and Mrs Spicer are little more than phantoms, eternally attached to the scenery of an unrepeatable event. We know almost nothing about George Spicer. We do not know his age. We do not know even the name of his wife. We do, however, know where the couple lived in London. It seems a strangely apt coincidence that the man whose first thought on seeing something in the road ahead was of 'a dragon or pre-historic animal' had not only seen *King Kong* but also lived by St George's Road.

3

The Sea-Serpent Man

Let us hope that, one day, its existence will be more definitely established by the capture of an actual specimen; or, equally to the point and far better, by a photograph or film of one.

Rupert Gould, *The Case for the Sea-Serpent* (1930)

Sometimes prominent figures in the Loch Ness story claim that they initially approached the Loch Ness mystery as impartial, wholly objective investigators who were then finally won round to the case for a monster by the sheer weight of the evidence. This is nonsense, of course. Monster fever requires a temperament moulded long before ever first catching sight of the dark waters of Loch Ness.

Rupert Gould supplies a prime example. He prefaced his classic book by presenting himself as a sturdy sceptic, initially convinced that the monster amounted to nothing more than 'some well-known sea creature which, in some unexplained manner, had made its way into Loch Ness'. He even pre-empted arguments which sceptics would revive decades later:

A large sturgeon, for example, a beluga or a seal, suddenly appearing in a land-locked basin where nothing of the kind had ever been seen before, would naturally give rise to reports whose surprising details sprang from the attempts of honest onlookers to describe something which, while familiar to coast-dwellers and to scientific men, was outside their own experience.

But Gould didn't speak to anyone but believers and eye-witnesses on his first and seminal trip to Loch Ness. Before he even reached the loch he stopped off in Edinburgh for two days, where he conferred with that ardent promulgator of the monster, Mr P. G. Stalker, journalist. Stalker's media role in promoting the idea of a monster in Loch Ness in 1933 was second only to that of Alex Campbell, whose fortuitous September 7 sighting reinforced Stalker's enthusiasm. Gould pored over newspaper reports of sightings and drew up a list of eye-witnesses he hoped to interview. He then set off for Loch Ness.

In *The Loch Ness Monster*, Gould claims still to have been imbued with scepticism when he arrived at the loch. Here, Gould is not only deceiving his readers, he was surely also deceiving himself. He patently had no interest in interviewing sceptics, such as Captain John Macdonald, who had told the press he had 'a close and intimate experience of the loch for well-nigh seventy years' and had never even heard of the monster, let alone seen it. Macdonald was in no doubt at all that those who reported an 'awful commotion' in Loch Ness were merely seeing 'sporting salmon in lively mood'.

This type of sceptical analysis Gould (whose experience of Loch Ness consisted of just two circumnavigations on a motorbike) haughtily dismissed as 'A simple explanation – the product, apparently, of a simple mind.' The word 'simple', of course, also means 'mad', or what would in Gould's lifetime have been defined as 'retarded'. This uncharacteristic sarcasm suggests that Gould's commitment to the monster was as much emotional as coolly rational. And though he sarcastically mocked those who believed that the monster and the 'commotion' it created had mundane, everyday explanations known to those who were familiar with the surface of Loch Ness, the last laugh belonged to the sceptics. The sceptic who aroused Gould's wrath pointed out the role of calm, clear days in the phenomenon's manifestations and the radical limitations of eye-witness testimony beyond 'half-a-mile' range. The passage of time would strengthen this kind of sceptical assessment of sightings, just as the monster of Gould's book would require savage revisionism in order to keep it alive in the second half of the twentieth century. Monsters which moved at 'some 13 knots', had eight humps and created 'a very violent commotion in the water' were quietly dropped from the case for Nessie. What this signified about eye-witness testimony was never considered or discussed.

Gould was a man passionately interested in enigmas, and not from a sceptical perspective. In 1928 he published *Oddities: A Book of Unexplained Facts*. This was an anthology of mysteries – 'incidents which have not, at present, been satisfactorily explained'. The mysteries included the unidentified creature responsible for 'the Devil's Hoof-Marks' which were made in the snow across Devonshire in February 1855, paranormal happenings in a churchyard vault in Barbados, and sightings of the mythical planet Vulcan. A year later he published a sequel, *Enigmas: Another Book of Unexplained Facts*. The following year, 1930, saw publication of Gould's *The Case for the Sea-Serpent*.

Exactly a decade later, in 1940, a then rather minor and commercially unsuccessful writer who went by the name of George Orwell enviously wondered what it was that made the big-name novelist Charles Reade so amazingly popular with so many readers. He noted that Reade's historical novels were crammed with the fruits of his research and furnished with lavish, factual detail. Orwell decided that that it was 'charm' which made Reade's fiction so compellingly readable, adding, cuttingly, that it was 'the same charm as one finds in R. Austin Freeman's detective stories or Lieutenant-Commander Gould's collections of curiosities – the charm of useless knowledge'.

The Loch Ness Monster is a classic of the 'useless knowledge' genre. It assembles 'Statements by fifty-eight witnesses' who each testify to having seen a large, unknown animal at Loch Ness. This inventory of wonders much resembles George Orwell's laconic description of a narrative comprised of 'dates, lists, catalogues, concrete details, descriptions of processes' – an encyclopaedic accumulation of 'disconnected information' duly transfigured by 'a lively narrative gift'.

In reality no one could have been more predisposed to the notion of a mystery animal in Loch Ness than Rupert Gould, and that bias was surely reinforced long before he ever reached Inverness. Philip Stalker, the man he conferred with in Edinburgh, was both a passionate believer in the monster and a huge fan of Gould's *The Case for the Sea-Serpent*. Indeed, Stalker even cited Gould's book when, in October 1933, he broadcast his belief in the monster's existence on BBC radio. Stalker's theory that a sea-serpent had swum up the River Ness into the loch was a thesis that Gould's book on the monster, published some eight months after that broadcast, duly endorsed. One might also ask why, if Rupert Gould really approached Loch Ness in the spirit of sturdy scepticism that he afterwards claimed, he had taken with him to Scotland a copy of his own book on the sea-serpent. His mind had plainly been fixed on a possible sea-serpent explanation long before he ever saw the loch. It was also disingenuous of him not to mention in his monster book Stalker's fervent belief in sea-serpents or Stalker's admiration for *The Case for the Sea-Serpent*.

Something I overlooked when writing *The Loch Ness Mystery Solved* (and which no one else has ever noticed or commented on) was Gould's extraordinary admission in Chapter Three of his book that he actually showed his copy of *The Case for the Sea-Serpent* to Loch Ness monster witnesses in order to clarify some of his drawings illustrating what they claimed to have seen.

> I used its illustrations as a means by which witnesses who could not draw might be able to indicate something to me which more or less resembled what they described; and I consider this was a very natural proceeding. If, for example, I were an insurance official, going to interview a witness who had seen a car accident but could not tell the make of the car, I should certainly take an illustrated catalogue of cars with me.

This is self-evidently spurious logic. Using sea-serpent pictures to help monster eye-witnesses shape their pictorial image of the mystery animal they claimed to have seen was blatantly manipulative, no matter how much Gould pretended otherwise. His normally meticulous attention to detail deserted him at this point. Which witnesses were helped by which pictures? Gould doesn't say.

'My change of opinion was a gradual process', Gould insists in his Introduction, but this sounds much more like self-deception than what actually occurred. Before he had even arrived at the loch his views on the Monster were shaped by conversations with Philip Stalker and existing press coverage. Once there, Gould's personal knowledge of Loch Ness was astonishingly superficial. He rode round the loch twice on his motorbike, talked to eye-witnesses, showing some of them his *Case for the Sea-Serpent*, and then went back to England to write his book. As is always the case with the Loch Ness monster, it's the 'soft' eye-witness testimony which seemed most persuasive, not the 'hard' evidence of photographs and film. 'The witnesses, almost without exception, impressed me very much indeed', he explained.

Gould was open-minded enough to contemplate the possibility that he had 'assisted various honest but self-deluded persons to create a zoological myth' – which, of course, is exactly what he did do. If he had not written his pioneering book it is perfectly possible that Nessie might never have been reborn and would have become as extinct as that other contemporary animal wonder, Gef the talking mongoose. However, Gould's preferred conclusion, inevitably, was that the evidence all pointed in the direction of 'a very singular spectacle – that of a living creature, unknown to science, disporting itself in a Scottish loch'.

Gould's extraordinary *volte-face* over the Spicer land sighting exposed the shakiness of his analysis. But even without such devastating revisionism, *The Loch Ness Monster and Others* had some contradictions of its own. The absence of communication with Hugh Gray and R. K. Wilson is telling. And what about that erroneous 'April 1, 1934' date for the Surgeon's photograph? The location of 'April 1' at the end of the line might simply indicate that the second digit fell off during the typesetting process. But that is the kind of error which page proofs are designed for. Not only was the date not corrected (and Gould seems to have been a meticulous proof-reader) but he allowed it to stand when he later re-read and annotated the book, correcting errors and making marginal comments. It is all the odder when one bears in mind that, between publication of *The Loch Ness Monster and Others* and his later annotations, Gould published an essay specifically devoted to the topic of 'Mistakes and Misprints'. It includes a discussion of technical errors involving bars of type-metal and linotype operators.

It is certainly noteworthy that Gould stuck with the date that signifies All Fools' Day – a day for pranks, practical jokes and colourful misinformation. And though Gould pronounced Hugh Gray's photograph 'undoubtedly genuine', he withheld such praise from his description of the Surgeon's photo. Shrewdly (from a sales perspective) he gave it prominence by making it the Frontispiece to his book. But Gould's comment that to get such a picture as the latter 'requires not only great patience but – as I am sure Mr. Wilson would admit – a great share of good fortune' can be interpreted equally as a neutral observation or as one laced with irony and scepticism.

4

Campbell Soup

Dinsdale and Holiday both take pains to claim him as a collaborator and speak of him almost as if he were their personal guru – and the monster's as well.

Victor Perera, *The Loch Ness Monster Watchers* (1974)

In four short years the fortunes of Alex Campbell, water bailiff, journalist and resident of Fort Augustus, were transformed. Constance Whyte's *More Than a Legend* (1957) was the book which woke the Loch Ness Monster from a long sleep and persuaded a new, younger generation (including me) that there really was something worth investigating at Loch Ness. But Alex Campbell was barely mentioned in this book. He was marginalised as a very minor eye-witness. Twenty-three years earlier, Rupert Gould had even used two sightings by Campbell as evidence of how easily an eye-witness might be fooled by a combination of heat haze and a line of cormorants.

Everything changed in 1961, with the publication of *Loch Ness Monster*. Tim Dinsdale opened his book by giving pride of place to a sensational sighting which had occurred on a warm June day in 1934:

As the mist shredded away under the warm sunlight I witnessed the most incredible sight I have seen in my forty years as a water bailiff on Scotland's biggest Loch. Something rose from the water like a monster of pre-historic times, measuring a full thirty feet from tip to tail.

Dinsdale erupted from nowhere to become a Loch Ness superstar. As he moved centre stage he brought an ally with him in the shape of Alex Campbell, reborn as both monster guru and classic eye-witness.

Dinsdale had every reason to be grateful to Campbell as an inspiration. It was the feature on Campbell's sighting of the Loch Ness Monster in *Everybody's* magazine (February 21, 1959) which first caught his eye and transformed him into a man who, quite literally overnight, became obsessed with this legendary beast. A little more than a year later he was at Loch Ness for the first time, sitting in Campbell's home at Fort Augustus, discussing Nessie and absorbing the wisdom of this local expert. It is scarcely a coincidence that within 48 hours of that thrilling meeting the impressionable Dinsdale saw and filmed the monster twice.

The following year Dinsdale's book enshrined Campbell's sighting as a classic. He not only opened *Loch Ness Monster* with it, but repeated it in a later chapter devoted to important sightings. Dinsdale solicited his own account of the wondrous 1934 sighting, which Campbell was happy to repeat and write down for his number one fan, with the added bonus of a sketch.

Alex Campbell was an icon requiring particular attention in *The Loch Ness Mystery Solved*'s general demolition project, both as the man who first publicised the existence of a Loch Ness Monster and as a respected eye-witness who testified to numerous encounters with the legendary beast. My book devoted a chapter to him, focusing on three particular aspects which all the previous books had ignored. These were his early role in inventing and promoting the monster, secondly the numerous inconsistencies surrounding his classic eye-witness sighting (not least his retraction of that sighting in 1933, recorded by Rupert Gould but studiously ignored by all later monster authors), and finally his record as a man who, remarkably, claimed to have seen the monster on eighteen separate occasions.

Even today Alex Campbell remains something of an enigmatic figure. It is obvious that he passionately believed that Loch Ness contained 'a fearsome-looking monster' which had been there 'for generations'. He lived beside the River Oich at Fort Augustus, in a house occupied by generations of Campbells since the family built it in 1710. He told Victor Perera that he had acquired his belief in the monster from his father, 'who had seen a large creature that caused a tremendous wash when it dived'. What this large creature looked like is not described. His father referred to it as the water horse and it had been known by this name in the Campbell family 'for many generations'. But, oddly, Alex Campbell's brother, Colin, who was convinced that St Columba's ghost ship sailed the loch, did not believe in the monster.

In 1962, when Maurice Burton achieved some prominence as a critic of the Dinsdale film and as a sceptic of multi-humped monsters which created great commotion, 'A.M. Campbell' stepped forward to defend his cherished beast. Now he revealed that one of his 'own forebears' – not identified – had been told as far back as 1802 of 'a strange animal in the loch'. The eye-witness on that occasion was crofter Alexander MacDonald of Abriachan, who believed that the creature was 20 feet long and resembled a giant salamander:

> he could see that it propelled itself with things like short legs and the movement was jerky. Then it turned off for no apparent reason and made off towards deeper water, finally submerging with a great upheaval some five hundred yards off-shore.

Alexander MacDonald's monster exhibits behaviour curiously like that of the monster sightings which Burton's effervescent vegetable mat theory was designed to rationalise. MacDonald's monster's zig-zag course might also be interpreted as an endorsement of the Dinsdale film.

Finally, MacDonald identified his monster as a salamander based on an illustration he'd seen, which replicates Campbell's own identification of the monster as a plesiosaurus after consulting a dinosaur book. Moreover, Alexander MacDonald's sightings satisfyingly helped to put in his place that other Macdonald, the sceptical ship's captain and MacBrayne's supervisor, who back in May 1933 had imperiously crushed the fantasies of the local journalist with the authority of his vast experience of Loch Ness.

This story first surfaced in the *Northern Chronicle* on August 12, 1933, and was quoted by Rupert Gould. But in this earlier version Alexander Macdonald (sic) is described not as a crofter but as a mason, and his sightings occurred not in the early years of the nineteenth century 'on fine summer days as he tended his sheep' but 'some forty-four years ago', i.e. around 1889. This Alexander Macdonald 'often saw a strange creature disporting itself on the loch in the early hours of the morning'. He referred to it as the 'salamander'.

It's obvious from the style and the publication that Alex Campbell wrote the *Northern Chronicle* piece and it is equally obvious that he later recycled it for his *Scots Magazine* feature twenty-nine years later.

Where he obtained the story from in the first place is uncertain. The hesitant note of the report ('it appears that some forty-four years ago') suggests both an anecdote from a third party and one only recently received. Had Campbell known of it before he would surely have trumpeted it weeks earlier, when the first wave of local sceptics had made their views known.

Intrigued by this ancient eye-witness cited by Campbell, I searched through the old graveyard at Abriachan hoping to find out more. But crofters, it seems, go to unmarked graves. There was, however, an impressive and expensive pink marble gravestone which bore the name Alexander MacDonald. His dates would fit sightings around 1889 and he did indeed die 'a good many years ago'. The gravestone defines him as a builder, which is reasonably close to the profession of mason ('a person skilled in cutting, dressing, and laying stone in buildings'). But MacDonald is a very common surname in this part of the world, so it may simply be coincidence.

From a sceptical perspective the interesting thing is that the glaring contradiction between the two versions publicised by Campbell passed without notice or comment. There's a curious parallel between Campbell's Monster sighting, which was rewritten as a line of cormorants, and the *Northern Chronicle* report which, three decades later, was deconstructed and rewritten in a new version.

Campbell's 1962 article supplied one other pre-1933 witness: James Rose, who died in 1904 and who allegedly in 1896 saw, along with unidentified companions, 'the familiar upturned boat tearing along the loch's surface'. But it is curious that Campbell made no mention of this local eye-witness in 1933. Why wait until 1962 to release this thrilling evidence to the world?

That Campbell is an unreliable source where historic eye-witness testimony is concerned is indicated by his remarkable assertion that 'as a girl' his maternal great-great-great grandmother had watched the Battle of Culloden. This is an implausible claim. The battle was an ad hoc affair, fought on a remote boggy moor in squally rain. It was a fast-moving confrontation, spread out over an area of moorland and walled enclosures, and it was all over inside an hour. There were no viewing areas for civilians, least of all local children.

Alex Campbell seems to have been unaware of any water kelpie tradition *directly* associated with Loch Ness, or even the more general material cited by Roland Watson in *The Water Horses of Loch Ness*. Had there been a tradition it is obvious that he would have energetically publicised it in 1933.

Alexander Macmillan Campbell (1901-1983) began working as the local Fort Augustus correspondent for the *Inverness Courier* in 1919, when he was about eighteen years old. He got the job because he was replacing his father. This is interesting because, if there was a family tradition of unknown animals in the loch, then his father would surely have wished to publicise it. Finding copy in a place as sleepy and tranquil as Fort Augustus cannot have been easy. But no one has so far found any references to monstrous manifestations in Loch Ness penned by Campbell senior. And Campbell junior, as far as we know, did not write about anything odd happening in the loch until August 27, 1930 – some eleven years after beginning his career as a stringer. In the *Courier*'s rival paper, *The Northern Chronicle*, on August 27, 1930, there appeared a report about three fishermen who had witnessed 'a great commotion with spray flying everywhere' followed by something which approached with 'a wriggling motion'. The anonymous item was almost certainly by Campbell and it leaves many questions unanswered. Was Campbell actively looking for evidence of a monster, or did this event trigger his interest? It would be another three years before there was another local sighting. This time the journalist made a poetic connection between two different imaginary animals – a 'fearsome looking monster' and the water kelpie.

Campbell's chief weapon was his anonymity. He poured out scores of stories for the *Inverness Courier* and the *Northern Chronicle* without ever having to identify himself. 'Every PR adviser to whom I have spoken agrees that the best PR conceals its own hand', writes the investigative journalist Nick Davies in his blistering analysis of how modern British newspapers distort, fabricate and mislead. Alex Campbell provides a staggering example of the truth, power and effectiveness of the simple reality that the best 'pseudo-event' disguises its origins.

From day one Campbell was the gatekeeper of knowledge and the man who filtered eye-witness testimony. And right from the start he was a totally unreliable conduit for accurate information. His legendary news report of May 2, 1933, began with the bogus claim that Loch Ness had 'for generations' been known as the home of 'a fearsome-looking monster'. Its second false statement was that there had been a new sighting of 'the beast' on 'Friday of last week' (i.e. April 28). It was, if Rupert Gould is right, two weeks earlier, on April 14. The third false statement was that 'a well known business man' and his wife had watched as 'the creature disported itself, rolling and plunging for fully a minute, its body resembling that of a whale'. In fact the husband was driving and did not see the monster. All he saw, as Gould discovered, was 'the final commotion, and a noticeable "wash" which came rolling on to the shore after X had sunk'. The fourth false statement was that when first seen the disturbance was 'fully three-quarters of a mile from the shore'. But the sighting took place opposite Aldourie Pier, where the loch is only half a mile wide. When questioned by Rupert Gould, the witness said it was 'about 100 yards from shore'. The fifth false statement is that 'neither seals nor porpoises have ever been known to enter Loch Ness. Indeed, in the case of the latter, it would be utterly impossible for them to do so.' In fact a school of porpoises were supposedly observed in Loch Ness in September 1914 and sightings were reported both in the national press as well as the local *Northern Chronicle* (September 16, 1914). Unusual events involving unexpected animals were reported from Loch Ness long before 1933, which is another reason why the Nessie 'tradition' lacks all credibility.

Campbell's seminal 'monster' news report was a classic instance of what Nick Davies defined as 'Flat Earth News' – or what in the year 2017 would be called 'fake news'. It was propaganda and spin masquerading as objective neutral reportage. Davies identifies a number of stages in the success of Flat Earth news reports. Firstly, there is 'an unreliable statement' which is not subjected to proper critical scrutiny. Secondly, the agency responsible for the unreliable statement is concealed, masking the fact that it has been manufactured, usually for 'commercial or political benefit'. Finally it is fed 'into the arteries of the media through which it then circulates around the whole body of global communication' without ever being checked.

Davies is writing about the fast-moving early twenty-first century media but his analysis is plainly relevant to the strange birth of the Loch Ness Monster. Campbell's numerous 'unreliable statements' were, however, not motivated by a desire for personal commercial gain (others would reap the financial rewards of monster fever) and the story had no relevance to local politics. However, there were surely strong ideological and psychological motives driving Campbell's ceaseless activity on behalf of the beast. It is not easy to pin down what personal factors lay behind his campaigning for the simple reason that he is a mysterious individual whose personal history is largely unknown. But in its widest dimension the monster's existence expressed a rebellion against modernity. It was the revenge of folklore upon science and established knowledge.

But Campbell could not have done it all on his own. Firstly, he required witnesses to the miracle. His first attempt to publicise a mystery fell flat and he had to wait three years before another opportunity occurred. Once he had found fresh witnesses it took several months before the Flat Earth News industry amplified the story. It was the editor of the *Scotsman* who first scented major news in this silly-season story in the provincial Highland press. The journalist he despatched, Philip Stalker, happened to be a man who greatly admired Rupert Gould's *The Case for the Sea-Serpent*. Arriving at Loch Ness, Stalker was quickly persuaded by the amazing evidence of two eye-witnesses – Alex Campbell and Commander R. A. R. Meiklem, who lived nearby each other at Fort Augustus. Meiklem was also a believer in sea-serpents. These mutually reinforcing narratives were given great prominence in the *Scotsman* and were then amplified by Stalker on BBC national radio and in the pages of the corporation's magazine *The Listener*. This immediately attracted the attention of popular English dailies like the *Mail* and the *Express*, as well as the interest of Rupert Gould. A tiny snowball had started to roll and grow in size.

At this point it is necessary to reflect on the monster sighting, reported by Philip Stalker in the *Scotsman* (October 17, 1933). It was given to him by 'a man who up to that time refused to believe of the existence in the loch of anything other than a seal or large marine animal of some kind'. This unnamed eye-witness reported sighting a creature 'fully 30 feet in length'. Its form 'was like that of a plesiosaurus'.

It did not become clear who this witness was until Rupert Gould published his book the following year. In the section devoted to sceptical explanations for monster sightings Gould quoted from a letter dated October 28, 1933, 'addressed to the Ness Fishery Board by Mr. A. Campbell, water-bailiff at Fort Augustus'. This described two recent sightings by Campbell. In the first (September 7, 1933) he described 'a strange object on the surface' which 'seemed to be about 30 feet long' with a head 'fully 5 feet above the surface of the Loch' which 'it kept turning'. This was the anonymous sighting reported by Stalker. However, as Campbell explained to his employers, he had 'last Friday' (presumably October 20) witnessed 'something very like what I have described' (i.e. on September 7). But as the mist thinned he quickly discovered that the 'Monster' was simply a line of cormorants, strung out behind a 'head' which was actually 'a cormorant standing in the water and flappings its wings, as they often do'.

As I wrote in *The Loch Ness Mystery Solved*:

> Campbell's motive in writing this letter remains obscure, but on the evidence available it would appear that his formidable role in promoting the monster had come to the ears of his employers. The Ness Fisheries Board, it seems, was not amused.

In other words, Campbell was worried about his job. A water bailiff was supposed to be the representative of authority, carrying out his duties with sober diligence and good order. A primary role was to police the loch, ensure that restrictions on fishing were being observed, and crack down on unlicensed fishing. The water bailiff was not someone who was supposed to see a thirty-foot monster resembling a plesiosaur. Disreputable stuff like that might lead to jokes involving whisky.

In small-town Fort Augustus and its environs Alex Campbell would not have been liked by everyone, including those who could not afford a licence or who saw no reason to fork out good money to enjoy a spot of fishing in such a massive body of water. From this perspective Campbell was merely a vexatious busybody. One gets a brief glimpse of how zealously he performed his role at this time in the anecdote about him arriving on the scene while Marmaduke Wetherell and his son Ian were photographing their toy submarine fake monster.

Although the context remains impenetrable it is obvious that someone with a grudge tipped off the Ness Fisheries Board about Alex Campbell and the Loch Ness Monster. Whether or not this person knew that Campbell was the unnamed eye-witness cited in the *Scotsman* (October 17, 1933) will probably never be established, but plainly the water bailiff believed that this was what had endangered his position with the Ness Fisheries Board. Campbell had antagonists in the *Inverness Courier* office as well, judging by the satire at his expense which appeared in that newspaper on August 11, 1933.

What is one to make of this episode, other than the obvious one that Campbell was seeking to deflect whatever information had come to the ears of his employers? There are two obvious interpretations. His September 7, 1933 sighting could be regarded as genuine and his supposed October 20 cormorants sighting as entirely fictitious and fabricated to humour the Ness Fisheries Board. Alternatively, as Rupert Gould believed, it could be a case of someone genuinely believing they had seen a Monster, but who later perceived that they had been misled as a result of fresh understanding of the behaviour of known species on the loch's surface.

Henry Bauer states that 'Alex Campbell once realized that one of his dozen-and-a-half Nessie sightings had actually been cormorants'. But that doesn't explain why this sighting – Campbell's second – was *identical* to his first, or why, having convincingly deconstructed his original thirty-foot monster, he then reconstructed it many years later, with embellishments.

The affair remains a murky one. It may be the case that Campbell gave a copy of his letter to Gould in a campaign to restore his good name with the Ness Fisheries Board. If so it was a futile manoeuvre, since by the time *The Loch Ness Monster and Others* was published in 1934, the hoo-ha had blown over. Alternatively Gould may have obtained the letter from the Ness Fisheries Board when he arrived at Inverness in mid-November. The Board gave Gould permission to make use of the letter; so, too, did Campbell. Either could have been the source.

Gould also had contact with W. U. Goodbody, who was a member of the Ness Fishery Board and who lived at Invergarry, some eight miles south-west of Fort William (and connected to it by passenger train until the line closed on December 1, 1933). But this evidently only occurred after Goodbody's sighting of a multi-humped monster on December 30, 1933. Goodbody believed that what he had seen fitted the theory that the monster was a giant squid.

Unfortunately – the Loch Ness story will forever be a ragged and inconclusive narrative – the original letter has been lost. Judging by the ellipses the text published by Gould is an edited account, with three sections of unknown length omitted,

This episode has always been a curious one, not least because later writers on the monster studiously averted their eyes from the glaring contradiction of the two Campbell sightings reported by Gould. Tim Dinsdale, Nicholas Witchell and Roy Mackal simply blanked it. The 'cormorant' monster melted away, never to be mentioned again. This episode displayed the monster fraternity's unwillingness to confront contradiction and negative evidence. What was sought was never understanding but only *verification*.

Decades later the original sighting was restored to its former glory, with colourful additions. In the Gould versions the first Monster was seen only when 'The light was very uncertain, there being a fairly thick haze on the water', whereas the cormorant-monster was quickly identified as the mist thinned. Twenty-six years later Campbell conflated both versions, reconfiguring them as a dazzling spectacle involving a creature which 'rose from the water like a monster of prehistoric times'. The date changed to 'a June morning in 1934'.

As far as Rupert Gould was concerned Alex Campbell's two sightings were merely a minor example of how someone who stood at the lochside hoping to see the monster could easily be fooled by birds, if the viewing conditions were suitable. There the matter ended until *More Than a Legend* appeared in 1957. Twenty-four years had passed since Campbell's two 1933 cormorant-monster sightings. In the main body of her book Constance Whyte mentioned him directly only twice. These were very brief references to his seminal May 1933 *Courier* report and as someone who 'has seen the Monster at least six times'. She was evidently unaware who the 'A.C.' was who was mentioned in connection with two other sightings, including one from September 1933 (which was plainly the first of the two sightings described by Gould, even though the date was different).

Appendix A of Whyte's book lists a sighting in the 'Late 1930s' by one 'A.C.', who saw the head and neck of the monster apparently 'covered with some entangling substance, from which the creature had to shake itself free'. There is another sighting attributed to 'A.C', which is basically Campbell's September 7, 1933 sighting, with minor variations. However, perplexingly, it is precisely dated as having occurred on September 22, 1933. Whyte mentions this last sighting in a footnote, in connection with 'the treatment, amounting almost to persecution' which some witnesses were subjected to. This footnote draws on an interview with 'A.C.' by Dom Cyril Dieckhoff, who noted the eye-witness's extreme reluctance to be identified by name. Whyte does not seem to have realised that this acutely anxious individual was none other than Alex Campbell, which suggests that her memory of the contents of Gould's book was not what it should have been.

Two years after this book appeared Campbell stepped forwards to claim he had had a sensational experience a quarter of a century ago. His colourful description of 'the most incredible sight I have seen in my forty years as a water bailiff' published by *Everybody's* magazine was yet another version of his September 7, 1933 sighting, but now the date had changed again. What was described by Whyte as having occurred on September 22, 1933, was now identified as having taken place on 'a June morning in 1934'. When he repeated his account for Tim Dinsdale

Campbell thought it was 'May, if I remember aright'. Slight variations in dating can be excused on the grounds of age and fading memory, although Campbell seems to have owned a copy of Gould's book and surely also purchased Constance Whyte's, both of which should have served as a reminder.

But it wasn't just the date of his original sighting on September 7, 1933, which radically changed. So, too, did the details. In the very first version, given to Philip Stalker, Campbell said he saw the monster *in the afternoon*. He described seeing 'a creature raise its head and body from the loch, pause, moving its head – a small head on a long neck – rapidly from side to side, apparently listening to the sound of two drifters coming from the Caledonian Canal, which was out of its sight'. The monster took fright and sank from view. Stalker, a keen believer in sea-serpents, wrote that Campbell's description was reminiscent of a plesiosaurus. When shown a picture of one, Campbell confirmed the resemblance.

Stalker reported that his unnamed witness was a man 'who up to that time had refused to believe of the existence in the loch of anything other than a seal or a large marine animal of some sort'. Here, Campbell is directly caught out as a liar, using the shield of anonymity to conceal the fact that he had both invented the concept of a monster-haunted loch while simultaneously expressly denying that seals ever got into the loch. For him to pass himself off as previously a sceptic illustrated his mendacity.

The version of the sighting contained in the letter to the Ness Fisheries Board contains two key differences. Now Campbell's sighting occurs not in the afternoon but 'at about half-past nine in the morning'. Secondly, the 'monster' does not appear from the depths but is already 'on the surface' when he spots it. There is additional detail: the light is poor and there is 'a fairly thick haze' on the loch. The sun is shining directly into his eyes, making visibility 'very bad'. The 'monster' is about 600 yards away. The head is five feet above the loch surface.

But there is also a detail in the *Scotsman* report which is omitted from the Fisheries letter. Campbell told Stalker that when the animal was at the surface 'he could see the swirl made by each movement of its limbs, and the creature seemed to him to be fully 30 feet in length'. This implicitly indicated paddles or flippers and supplied an exciting endorsement of the living plesiosaur explanation which Stalker was plainly keen to suggest for this sighting.

By the time Campbell retold this sighting to *Everybody's* magazine the encounter was wondrously transformed. He is no longer stationed further along the river bank, watching. Instead his sighting occurred as he emerged from his cottage on the banks of Loch Ness. There is no thick haze or poor light but just 'early morning mist' which was 'clearing fast'. Instead of being dazzled by the September sun shining directly in his eyes, it is simply 'a June morning' of 'warm sunlight'. As the mist 'shredded away', the monster made its appearance. It 'rose from the water like a monster of pre-historic times'. It measured 'a full thirty feet from tip to tail' (although how Campbell knew there was a tail, which must have been underwater, is not explained). This pre-historic monster had 'a long sinuous neck and a flat reptilian head'.

He was close enough to observe that 'Its skin was a greyish black, tough looking'. Behind that, where the neck joined the body, 'was a giant hump like that on a camel, though many times bigger'. It was unmistakeably the Loch Ness Monster, 'real and tangible'. For several minutes it lay there contentedly, basking in the early sunlight'. Then two herring drifters approached the loch from the nearby Caledonian canal.

In the *Scotsman* version of the September 1933 sighting the creature was observed by Campbell to 'raise its head and body from the loch' (ambiguous phrasing, which could indicate either surfacing into view, or being already present at the loch surface and then raising its head and stretching its body upward). The animal then paused and moved its head and neck 'rapidly from side to side'. This seemed to be a nervous reaction to the noise of two herring trawlers approaching the loch from the Caledonian canal. The vessels were out of the monster's sight but the noise and disturbance were sufficient to frighten the animal, which promptly submerged.

The Fisheries Board letter contradicts this. In this version the monster seemed to be *watching* the two drifters as they passed out of the canal entrance and into Loch Ness. It responded by 'turning its head and also its body very quickly' for some sixty seconds. Then the object 'vanished as if it had sunk out of sight'.

In the *Everybody*'s version it is implied that noise of the drifters' approach was what disturbed the monster, which then 'lowered its long neck and dived'. A fresh detail was added. As the monster dived it caused 'a turmoil of water' creating 'a miniature tidal wave'. In addition to these three versions, there are at least three more. The first is Campbell's letter to Tim Dinsdale, dated October 16, 1960. This adds yet more detail. Now he explains that he was standing at the mouth of the River Oich when 'a strange object...seemed to shoot out of the calm waters almost opposite the Abbey boathouse'. It had a 'swanlike neck' which 'reached six feet or so above the water'. The body was 'a darkish grey glistening with moisture'. It was '*at least* 30 ft. long'. Campbell was confident of this estimate because he mentally placed 'two ordinary rowing boats of 15 ft. overall length end to end'.

The animal sensed the approach of the two trawlers approaching down the Caledonian canal. He saw it 'turns its head in an apprehensive way, this way and that'. It then 'sank rapidly out of sight, lowering the neck in doing so, and leaving a considerable disturbance on the mirror-like surface of the loch'. The animal was 'some 400 yards' from where Campbell was standing, 'possibly less'. He had 'a very clear view of it which lasted several minutes'.

The next version is an account reproduced by the paper manufacturers Wiggins Teape, in association with the Loch Ness Investigation. The company produced a folder of samples of its Orbit brand to display the different types of paper. One of these samples reproduced the only handwritten account by Campbell ever published in facsimile. It comprises a single page signed statement and incorporates a sketch in Campbell's hand. The statement is undated and begins, 'This was my best sighting'. It implies it was given in connection with a verbal account, since it goes on to say, 'I was standing as stated, as the mouth of the River Oich when I noticed the creature on the surface of Loch Ness almost opposite the Abbey Boathouse.'

In this version the monster 'seemed nervous – head turning this way and that'. Campbell was sure this behaviour was in response to the beat of the engines of two small trawlers approaching along the Caledonian Canal. 'At that time', he explained, 'the trawlers were not within either the object's line of vision or my own'. But when the first trawler appeared 'it dived head first as soon as the first vessel came into its view and mine, simultaneously, that is'. His sketch, he wrote, showed 'very clearly what the creature looked like'.

This sketch showed a distinctly bird-like head and neck (marked as being six feet high) attached to a single low broad hump attached to a second much shorter and flatter hump, with an overall length of thirty feet. 'No eyes were visible, or flippers' Campbell added by way of conclusion, 'or anything else that might give one some clue as to its means of propulsion'. The statement is signed 'Alex M. Campbell'.

This sketch of the monster appears to be the source of the

illustration produced by Tim Dinsdale in the first edition of his book *Loch Ness Monster*. However, although captioned by Dinsdale as 'Alex Cambell's sketch', it has plainly been re-drawn and 'improved' by Dinsdale, as I demonstrated in *The Loch Ness Mystery Solved*. However, puzzlingly, Campbell's account of his sighting is quite different to the text reproduced in *Loch Ness Monster*, which Dinsdale states is taken from a personal letter dated October 16, 1960.

Campbell appeared in person in the 1973 Walt Disney film *Man, Monsters and Mysteries*. Standing on the river bank he told his story:

It was from this point I had my first and best sighting in the month of May, 1934. Standing here one lovely summer morning, sun shining brightly, loch flat calm… I saw this huge animal, thirty-foot body, head turning like so [from side to side], and the neck six feet above water. There were two small trawlers coming through the canal about to come into Loch Ness and I'm positive the animal heard the beat of the engines. Well the first trawler came out and as soon as it came into the animal's view and mine – terrific dive and there was a terrific upheaval in the water. That was my best sighting out of eighteen.

It was around this time that Campbell was visited at home by Victor Perera – an enthusiastic and inquisitive American tourist, who had read two books about the monster and was keen to learn more from the experts. Campbell recited his basic narrative but once again there were variations. Now the sighting occurred at 8am. It was a beautiful, bright morning. An object shot out across the flat, calm surface 'from near the abbey boathouse'. It created a wash 'about three feet high'. Then a neck appeared: 'It was slender and long – I would say, swanlike – and reached about six feet above the surface.' The body was glistening wet, darkish grey in colour, and at least thirty feet long. Then the trawlers approached and the animal turned its head 'this way and that, as if in apprehension'.

Then it sank rapidly out of sight, lowering its neck and creating a great commotion on the surface. The animal was about four hundred yards from where I stood, about two hundred fifty from the abbey boathouse, and I had a very good view of it which lasted several minutes.

In this version there was no mist. Everything was crystal clear.

What, then, is one to make of Campbell's retraction of his September 1933 sighting and its later reappearance as a genuine one, with a number of variations?

To the monster's number one contemporary fan, Roland Watson, the answer is perfectly simple. Campbell's original sighting was an authentic one and the water bailiff is a man monstrously misrepresented by sceptics such as myself. In a series of three features published in 2017 on his Loch Ness Monster blog, Watson sets out the case for Campbell. In the first one he begins by setting up a straw man which he then proceeds to knock down. This consists of an anonymous 'letter from Loch Ness' which was published in the *Scotsman* (September 6, 2003), by someone who claimed to have been a confidante of Campbell's. This 'letter' is an error-strewn piece which is plainly a work of fiction by someone who very obviously was not a dear friend of Alex (who by this time had been dead for twenty years). I had never heard of this 'letter' and no Nessie sceptic has, as far as know, ever bothered to cite it.

In his second piece Watson discusses the 1933 sighting that was retracted and writes:

> you know, it is rather a pity that all these sceptics who were at the loch at the same time as Alex Campbell never seemed to bother to ask the man about this conundrum. Certainly there is no written record anywhere I can see.

That's an easy one for me to answer. Leaving aside the rather obvious reality that many of today's sceptics were yesterday's believers (Ronald Binns, Dick Raynor, Nicholas Witchell, Ivor Newby etc), I simply *didn't know* about Campbell's *volte-face* as reported by Rupert Gould. This was for the simple reason that *The Loch Ness Monster and Others* was, in my younger days, an exceptionally rare book. It has never been republished in Britain since the first 1934 edition. My bibles as a young monster hunter were Whyte's *More Than a Legend* and Dinsdale's *Loch Ness Monster*. I had never read Rupert Gould's classic text during any of my trips to Loch Ness before publication of *The Loch Ness Mystery Solved*. It was not a book to be found in public libraries.

I did not obtain and read a copy until late 1981. The first time I heard about Alex Campbell's strangely contradictory sighting was in the late 1970s, long after the golden age of monster surveillance was over. And although Gould's book was republished in at least one

American edition, none of the Americans I met at Loch Ness possessed a copy or ever mentioned it. Before the arrival of the internet, American publications were infinitely remote and exotic. Watson's insinuation that sceptics such as me never had the courage to knock on Campbell's door and interrogate him is therefore wholly baseless.

Watson's second point concerns Campbell's motive in retracting his sighting. He asks 'why was this so called self-publicist and monster-pusher suddenly turning witness for the prosecution and playing the sceptic?' He states:

> Nessie sceptic, Ronald Binns, dismissively says that Campbell wrote to the Board for *'some obscure reason'*. If he had temporarily suspended his zeal to nail Campbell, it would be obvious to him why Campbell wrote this letter – he was afraid of losing his job!
>
> Author Ronald Binns swerves round the issue of the strange letter to the Fishery Board. Gareth Williams gets closer with his speculation about tensions between the two parties.

This is a misrepresentation which misleadingly introduces a bogus direct quotation. Let me repeat what I wrote in *The Loch Ness Mystery Solved*:

> Campbell's motive in writing this letter remains obscure, but on the evidence available it would appear that his formidable role in promoting the monster had come to the ears of his employers. The Ness Fisheries Board, it seems, was not amused.

If Watson cannot understand the thrust of that (which evidently he can't), it reflects on his interpretive skills, not mine.

He continues by describing how Philip Stalker's report of Campbell's September 1933 sighting, first reported in the *Scotsman* (October 17, 1933), was repeated on November 15. On this occasion the story was accompanied by an illustration, which Watson reproduces on his blog. He comments:

> This is the earliest sketch of Campbell's monster and therefore should be taken as the most accurate. But, strangely, Binns rather pointed out another sketch done much later in 1970 as being *'bird-like'*. I prefer sketches done four weeks later rather than forty years later. Can't imagine why Binns preferred to go with the 1970

version ...

Tiresome nonsense like this is one reason why I have never once contributed to the great Loch Ness Monster on-line debate, which rages on Facebook, in comments boxes on websites and even in Amazon reviews. Devoting time to rectifying this kind of misrepresentation brings to mind the well known cartoon about the man hunched over his computer screen telling his female companion he can't come to bed because someone has said something wrong on the internet which he needs to correct.

If Roland Watson has discovered the earliest pictorial version by Campbell of his September 1933 sighting, then this is a welcome discovery, for which he is to be congratulated. However, I note that he does not reproduce the original full article in facsimile, only the sketch. He does not explain why the number '3' is attached to it (which implies there were at least two other accompanying Nessie sketches). His description of it as 'the earliest sketch of Campbell's monster' contains an ambiguity which he does not acknowledge. Is this a sketch *by* Campbell or is it someone else's version of what the witness described? Watson doesn't say. The distinction is an important one, since writers such as Rupert Gould, Constance Whyte and Tim Dinsdale all felt the need to mediate and filter original eye-witness testimony. Dinsdale can certainly be convicted of 'improving' eye-witness sketches to make them conform more to his own mental monster. Gould was undoubtedly guilty of the same urge.

Watson refers to 'the 1970 version' of Campbell's sketch but supplies no authority for his confident dating. Wiggins Teape *published* the sketch around this time, but when it was originally drawn is, as far as I'm aware, unknown. Tim Dinsdale's drawing of Campbell's 'monster', published in 1961, appears to be based on the one reproduced by Wiggins Teape, which would indicate a date at least ten years earlier.

Watson remarks sarcastically, 'Can't imagine why Binns preferred to go with the 1970 version ...' The answer is perfectly simple. I had never before seen the sketch he published on his blog on March 29, 2017. Nor, I'm sure, had anyone else. If Nicholas Witchell had known of this image I'm certain he would have been very pleased to use it in *The Loch Ness Story*. I don't doubt there's a lot of material out there in newspaper archives which was missed by those of us writing books before the arrival of the internet, online archives and search engines.

Watson's insinuation that in 1983 I *deliberately* chose not to use this newly discovered image is not only baseless but rather ironic, since he himself chooses to deny readers of his blog information which would allow them to make up their own minds. He does not reproduce Campbell's bird-like sketch or Dinsdale's version, which I used side by side to show how Campbell's own drawing of his 'monster' was compatible with a cormorant and to demonstrate how Dinsdale had 'improved' it, making it bigger and more classically monstrous in appearance.

The new sketch which Watson has discovered is perfectly compatible with the cormorant explanation. It is interesting to compare it with Dinsdale's re-drawn Campbell 'monster', which has a slender neck, a small head which is pointing slightly upward, and a massive body comprised of two joined humps. Dinsdale's grossly exaggerated version is plainly influenced by the Surgeon's photograph, but of course this iconic image of what the Loch Ness Monster should look like *did not yet exist* when the Campbell monster sketch was published in the *Scotsman* on November 15, 1933. This first version, interestingly, has a short stubby neck and an oval featureless head.

Watson goes on to criticise and quote 'another sceptic', but he shields his readers from such trifles as the name of this sceptic or where that person's sceptical interpretation might be found and read. Ultimately a web post like Watson's simply becomes an echo chamber in which the only voices to be heard are those of the blogger and his shrill chorus of supporters.

In a third, surprisingly intemperate article, Watson angrily defends Campbell from the charge that he was 'unreliable and possibly even untruthful'. He writes: 'Binns' tactic is psychological as he attempts to make Campbell look small in the eyes of the readers by criticising anything about him. It's a filthy tactic.' This is a distinctly unhinged reading of Chapter Five of *The Loch Ness Mystery Solved*, which simply points out, rather gently, all the inconsistencies surrounding Campbell's role in the Loch Ness story.

There are numerous contradictions and inconsistencies of detail between the many versions of Campbell's classic sighting, as anyone who cares to write them down side by side can discover for themselves. In *The Loch Ness Mystery Solved* I pointed out that Campbell had claimed eighteen sightings of the monster, a remarkable statistic when compared to the barren results obtained by others. Campbell claimed some very close encounters, yet he never once took a single photograph despite his amazing success rate. Watson's way around this difficulty is to claim that, because details of all these sightings are lacking, there must have been only 'about three visual sightings of note'. This is sheer speculation. Of course, even if it *were* true it wouldn't explain why Campbell failed to take any photographs or why his admirers did not request key details of these sightings (date, location, description of the Monster, and so on). Only one of Campbell's eighteen sightings was accompanied by a sketch.

3. The view from the road outside Alex Campbell's cottage. The entrance to the River Oich, with Loch Ness in the distance.

Most importantly of all, it is noticeable that Watson nowhere addresses Philip Stalker's devastatingly revealing description of Alex Campbell as 'a man who up to that time [September 1933] refused to believe of the existence in the loch of anything other than a seal or large marine animal of some kind'. It is hard to see how Stalker could have misunderstood Campbell on this point. The only conclusion which can be drawn from this episode is that Alex Campbell was indeed someone prepared to mislead others in order to promote his Monster.

Where Campbell's two versions of two sightings are concerned it is plain that *something* happened, but *what?*

Gould, who interviewed Campbell face-to-face, remarked that 'the element of "expectant attention" was, in my opinion, certainly present'. This is an intriguing observation because it suggests that Campbell, having invented the Loch Ness Monster, was then startled by the growing evidence for his private fantasy. He began to believe in his own fiction. He started watching the loch keenly. And in due course his surveillance was rewarded. *Expectant attention plus distant unidentifiable object equals Monster*: the recurring formula.

But Campbell then, perhaps, *unlearned* his sighting, just as Dick Raynor did some half a century or so later. In 1967 Raynor believed he had filmed a large unknown animal slicing through the loch surface, then crash-diving as *Scott II* arrived on the scene. So, too, did we all. But long experience of phenomena on the loch eventually suggested an alternative explanation. In June 1981 Raynor witnessed 'a family group of mergansers' behaving just like the 'monster' in his film.

What strikes me about Campbell's parallel deconstruction of his own sighting is just how *plausible* it is. He was a man who had learned how cormorants behave. He was also acquainted with the strange, magnifying effect of heat haze.

Later, when the Monster showed signs of resurrection, he helped it take flight with a resurrection of his own. His ancient cormorant sighting was reborn in its original monster format. It was May 2, 1933, all over again – only this time Campbell wasn't exaggerating someone else's sighting, he was reinventing one of his own. He also helped whet the appetites of others with inspiring news of his own encounters with the beast. In the first 24 years he had six sightings. Over the next 15 years he had twice as many. But on none of these occasions did he ever take a photograph, of anything – not even a wake.

To visit the site of Campbell's first sighting is enlightening, even though today it is obviously different in some ways to how it would have been in 1933. His perspective as an observer was a poor one, since he was standing beside the river, with a highly compressed view across the loch. He claimed the beast was 600 yards away (later reducing the figure to 400 yards). Accurate estimates of distance are notoriously unreliable in this kind of context and the location of his 'monster' is far from clear. It seems to have been first seen by Campbell at a point beyond the canal entrance but some distance from the shoreline beside the Abbey grounds.

Campbell's 'monster' is entirely consistent with his own

deconstruction. Standing beside the river, gazing towards the loch, eager to see the Monster, he saw a black shape cruise out from beyond the second of two promontories which obstructed his view of the south-west aspect of Borlum Bay. The sun was shining in his eyes, making identification difficult. The loch was flat calm and there was a morning mist across its surface. As the putative 'monster' moved out into the main body of the loch it was disturbed by the noise of two trawlers approaching from the nearby canal. The animal moved its head, trying to locate the source of the disturbance. Then, as the trawlers came into view, it dived (or *seemed* to dive, like the distant object[s] in the 1967 Raynor film, which quite possibly did not in fact dive but rose up from the loch surface and flew away, unseen against a dark background).

All of this is entirely consistent with one or more cormorants swimming out from beyond the Abbey boathouse. Campbell did not have binoculars with him. His explanation of the monster's head and neck as 'a cormorant standing in the water and flapping its wings' will persuade anyone who has seen this happen.

Alex Campbell's two radically conflicting versions of two apparently identical sightings perfectly illustrate how the case for a Monster based on the perception of unidentified phenomena can be deconstructed with a convincing naturalistic explanation. The man who invented the Loch Ness Monster was also among the first truly to understand one of its many identities.

5

Pictures of Nessie

It was a sorry piece of illustration of the old-fashioned sort, lacking definition and finish, but effective notwithstanding; for it was evidently the reproduction, through a cheap and imperfect process, of a photograph.

Erskine Childers, *The Riddle of the Sands* (1903)

The Hugh Gray Photograph

The Hugh Gray photograph remains the most ambiguous and contested of all the classic photographs. The contours of the dark serpentine figure in the image are hard to determine because it is blurred by areas of whiteness which might be light fogging, lack of focus, water spray or double exposure. Maurice Burton supplied the best description of any monster author when he wrote that the Gray photograph

> lacks definition but there is in it a dark, somewhat S-shaped object partially obscured by mist-like curtains rising almost vertically from its sides. There is also, on the far side of the object, a good deal of ill-defined patches of white that might be surf or foam.

The abstraction and imprecision of the image actively invites speculative interpretation. The original negative has to date never been located and is presumed lost. Conventional wisdom asserts that the image has not been touched up and was published uncropped (although where Nessie is concerned it is not exactly unknown for conventional wisdom to turn out to be false). The camera model which Gray used is also not known and has not survived, although it was apparently some kind of simple box camera.

Gray claimed to have been walking along the ridge which runs beside the shoreline west of the River Foyers as far as the cemetery. In December 1933, after selling the photograph to the Scottish *Daily Record*, he made the following statement:

> The loch was like a mill pond and the sun shining brightly. An object of considerable dimensions rose out of the water not so very far from where I was. I immediately got my camera ready and snapped the object which was then two to three feet above the surface of the water. I did not see any head, for what I took to be the front parts were under the water, but there was considerable movement from what seemed to be the tail, the part further from me. The object only appeared for a few minutes then sank out of sight.

Nowadays even the location of the sighting is contested. In his book *The Great Orm of Loch Ness* Ted Holiday confidently marked it with an 'X' on his map of Foyers, and from the perspective of the 1960s there did indeed seem to be only one location which allowed an unrestricted view of the loch. This was where the path terminated at a small steep headland just west of the Jane Fraser monument. In 1960 Tim Dinsdale visited Hugh Gray and was taken 'to the exact spot' from which he claimed to have taken his photograph. Maddeningly, Dinsdale did not indicate on his map of Foyers where that location was. Today, in the second decade of the twenty-first century, it is impossible to get an unrestricted view of Loch Ness from anywhere along this path, because of all the trees which have grown up along the lochside.

Ted Holiday wrote that Hugh Gray had already seen the Monster on a previous occasion and that he was carrying his camera in hope of getting a picture of the animal (though he supplied no source for these assertions). Gray told a reporter: 'I had hardly sat down on the bank when an object of considerable dimensions rose out of the loch two hundred yards away. I immediately got my camera into position and snapped the object which was two or three feet above the surface of the water. I did not see any head but there was considerable motion from what I thought was the tail. I cannot give any definite option as to its size or appearance except that it was of great size.'

Tim Dinsdale, who interviewed Gray some 27 years later, supplied a slightly different account: 'suddenly, about a hundred yards offshore he saw a great upheaval of water, and then a tremendous disturbance and splashing, caused by some huge animal thrashing about. He estimated he could see about 40 ft. of it – a thick rounded back, and what appeared to be a powerful tail.' After talking to Gray, Dinsdale was convinced of his veracity. He concluded that Gray's description of the episode 'fitted the facts recorded by Mrs. Whyte in every detail'.

Constance Whyte had interviewed Gray in May 1955:

> He was looking down from a height of 30 feet or so when suddenly there was a terrific upheaval of the water followed by a terrific commotion about a hundred yards out, and about 40 feet of a thick rounded back and a powerful tail came in sight but the head was submerged... The creature lashed about furiously and was so enveloped in spray that further details could not be distinguished... Because there was so much splashing and also because he was busy with the camera, Mr Gray did not have the opportunity to observe the creature closely.

When pressed to supply further details, Gray said that the size was 'very great' and that the phenomenon 'was a dark greyish colour, the skin was glistening and appeared to be fairly smooth'.

Gray told Whyte that the occasion on which he took his photograph was his first sighting, but that he had since seen the monster a further five times. Gray mentioned to Dinsdale how he had seen the monster's wake on 'several' occasions: he 'described in graphic terms the extraordinary bow wave building up, rushing down the loch at extraordinary speed, *without anything visible* making it'. This last aspect, italicised, was something Dinsdale was keen to stress, since it helped to validate his very questionable insistence that the mystery object in his own 1960 film could be seen to submerge. Neither Whyte nor Dinsdale seem to have recorded the detail of Gray's other monster sightings, or if they did they never published them. There is a strange lack of curiosity among the monster faithful regarding key witnesses in the Loch Ness story who claimed multiple sightings. The most notorious example is Alex Campbell. In the vast literature about the Loch Ness Monster there is no complete list of the sightings claimed by Gray and Campbell. We do not know what it was they saw, or where they saw it, or when they saw it. No one thought to ask them. The Loch Ness story is one which will always remain inconclusive where certain key individuals are concerned.

In *The Loch Ness Mystery Solved* I suggested that Gray's

photograph was a hoax. It could not have been taken from that ridge at a distance of 100-200 yards on a simple box camera without capturing the shoreline and its foliage in the foreground (or indeed much more of the loch surface). The scale is all wrong. The only way round that objection would be if the image had been cropped by the *Daily Record* – something which has always been denied. Secondly, it is an amazing coincidence that on Wednesday, November 29 the *Inverness Courier* reported Lieutenant Commander Rupert Gould's amazing conclusion that Loch Ness contained a sea-serpent and just two days later, on Friday December 1, Hugh Gray's brother took a roll of film which purported to show this creature into an Inverness chemist. Significantly, the shape of the object in Hugh's photograph is *serpentine*. Finally, I queried what the connection might be between Hugh Gray and the Alex Gray who, earlier that year, had floated a barrel in the loch and sought to catch the monster using baited hooks. Were they brothers?

Interpretation of the image has been very varied. Rupert Gould's view that it was 'undoubtedly genuine' was duly echoed by Whyte and Dinsdale and later Nessie enthusiasts. Even Maurice Burton accepted Gray's probity, but he detected 'signs of a great deal of turbulence' which reinforced the 'reasonable' conclusion that what the photograph showed was a 'tree trunk buoyed by the gases of its own decay'. Later he changed his mind and decided that it showed an otter. Steuart Campbell suggested that Gray was not truthful about either his distance from the object or its size: 'The geometry of the picture indicates that the camera was at an angle of about 12° to the plane of the water, and that Gray was much closer to the object than he admitted.' In short: what was photographed was no monster.

Campbell seems to have been the first person to publicise the theory that what was photographed was 'a Labrador dog swimming towards the camera with a stick in its mouth'. More recently Darren Naish has argued that the image involves 'possible double exposure' (which is plausible, since waves can be seen showing through what might be interpreted as the torso of the Monster) and that the object photographed was actually a swan. But Roland Watson, who is offended by the suggestion that a well-respected local man such as Gray could have been capable of fraud, insists that it does show the monster, and that at the right end of the object an eye and an open mouth can be identified.

Such is the ambiguity of the image that all three interpretations seem quite convincing when viewed in isolation. I have no problem at all seeing the Labrador dog or the swan or the monster with a gaping mouth. But I am not myself persuaded that any of those explanations holds the solution to the image. Context is everything where the Loch Ness story is concerned. Two reasons for doubting Gray's veracity can be found in the literature of the believers. The first is found in Gould.

Rupert Gould illustrated his pioneering monster book with photographs by Gray and R. K. Wilson and a frame from some film attributed to 'Messrs. Irvine, Clinton and Hay, of Scottish Film Productions Ltd.' Gould was meticulous in tracking down eye-witnesses and getting them to describe their experiences. No one ever seems to have noticed that this attention to detail vanished when it came to the evidence supplied by photographers. This is unlikely to have been laziness on Gould's part. A more probable explanation is that none of these photographers wanted to discuss their pictures with him. In retrospect it is rather obvious why R. K. Wilson would have chosen to avoid at all costs interrogation by such a relatively knowledgeable inquisitor as Lieutenant Commander Gould.

Hugh Gray's address was published in the national press ('The Bungalow, Foyers') and Gould found the photograph 'both interesting and undoubtedly genuine', which makes it all the odder that he supplies no detail about the circumstances of its taking, other than the day, the distance and a location given as 'near Foyers'. For a man with a mania for fine detail this vagueness is peculiar. Reticence on Hugh Gray's part seems a far more likely explanation than lack of interest on Gould's.

The other peculiarity is the unexplained transformation in Tim Dinsdale's attitude to the photograph. In *Loch Ness Monster* he describes meeting Gray and being bowled over by his obvious sincerity. Gray spoke 'with complete conviction' and Dinsdale had no doubt whatever that his camera had captured 'some huge animal thrashing about'. But twelve years later, in *The Story of the Loch Ness Monster*, Dinsdale's tone is noticeably cooler. He conceded the possibility that the photograph might have been 'touched up to create the impression of spray' and concluded that 'There are other features in it which are peculiar'. It is a less than enthusiastic endorsement.

Is the Hugh Gray photograph a fake? My own view remains that yes, it is. The object in the picture probably owes something to the giant eel hypothesis which was popular in the local and national newspapers of 1933. The photograph may well have been inspired by the publication on Wednesday, November 29 of a report in the *Inverness Courier* that Commander Rupert Gould had investigated the sightings and concluded that Loch Ness contained a sea-serpent. Since it was just two days later, on Friday December 1, that Hugh Gray's brother took a roll of film purporting to show the monster into an Inverness chemist, my guess is that the Hugh Gray photograph was actually taken on the intervening Thursday, November 30, and not, as he claimed, eighteen days earlier.

The one thing which is indisputable is that the object in the picture is *serpentine* in shape. The difficulty lies in establishing its outlines. Whatever it was that Gray photographed it was surely an artefact, not a living animal. I don't believe he took his photograph from the path that runs west of the River Foyers to the Jane Fraser memorial. Like Steuart Campbell, I believe that the object is very much closer to the camera than Gray claimed, and very much smaller. It was probably less than a yard in length, photographed in shallow water and just two or three yards from the camera. Since Gray was a fitter at the Foyers aluminium factory he probably had little difficulty in constructing a model monster. The components of his fake monster remain unidentifiable, although I think it helps to tip the photograph on its side, so that the tail/neck at the left of the image appears at the top. Looked at from this perspective the object looks more rigid – I can see a tiller, the wing of a model aircraft, a paddle... The clue to the object's identity, I suspect, lies in those two mysterious blobs located on the dark spine of the model. Ted Holiday was quick to identify them as 'lateral organs of the Orm' but to my mind they are much more indicative of some piece of machinery or metallic material used to concoct the 'monster'. Perhaps one day someone will persuasively identify what they are.

Tim Dinsdale believed that he had. He discussed the Hugh Gray photograph one final time in his last book publication, the fourth edition of *Loch Ness Monster* (1982). Here he describes how, when he held the image at arm's length, he 'noticed that the two bulbous objects at the side of the "sinuous shape" looked very much like hard-hatted divers helmets! Once seen in this light it is difficult to ignore the similarity, which is sufficiently real to cause doubt...'. This is not an analysis I find persuasive. As Dinsdale admits, the notion that Gray *unwittingly* photographed divers at work can be ruled out. But a hoax involving two divers and a fake monster of very substantial dimensions seems to me far less plausible than that the Gray picture involved a small model photographed at close quarters.

When Hugh Gray took his hoax photograph I am quite sure he never anticipated the consequences. At the time it must have seemed like a harmless prank. Selling the print to a Scottish popular newspaper must have earned Gray an agreeable sum which probably compared very favourably to his wages as a fitter in the local aluminium factory. It was all just a bit of innocent fun. A bogus monster picture harms no one. And then came the unexpected consequences. Suddenly he was up before the local establishment, being interrogated. On December 6 'he was interviewed at Foyers by Bailie MacKenzie (now Sir Hugh MacKenzie, C.B.E., J.P.), Mr Peter Munro representing the British Aluminium Company, and a member of the staff of the *Daily Record*'. He was obliged to make a statement. Things were suddenly starting to spiral out of control.

Viewed from a sceptical perspective, Gray's statement has some curious features. He saw the monster for 'a few minutes' – a generous length of time, which would make any modern monster-watcher throb with joy. But instead of referring to the animal he claims to have seen, Gray refers only to 'An object... the object... The object.' This can be interpreted as an admirable reluctance to speculate or as slippery equivocation by a hoaxer, according to taste. Significantly, R. K. Wilson was equally evasive and reluctant to say that the object in his photograph was an animal. When pressed further, Gray declined to estimate the size of the object, saying only that it was 'very great'. He also added that it was a dark, greyish colour with glistening skin and 'appeared to be fairly smooth'. For someone who was relatively close to the monster and who watched it for several minutes, *he says nothing which is in any way illuminating.*

To Roland Watson the suggestion that the picture is a hoax involves an unwarranted assault on the reputation of a churchgoer and a widely respected local man. He may of course be right, but I do not myself share his rosy view of humanity. It is a common feature of modern life that respected individuals (even churchgoers and priests) sometimes turn out to have a very dark side indeed. The admiration of one's peers is no guide to individual probity. The greatest serial killer in British history turned out to be a much-admired local doctor.

Gray himself is a shadowy figure, about whom little is actually known. Gray could scarcely have foreseen that he would become an historic figure in a global legend, or that decades later people like Tim Dinsdale would come knocking on his front door. The extraordinary saga of the Cottingley fairies shows how a small, innocent prank can have substantial, enduring and wholly unwelcome and unforeseen consequences.

It should also be remembered that when Gray produced his image there was no consensus about what the Loch Ness monster looked like. The iconic image of the monster (the Surgeon's) did not yet exist. Gould's book on the monster, packed with illustrations, was not yet written. Towards the end of 1933 there was a clutter of incongruous and contradictory sighting reports but no pictorial clues and no template monster. The plesiosaur-style monster equipped with four flippers, a long neck and a small head had yet to become the defining image of Nessie. For a hoaxer, this would raise the question of what shape the monster should actually take. Hugh Gray's ambiguous, serpentine monster perfectly fitted the bill for that moment in time.

Of course the final impediment to accepting the veracity of Hugh Gray and his photograph is simply that no one has taken a photograph which remotely resembles his over the past 80 years at Loch Ness. No one nowadays sees huge creatures displaying forty feet of back thrashing around at the loch surface, creating immense turbulence. That kind of lively, jumbo Loch Ness Monster has long since gone out of fashion.

The Surgeon's Photograph

In discussing the Surgeon's photograph in *The Loch Ness Mystery Solved*, I concluded that, although the image had been subject to multiple interpretations, 'The available evidence points strongly in the direction of a hoax.' I wrote that the object pictured 'may simply have been a model which Wilson threw into the loch' and that it was 'possibly only ten or twelve inches in height'. I even made a simple model and photographed it to show how easy it is to reproduce a reasonable likeness of the image.

My opinion clashed with all the classic monster authors. Tim Dinsdale echoed the conventional wisdom when he asserted that 'the sincerity and integrity of the photographer could not be questioned'. In *Loch Ness Monster* Dinsdale devoted an entire chapter to the picture, modestly revealing that his personal technical expertise as a photographer and an engineer enabled him to perceive features in the image which other less well qualified individuals had failed to perceive. Dinsdale ruled out fraud: 'As a photographer I could see much that suggested it was not [a fake], from a purely technical point of view'. But there was more.

The detail in the picture was obscure, so difficult to see in fact I must have peered at it at least a dozen times before noticing anything unusual, and then only because I had held the photo away from me at arm's length.

He had spotted 'obscure marks' in the image. Only a certain sort of professional could understand their significance:

It concerned a fundamental physical law with which, as an engineer, I was familiar. Had I not been in this category of persons I could not have known what this point, or the secondary meaning, was. Altogether the subtleties involved in the picture proved beyond doubt that it was genuine.

More sustained peering yielded 'three other significant features in the picture which had previously escaped attention'.

Dinsdale magisterially concluded that, not only did the object match important aspects of eye-witness sightings, but that part of the two forward flippers were protruding above the loch surface around the neck. Further back, 'it is possible to make out a second smaller ring of ripples, caused by some disturbance well to the rear of the neck…this proves irrefutably that with the neck appearing in the position shown, there is also a part of the animal underwater, considerably behind it'.

In *The Loch Ness Mystery Solved* I concluded that the Surgeon's photograph was probably a hoax. Among those untroubled by this possibility were Paul LeBlond and Michael Collins of the Department of Oceanography at the University of British Columbia, who four years later presented a paper to a meeting of the International Society of Cryptozoology. 'The Wilson Nessie Photo: A Size Determination Based on Physical Principles' asserted that the size of the object in the photograph could be determined scientifically through a calculation involving the surface disturbance and wind speed. This enabled comparisons to be made which resulted in an objective estimate of the object's height above the water surface as being 1.2 metres (four feet).

The passage of time has demonstrated just how comically deluded Dinsdale, LeBlond and Collins all were in their supposedly scientific analysis of an image which we now know was indeed a hoax.

To underline my argument that the Surgeon's photograph might simply feature a model some ten or twelve inches in height, I constructed a look-alike model and photographed it in the loch (Plate 3,

The Loch Ness Mystery Solved). This turns out to have been an amazingly percipient piece of guesswork. Thanks to David Martin and Alastair Boyd, we now know that all along the most impressive and influential Nessie photograph in existence did indeed involve nothing more than a model some twelve inches in height. Whereas my model Nessie involved the cardboard outline of a head and neck, cut from a cereal box, stuffed into the neck of an empty Perrier glass water bottle and wrapped in black polythene sliced from a garbage bag, the Surgeon's monster was altogether more sophisticated. My own model Nessie was a fairly crude construction, knocked together in ten minutes. By contrast Christian Spurling, who manufactured the Wilson 'monster', possessed real flair as a craftsman. It took him 'about eight days' to create his miniature monster. Spurling's creative skill lent the finished product a grace and conviction which gave it enormous appeal as an image of a strange, unknown animal.

4. Message in a bottle. The 'Perrier' Monster (1981)

'The life of a deliberate hoax is usually short,' wrote Rupert Gould, revealing that his understanding of hoaxes was somewhat inferior to his knowledge of the marine chronometer. The famous Cottingley fairy photographs were taken in 1917 and 1920 and as late as 1976 Elsie

Wright and Frances Griffiths were still denying that they were faked. It was another seven years before the by-now elderly pranksters finally confessed. Similarly, the 1934 Surgeon's photograph hoax was exposed only after sixty years, and also involved a confession from someone who didn't have long to live.

The investigation carried out by David Martin and Alastair Boyd unpicked the unexpectedly complex chain of events which lay behind a photograph which, ever since 1934, had provided the single most compelling piece of evidence for the existence of the Loch Ness monster. Their findings, published in the *Sunday Telegraph* (March 13, 1994) were devastating.

As they explained, this stunningly successful hoax was masterminded by Marmaduke Wetherell, hitherto a somewhat marginal figure in the Loch Ness story. His stepson, Christian, created the fake Nessie using plastic wood and a clockwork toy submarine purchased from the Richmond branch of Woolworth's by Wetherell's son, Ian. Christian explained that, although the construction of his monster involved 'sheer imagination', he felt it should look 'like a sea-serpent'. Ian Wetherell then photographed the model at Loch Ness at close quarters, on a Leica camera. Someone – possibly Maurice Chambers – then 'changed the prints from 50mm to quarter-plate' and R. K. Wilson then duly took the credit for photographing an unknown animal in Loch Ness.

The Martin and Boyd investigation is illuminating in a number of ways, apart from their exposure of the convoluted story behind the hoax. One is the way in which a somewhat arbitrary prank snowballed in a wholly unanticipated way. By the end of 1934 the Loch Ness monster appeared to be close to extinction – a silly-season story which had begun to lose its news value. No one could have anticipated how it would be massively reborn a quarter of a century later. Those involved in the hoax forgot about it and got on with their lives, unaware that the photograph would generate commentary that would endure for decades. Those who knew the truth about this image were oblivious to the great Nessie subculture.

Writing *The Loch Ness Mystery Solved*, I had discovered that by going back to the files of the *Inverness Courier* a very different picture of events in 1933 emerged to that conventionally given in classic monster books. I also pointed out that the Loch Ness story was riddled with inconsistencies and contradictions which were never acknowledged or discussed by monster buffs. My co-author Rod Bell had always been astonished by the way in which Alex Campbell had explained his 'plesiosaur' monster sighting as involving the misperception of a group of cormorants, only to subsequently reinvent it later as an authentic monster sighting. Nowhere in monster literature had anyone acknowledged or commented on this glaring contradiction. No one had ever challenged Campbell about the inconsistencies surrounding his classic sighting. Throughout his lifetime he enjoyed the role of monster guru, with a succession of admirers making their way to his door in search of enlightenment and invigoration.

In their pursuit of the truth behind the Surgeon's photograph, Martin and Boyd similarly discovered just how inward-looking and sloppy monster literature had been, complaining that 'it is obvious that time and time again the same information has simply been lifted from one text to the next without any true research into the facts between the individual publications'. Over two pages they list the radical inconsistencies between Wilson's account as given to the *Daily Mail* in April 1934 and the versions which appear in books by Constance Whyte and Nicholas Witchell. The contradictions extend to eleven different aspects of Wilson's supposed sighting. They also raise unanswered questions about why, when previously unknown evidence that the picture was a hoax came privately to the attention of certain monster authors, they blanked it out. Even more astonishing is how on December 7, 1975, the *Sunday Telegraph* published the claim that a classic Nessie photograph was a hoax involving a toy submarine, this remarkable revelation was simply ignored by the monster fraternity. (I was abroad for most of 1975, including December, so I never knew about this item. Not that I would normally have bought this particular newspaper, preferring the *Observer* and the *Sunday Times*.)

My own research concentrated on 1933 and went no further. When Alastair Boyd researched publications for the year 1934 he came across a full, uncropped print of the Surgeon's photograph in the *Illustrated London News* (April 28, 1934). The full print is far less compelling than the conventional cropped version. As is so often the case, the truth about the Loch Ness monster can be found just as much in a library as at the loch.

In the face of the findings of Martin and Boyd the supposedly 'scientific' calculations of Paul LeBlond and Michael Collins collapsed like a house of cards. The object had not been photographed by R. K. Wilson, whose descriptions of the circumstances under which the photograph had been taken were false. The date and time when the photograph was taken could not be precisely determined, therefore calculations based on wind information for 7am on April 19, 1934, were meaningless. Even the precise location was unknown. The final nail in the coffin was the ease with which the photograph could be replicated at Loch Ness, using a model twelve inches high.

Boyd and Martin's account is both plausible and persuasive, and it has generally been accepted as an authentic account of how and why the Surgeon's photograph was created. However, a tiny minority of fringe dissenters continue to insist that Christian Spurling's confession was fraudulent and that he and Ian Wetherell fabricated the toy submarine story, 'seeking revenge upon Nessie for their father's humiliation'.

Karl Shuker argues that the circular ripples around the object contradict the claim that a moving toy submarine was photographed. He asserts that 'The type of clockwork toy submarine available at that time could not have supported such an unwieldy structure as a model of the head-and-neck without being in serious danger of overbalancing'. He also suggests that the second Surgeon's photo might well indicate that the object shown in the first picture was alive and had changed its position, and he suggests it is 'a notable mystery' that the 1975 'Mandrake' article revealing that 'the most famous Loch Ness monster picture of all time' was a fake attracted no further attention. Shuker also points to inconsistencies between what Ian Wetherell said about the construction of the model monster and Christian Spurling's account.

The variations between what Wetherell said and what Spurling said have an obvious explanation. By the time David Martin and Alastair Boyd were on the case the trail had gone very cold. Ian Wetherell was unavailable for interview because he was dead. Spurling seems to have been the one with the skill and the patience and the one who had most to do with building the model monster. But Spurling was not personally involved with photographing the model at Loch Ness, so his account is not a first-hand one. The precise circumstances of that event will now never be known – the date, the time, the location, or indeed how the ripples were caused. Nor, now, can the context, identity or purpose of the second photograph ever be confidently established. The solution to these riddles died with Ian Wetherell.

Many of Shuker's objections have in any case already been dealt with by Boyd and Martin in their well-researched book. The 'Mandrake' article never actually identified the photograph in question and in 1975 names like Ian Wetherell and 'Chambers, an insurance broker' meant nothing at the time to anyone interested in Nessie. If Wetherell and Spurling had really been engaged in a conspiratorial joint enterprise to discredit the Monster they would surely have had a second go at attracting publicity after the 'Mandrake' article failed to engage anyone's interest. The reality is that, after the spoof first succeeded in 1934, most of the participants then forgot about it. Only Wilson had to put up with the attentions of Nessie enthusiasts, and it is very revealing that he shunned them, beginning, most probably, with Rupert Gould.

Those most directly involved in the hoax were blissfully unaware of the developing Loch Ness Monster cult, with its experts and books and monster hunts. It is perhaps hard for anyone suffering from monster fever to realise that *most people actually aren't at all interested in the subject.*

The height of the object in the first photograph is unquestionably twelve inches, as is proven by the ease with which the image can be convincingly duplicated at Loch Ness using a model of this size. The calculations of LeBlond and Collins are worthless, since they are based on demonstrably false assumptions. Shuker's claim that the toy submarine would have overbalanced fails to consider Spurling's very specific memory of soldering a small strip of lead to the model to give it stability.

Remarkably, even the level-headed sceptic Steuart Campbell decided that the hoax story was bogus. In the original 1986 edition of *The Loch Ness Monster: The Evidence*, prior to Boyd and Martin's exposé, he argued that it was possible to calculate that the height of the object was some 70 cm and its distance from the camera was around 30 metres: 'This size is consistent with it being the tail of an otter. The shape is also consistent with this explanation.'

In the 1996 edition Campbell stuck to his original analysis. He contacted Alastair Boyd, asking how a model could create ripple rings and what explanation there was for the second photograph: 'Boyd declined to discuss the case with me or provide additional information.' He concluded, 'One may suspect that the story of a model is itself a hoax.'

What is portrayed in the second photograph is an enigma which will probably never be solved. However, the surface condition of the unidentifiable water surface is quite different to that shown in the first image. As for the circular ripples in the first, famous image, the precise circumstances in which the fake monster was photographed are unrecorded. The truth died with Marmaduke Wetherell and his son Ian.

But that the object was a toy submarine is beyond reasonable doubt. Probably the photograph captures it as it bobbed to the surface after being submerged.

Ironically, when Tim Dinsdale thought he could spot part of the two front flippers protruding above the loch surface forward of the neck, what he was actually seeing was *the front part of the submarine*. And in a comically deluded deconstruction of the object, Denys Tucker noted how the final proof that this was a living animal was revealed by the sheet of water 'cascading off the hump in much the same way as it does from the hull of a submarine'.

Quite.

My only regret where David Martin and Alastair Boyd are concerned is that they sold their scoop to the *Sunday Telegraph* in 1994 and did not publish their findings in book form for another five years. By this time the market for a book on this subject had gone cold, and they were obliged to self-publish a paperback only 100 pages in length. I can't help thinking they would instead have been better advised to write a full-length book about their sensational discoveries and sell the *Sunday Telegraph* exclusive rights to publish extracts prior to publication.

What is missing from their admirable but belated publication is any account of the long history of this iconic image in monster lore. It would have been interesting to trace the history of this image and the kind of analysis it provoked among Gould, Whyte, Dinsdale, Holiday and all the other commentators who felt they held the key to its interpretation. Looking back at the quantity of earnest, ingenious analysis this image of a modified toy submarine provoked is a monstrously revealing exercise.

Lachlan Stuart

James Carney's contemporary tourist booklet *The Loch Ness Monster* reproduces this 1951 photograph of three humps with a caption which asserts that Stuart 'later confessed that the "humps" were in fact floating bales of hay covered in tarpaulin'. This is misleading since there is no primary evidence of any such confession, merely a claim by local Loch Ness sceptic Richard Frere that Stuart had privately confessed to him. Roland Watson has made a very convincing case for doubting Frere's claim (which was first made decades after the photograph was published). It also has to be questioned if the objects seen in the image are free-floating, since aligning them would be extraordinarily difficult in the rough surface conditions shown in the picture.

If there was no such confession, why would Frere lie? One possible answer might be that, as a local resident with a distinctly proprietorial attitude to the loch, he was keen to discourage fresh waves of monster hunters from clogging up his cherished locality. Frere was not a reliable transmitter of information, as is demonstrated by his account of the St Columba water beast encounter, in which the animal 'swam off, with undulating humps'. Those humps belonged to Frere's imagination, not the text he was summarising. Here Frere mocks 'seekers after the True Monster', but not even the most fervent believer has ever distorted the Columba narrative quite like that.

In my younger days Stuart's picture was always my second favourite monster photograph. It is as iconic in its own way as the Surgeon's. There is something magical and other-worldly about those three mysterious stark black triangular humps, captured just off-shore at dawn in what is unmistakably Loch Ness. But although Stuart's 'confession' to Frere must be doubted, this is not to say that he photographed a monster. I had never actually bothered to investigate the location of this photograph until 1981, when I returned on a research trip to Loch Ness as part of writing *The Loch Ness Mystery Solved*.

On the day I rolled up to Whitefield, the surface of the loch had dropped, and I was stunned to discover just how shallow the water was along the length of shoreline where Stuart took his photograph. The giveaway evidence was the sight of rocks, much further out than I'd ever expected to see at Loch Ness. I took photographs of one for the book (plates 6(a) and 6(b)). I was amused to discover three years later that Steuart Campbell seems to have harboured doubts about my rock photographs: 'Binns appears to have found one out from the shore', he wrote, with an implicit note of scepticism. In reality my use of a telephoto lens simply created a foreshortening effect that made the rock appear mid-loch. It was another rather rudimentary example of how photography can deceive. A spectacular example of 'forced perspective' is shown in Karl Shuker's book *Mirabilis*, in which a monstrous cryptid called a gorgakh, alleged to feast on human corpses, was quickly identifiable as a dead pangolin held very close to the camera lens to make it seem enormous in comparison to the people behind it.

The complacent ignorance of some Nessie hunters is underlined by an episode from the nineteen-sixties described in David and Yvonne Cook's book *The Great Monster Hunt*. After an inconclusive sighting of a possible monster seen from their moving car on the south shore road beyond Dores, they described the event to LNI volunteers. David Cook thought they might simply have glimpsed rocks but his wife was convinced it had been the beast. One volunteer confidently told them it *must* have been the monster because 'There are absolutely no rocks showing above the water between Dores and Foyers. Not even one, much less the two humps you saw.'

This was complete nonsense. It's a very good example of the kind of misinformation related by enthusiastic believers whose ignorance of the loch's geography, habitat and history was far more comprehensive than they ever understood. In reality there are rocks at numerous locations along Loch Ness, including between Dores and Foyers, but their visibility is restricted by trees and bushes and varies according to the height of the loch surface, which is notoriously open to sudden and dramatic change after heavy rainfall.

The Stuart photograph was plainly influenced by the current conventional wisdom about the Loch Ness Monster, as enshrined in Rupert Gould's book. Gould was a confirmed believer in multi-humped monsters (including Mr Morrison's six humped monster and Mr Goodbody's remarkable eight humped beast) and it would not be until the decade following the Stuart picture that Peter Baker and his team would conclude that such phenomena were simply boat wakes misperceived by inexperienced and over-excited observers. Even today people still report and film 'monsters' which are very obviously wakes generated by boats.

As I argued in *The Loch Ness Mystery Solved*, the objections to the Stuart photograph are threefold. There is no wake, the angular humps are very slightly out of alignment (suggesting three separate objects) and, most tellingly of all, 'the objects photographed are extremely close to the shore and in shallow water.' This is not a quick, hurried snapshot of a moving object but rather an artfully posed picture. In my book I did not speculate what the three objects might be, although I thought it entirely possible that a rock might have been used as the base for at least one section of whatever Stuart and his associate Taylor Hay were using to simulate a monster – whether bales of hay wrapped in tarpaulin or some other materials. There may even have been two rocks used, but no more than that since three aligned rocks at this location would scarcely escape notice. Roland Watson is over-hasty in his dismissal of rocks and Nessie.

There are analogies with the Hugh Gray sighting. Despite a sensationally close sighting, Stuart was vague about the monster's appearance. He was interrogated by Maurice Burton, who reported that Stuart 'saw no feature that marked this object as an animal – and none shows in the photograph'. The picture probably originated as a harmless prank – with the added bonus of an agreeable cash payment from a national newspaper. What Stuart could not have anticipated was how matters would snowball, or that how his photograph would endure as a subject of fascination and speculation for decades afterwards. Constance Whyte was just one of many pilgrims to the Stuarts' rented cottage. She reported how his wife's attitude was 'a mixture of boredom at the constant intrusions and incredulity that the matter could be of so much interest'. In due course the couple left Loch Ness and vanished into obscurity – yet another story left incomplete and open-ended.

The Cockrell Photograph

In 1958 H. L. Cockrell's photograph of the monster was splashed across the front page of the *Scotsman* and subsequently reproduced in Tim Dinsdale's *Loch Ness Monster*. Several monster authors ignore it, which is odd, since from a believer's perspective the object portrayed perfectly fits the image of a long-necked creature with a humped back and is consistent with Cockrell's description of his encounter with a large swimming creature.

This lack of enthusiasm probably stemmed from Cockrell's own hesitancy about identifying his photograph as Nessie and his admission that, when he closed in on the location of his sighting, he found only a four foot long stick, around one inch thick. Roy Mackal concluded that Cockrell had indeed photographed a stick or log and attributed this episode to 'a combination of fatigue from three nights of activity on Loch Ness and a tremendous psychological bias of belief and expectation'.

In *The Loch Ness Mystery Solved* I observed that Cockrell's monster 'greatly resembles a floating stick; in some prints of the photograph it is even possible to see *through* the curving "hump".' I also dryly noted that the image supplied a 'convenient' climax to a series of articles which Cockrell was writing for the newspaper which published his photograph. Caution is always advisable when monster hunters contact the media announcing an impending expedition, then visit the loch and promptly have a sighting and obtain a photograph.

The image itself is problematic in so far as it exists in different versions (for reasons which probably have nothing to do with Cockrell). I contacted Cockrell when I was writing my book, asking permission to use his picture. He wrote back giving me details of the agency which was handling his photograph. The publisher paid the required fee (which I think was £50 – the going rate to reproduce a Nessie picture in a book in 1983) and the agency supplied a print. But the image supplied was radically cropped, and also lacked the white patch beside the central 'hump' which I interpreted as a gap in the object. The print used in Dinsdale's *Loch Ness Monster* is also cropped and is smaller than the one supplied to Maurice Burton for his book. Cockrell's 'monster' in Burton shows a white mark at the base of the putative hump; the same monster in Dinsdale does not.

The Cockrell photograph is actually the second of two images taken that morning. In 2016 the earlier picture was published for the first time, having been tracked down by Roland Watson. In a detailed analysis, using uncropped prints of both photographs, Watson makes the case for Cockrell having genuinely had an encounter with the monster. The object appears to have changed its position between the first and second photograph (although this is not in itself proof that it is animate, since the photographer had also changed his position on the loch).

Is it a living animal? What is odd is that the object shows no sign at all of leaving a wake or causing any kind of ripples at the surface, even though the loch was almost flat calm. Cockrell interpreted his photograph differently:

> The film showed quite a large affair which had a distinct wash. There was no reason for this wash as the picture also shows the water mirror calm when the snap was taken by the reflection of the hills. What caused the wash? Could it have been Nessie after all? I just don't know.

It is true that there are ripples in the foreground, where the loch surface reflects the sky, but they are most probably the result of wind action. The nearest ones do not align with the 'monster' but point ahead of it.

The object appears as inert as the objects portrayed in the Lachlan Stuart and Peter O'Connor photographs. Cockrell's putative monster in fact bears some resemblance to two original photographs used in *The Loch Ness Mystery Solved*. One shows a log floating in Loch Ness, the other an otter gliding along at the surface (Plates 13 and 15(a)). The otter creates surface turbulence and a wake; the log, of course, does not. Watson, however, believes that surface disturbance can be perceived in the Cockrell image, but this strikes me as a wholly subjective interpretation.

As the foremost contemporary proponent of actually existing monsters in Loch Ness, Roland Watson is naturally indignant about my sceptical readings of the classic photographs. However, he is occasionally careless in his critiques. For example, he says:

Going back to log theories, by proposing that a log was behind the photo, Ronald Binns was basically accusing Herman Cockrell of being economical with the truth (because he only reported a puny stick).

In fact I made no such accusation, nor did I ever use the word 'log' (unlike Roy Mackal, who did use it). What I actually wrote was:

His 'monster' greatly resembles a floating stick; in some prints of the photograph it is even possible to see through the curving 'hump'. Cockrell described how a squall blew up and he lost sight of the object. When he paddled to the spot he did indeed find a stick.

Cockrell's description of the monster's appearance – 'It looked slightly whiskery and misshapen' – is entirely consistent with the object having been floating débris from a tree, whether or not it was a large branch or even the trunk. Now that we have a second photograph of the object it reveals one thing, which is that *the object did not change shape in any way*. This rather underlines its inert quality. An object which looks like floating débris from a tree, which does not leave a wake and which does not change shape, is much more likely to be floating débris from a tree than the notoriously splashy, frisky, shape-shifting monster (or for that matter any aquatic animal).

Cockrell wrote:

There was a light squall out of the glen behind Invermoriston, and the object appeared to sink. When the squall cleared I could still see

something on the surface. I closed in again cautiously. It remained
motionless and I found it was a long stick about an inch thick.

This object, however, cannot have been the one which he photographed,
which is plainly much more substantial.

Cockrell's own hesitancy and diffidence about the episode was
perhaps the reason why even monster enthusiasts were reluctant to
endorse his photograph as unambiguous evidence of the monster. It
must surely have been a terrifying experience for a believer like
Cockrell. In such circumstances, from a moving kayak, a stationary
object might well appear to be in motion, or even moving towards the
observer. In his sceptical analysis of the image Roy Mackal makes a
good point regarding fatigue and expectant attention on the part of the
photographer. The episode is reminiscent of the time Adrian Shine was
rowing on Loch Morar when he thought he saw the huge back of an
animal moving away from the shore. It turned out to be a trick of
perspective involving a rock and Shine's own trajectory in a moving
boat. Sightings of monsters by eye-witnesses in moving objects,
whether cars or boats, all too easily involve misperception.

The sudden squall which Cockrell reported and which rendered his
encounter with the monster problematic is curiously symbolic of the
larger Loch Ness narrative. Revelation occurs but resolution is always
deferred, always inconclusive.

Macnab

Even in my days as a fervent believer I never much liked the Macnab
photograph (massively enlarged, it was on display in the LNI HQ
information hut and appeared on the front of the LNI membership
application form). To my eyes the monster seemed too big and the two
humps too mismatched to be The Real Thing.

Roy Mackal was the first monster author to cast doubts on Peter
Macnab's probity, enquiring why two different versions of the print
existed, with the second one apparently having involved re-
photography of a print rather than a fresh print made from the original
negative. Gareth Williams identifies other problematic aspects:

> It is not blurred, as might be expected using a 135mm telephoto lens
> with shaking hands, no tripod and a relatively slow shutter speed.
> Also, the two-humped 'Monster' looks blacker and more clear-cut
> than everything else.

Roland Watson is offended by the suggestion of fraud, arguing that a man of Macnab's social status had no reason to risk his reputation. He dismisses both the suggestion of jiggery-pokery on Macnab's part and the idea that what was photographed was merely a standing wave. He revives the old theory that the photograph actually shows two monsters:

> If the object is one creature then it is huge even by normal Nessie standards. A size of 60 to 70 feet would not be out of place. This is too much for some and so is rejected. However, it is clear to me from what I said above that this is in fact two creatures as the humps are out of alignment and the wave structure is different between the two. In that light, the bigger hump is about 30 foot long and the smaller one about 13 feet long which brings the total dimensions of these creatures within the historical record.

Macnab said he had taken a second photograph but had later destroyed it and the original negatives appear to be lost.

My own interpretation of this photograph is unchanged, in so far as I believe the object shown is nothing more than a wake. As I wrote in *The Loch Ness Mystery Solved* I was once on duty at the LNI camera site at Strone, in the garden of Basil and Winifred Cary, when three trawlers passed by in V-formation, heading for Fort Augustus. They were moving fast and creating huge wakes, which merged, with delightfully monstrous consequences. It struck me at the time how much the effect resembled the 'monster(s)' in the Macnab photograph. In retrospect I wish I had taken a photograph, but at the time I wasn't interested in negative evidence.

To my eyes the object in the Macnab photograph is plainly part of the right-hand arm of a wake from a vessel travelling west which has vanished from sight. Other water disturbance can be seen in the background (though Watson interprets these as residual wakes from other shipping which has passed by and which have nothing to do with the object photographed by Macnab).

The only question to my mind is whether or not Macnab manipulated the image simply by adjusting the contrast (which can indeed make a curling wave seem black and full-bodied, resembling the back of an animal) or whether he actively transgressed by doctoring the image with black ink.

Peter O'Connor

As an eager young monster hunter this was always my third favourite photograph (after the Surgeon's and Lachlan Stuart's). It looked just how the monster I believed in should have looked. Today, over half a century after it was produced, the startling object in the O'Connor picture has yet to be convincingly identified.

This is one of those photographs where context is everything. Just as Hugh Gray and his brother popped up with a serpentine Nessie photograph two days after the *Inverness Courier* reported Rupert Gould's 'sea-serpent' analysis, so Peter O'Connor stepped into the limelight with his picture just three days after Tim Dinsdale had appeared in the *Daily Mail* in the morning and on BBC TV in the evening. O'Connor's 'monster' was plainly inspired by the one Dinsdale claimed to have seen (which makes Dinsdale's assertion that the back of O'Connor's monster is 'exactly what I saw' deeply ironic).

Few believe the O'Connor picture to be anything other than a fake. The only mystery is what it was he employed to portray his sensational close-up 'monster'. Maurice Burton claimed to have found at the lochside evidence of material used by O'Connor to construct a model monster but his claim lacked credibility since he was patently unable to reproduce anything at all resembling the O'Connor photograph. More recently Dick Raynor has argued that O'Connor used a canoe for his monster's body. This is a plausible but not yet definitive analysis. The shape of the back of the 'monster' doesn't quite seem to match.

While writing *The Loch Ness Mystery Solved* I contacted Peter O'Connor. I received a longer letter back from him than I was expecting. He refused me permission to reproduce his photograph but insisted it was genuine.

The O'Connor picture remains an enigmatic image. Even for most believers it is just too good to be true. The photographer claimed that the monster glided past at a range of just 25 yards but there is not the slightest sign of a wake. The inertia of the object is, to my mind, the most telling contradiction of O'Connor's account.

It is significant, I think, that O'Connor subsequently became one of Britain's leading taxidermists. This rather grisly profession requires great skill in the reconstruction of dead matter to make it resemble a living animal.

6

Seals in Loch Ness

Seals have been observed in the river but only where it is tidal and never within miles of Loch Ness.

    Constance Whyte, *More Than a Legend* (1957)

In 1933 some leading zoologists were quick to identify the Loch Ness Monster as nothing more than a seal, 'in all likelihood, a large grey seal'. Rupert Gould noted that 'such seals have never been seen, hitherto, in Loch Ness' but conceded that the presence of such a creature could not absolutely be ruled out. Because seals were unknown in Loch Ness, their presence might well perplex an observer and 'might easily postpone its identification'. Moreover, several aspects of a seal's appearance and behaviour seemed to match reports from the loch:

> A grey seal has a long and surprisingly extensible neck; it swims with a paddling action; its colour fits the bill; and there is nothing surprising in its being seen on the shore of the Loch, or crossing a road.

But having conceded this much, Gould then proceeded to attack the seal theory with all guns blazing. The monster was *at least* 24 feet long – far too big for a seal. Besides, the head and neck were not remotely seal-like. Seals don't have tails, unlike the Monster, which Gould believed had a 'long tail'. A seal cannot bend its body into 'the line of humps so often observed'. The Loch Ness Monster 'often' manifests itself at the surface with 'a very violent commotion in the water' and displays 'a single large dark-coloured hump'. But a seal creates very little disturbance when swimming, and it displays its head, not its body. 'A seal has a powerful voice, and is not afraid to use it. No one has ever heard [the Loch Ness Monster] emit a sound of any sort.' What's more:

> The seal – an air-breather – usually breaks surface at short intervals in order to breathe. If once sighted, it could be followed with the naked eye for miles – since, even if swimming rapidly under water, it would probably come up every few hundred yards.

In a final crushing rejoinder to those sceptical zoologists, Gould cited eleven witnesses whose monster sightings appeared in his book. Every single one of them knew what seals looked like in water and every one of them told him they were certain that what they had seen was not a seal.

Constance Whyte reiterated many of these objections in *More Than a Legend*, and the seal theory faded from view. Even Maurice Burton, analysing the sighting of a witness who saw a mystery animal displaying 'a head the shape of a seal's head', was more inclined to perceive the behaviour of an otter.

The seal theory resurfaced in 1974, but in an unexpected form, when Peter Costello confidently identified Nessie as a new species of large, long-necked seal. 'It has reached the stage of giving birth in the water, which seals are only infrequently forced into doing', he helpfully explained. Costello derived his theory from his cryptid guru, the once-influential Belgian zoologist Bernard Heuvelmans.

When I wrote *The Loch Ness Mystery Solved* the conventional wisdom was that no seal had ever been seen in Loch Ness. My own personal experience of seals came from the Scottish coast. The seals I'd seen were in clusters. They bobbed up in groups. They were inquisitive and friendly and very obviously seals. How could anyone possibly mistake a seal for a monster? Gould was surely right.

The year after *The Loch Ness Mystery Solved* was published, half a century of received wisdom collapsed when a seal was spotted in Loch Ness. It was first seen on November 16, 1984, and it lived in the loch until June 11, 1985, when it was shot. This was the first authoritative record of a seal being present in the loch. Gordon R. Williamson subsequently wrote a paper about the episode, which observed: 'Fishermen's reports indicate that Loch Ness is visited by a seal approximately once every two years.'

Williamson found anecdotal evidence of seals being seen in the loch dating back to 1972 and concluded that 'seals have probably been visiting Loch Ness for thousands of years'. It is now a commonplace of sceptical analysis that seals form one part of the rich variety of miscellaneous phenomena which comprise 'the Loch Ness Monster'.

Daniel Loxton brings the record up to date and points out seal-like sightings which exist in the long inventory of Monster sightings. Adrian Shine has argued that the classic 1934 Margaret Munro land sighting involved a seal, although this interpretation inevitably reproduces the traditional dissension between scepticism and belief regarding perceptions of size and shape.

The classic sighting by Miss J. S. Fraser and three companions from the balcony of the Half-Way House tea room at Altsigh sounds very much as if the witnesses saw a seal. The Monster was observed for some ten minutes 'rising and sinking slightly from time to time…The head and neck rose almost vertically out of the water'. The creature exhibited 'what appeared to be a large glittering circular eye'. These descriptions are consistent with seal behaviour (the glittering eye was probably sunlight reflected off the seal's wet nose). Maurice Burton summed up sightings of this sort when he commented that the four witnesses 'saw an unfamiliar object at a distance of more than half a mile'. He also noted another potential source of error: 'the time that elapsed between the sighting and interview'. Of course a crypto-zoological literalist will dismiss such an explanation, by insisting that every detail given by the witnesses was precise. But, to a sceptic, what is more interesting is how the 'Monster' template was imposed on an unknown but explicable phenomenon by both the witnesses and by Gould.

My own knowledge and experience of seals is now much better than it was in 1983. Not all seals behave like the ones I saw off the Highland coastline. Seals can be shy, solitary creatures. Even at relatively close range they can look like black humps. When they raise their head and necks from the water they can indeed resemble Nessie. Like the monster they can drop abruptly from view. And seals on land don't always resemble the cuddly, whiskery seals of picture postcards.

Sometimes they look distinctly odd.

7

Not So Classical

'As I say, it's still there, so far as I know.'
  Rupert Gould, talking about the Loch Ness Monster (1937)

F. C. Adams (1934)

This photograph was first published (where else?) in the *Daily Mail*, August 25, 1934, attributed only to 'a visitor on holiday at Fort Augustus'. Forty years later Peter Costello identified the photographer as F. C. Adams, whereas Nicholas Witchell attributed it to one Dr James Lee. Classic authors like Constance Whyte and Tim Dinsdale make no mention of the photograph, which has largely been marginalised in Nessie literature. This was probably because there is no evidence it was taken at Loch Ness and it greatly resembles the dorsal fin of a large fish. This is not the head and neck of a monster moving to the left of the photographer but simply a fish swimming in the opposite direction. Doubts about the image are reinforced by the absence of any information about the photographer or the circumstances and location of the supposed sighting. In June 2016 Roland Watson published a substantial article describing his investigations into the background to the photograph, asserting that the animal portrayed cannot be, as some have suggested, a bottlenose dolphin. However, in November 2015 Gareth Williams' book *A Monstrous Commotion* was published, which identifies the image as showing the dorsal fin of a bottle-nosed porpoise – an identification made, authoritatively, by Professor David Sims of the Marine Biological Association, Plymouth. Since it seems very unlikely that there was a bottle-nosed porpoise in Loch Ness in the summer of 1934 this picture must therefore be identified as a hoax – a genuine photograph of a living animal fraudulently purporting to have been taken at Loch Ness for no other reason than to delude the gullible.

Jennifer Bruce (1982)

This photograph, taken by a tourist making her first visit to the loch, marked the beginning of a new genre of Nessie picture. This involved the casual taking of a landscape photograph which, when examined later, turned out to contain a mystery object presumed to be the Loch Ness Monster, even though nothing unusual had been observed at the time.

I had not seen this photograph when *The Loch Ness Mystery Solved* went to press, and when I did see it for the first time I was baffled by it. It shows what appears to be a sinuous head and neck protruding from the surface near Temple Pier. The photograph seems to have been taken from a lay-by. Steuart Campbell was equally puzzled. When *The Loch Ness Monster: The Evidence* appeared in 1986, his treatment of the Bruce photo was purely descriptive and offered no explanation of what it might show. This remained the case in the 1996 revised and updated edition.

The 'head and neck' seem altogether too sinuous for any type of aquatic creature – even Nessie. Whatever can it be that Bruce casually snapped? The answer, of course, is that the animal photographed wasn't *in* the loch at all but *above* it. What Jennifer Bruce inadvertently captured on film was simply a passing bird. This explains why she saw nothing at the time. The 'head and neck' is simply the silhouette of a wing. In an update to his book Campbell writes: 'It is now clear that the object is a bird, perhaps a gull, flying through the scene unnoticed as she took the picture.'

Roland Watson rejects this interpretation and asserts that the image doesn't match a flying bird. I think he is quite wrong here. What kind of bird it is is open to debate, as is its distance from the camera. But birds photographed in flight form all kinds of weird shapes when scrutinised frame by frame. This phenomenon also accounts for the high speed monsters of yesteryear. Fast-moving humps are simply *in flight*.

In 2016 Joline Lin described 'a brief and spontaneous moment' in which she saw 'a thin snake-like head emerging from the waters'. But her photograph suggests the silhouette of a bird in flight.

William Jobes (2011 and 2015)

Nessie photographs taken by William Jobes on May 24, 2011, and June 20, 2015, are reproduced in Malcolm Robinson's recent book, *The Monsters of Loch Ness* (2016). The earlier photograph shows a hump and what might be a protruding head, tail or fin. The spine of the hump appears uneven. It might be Nessie, some type of very large fish, or drifting débris. The photograph taken four years later shows a distant object of indeterminate shape, with a dark pole-like object leaning left, at an acute angle to the water. Jobes did not see the object when he took the photograph and only noticed it when he scrutinised the image later. To me it looks very much like the distant blurry outline of a windsurfer.

Jonathan Bright (2011)

The Jonathan Bright photograph, taken from the rear of a Jacobite Cruises vessel, has been interpreted as showing the monster's head, protruding from the surface. Bright explained how, examining photographs he'd taken on a trip to the loch in 2011, he suddenly spotted 'a strange-looking shade in the grey waterscape of waves'. It looked like an object, 'a head coming out of the water!'

> In fact it even appeared to possess the basic characteristics of the traditional Nessie – a straight neck, the dinosaur-like shape of the head and on the top, what looked like a pair of small horns or ears, bringing to mind the Kelpie or Water Horse of Celtic mythology.

The image has been duly greeted with rapture by the usual suspects. I must admit that at this point I start to get bored with the case for Nessie. The classic photos are *fun* to look at and to interpret. There's something of substance to argue about where Gray and Stuart and O'Connor are concerned. But the Bright picture sums up everything that's wrong with the photographic evidence of recent decades. In itself *it's just not very interesting.*

It's a wave formation. It's even a very common wave formation. Anyone can board a Jacobite Cruiser at The Clansman and take the same return trip to Urquhart Castle that Bright went on. Stand at the back and you'll observe exactly the same phenomenon that Bright photographed. You'll see a foaming propeller wake which flattens out the loch surface and streams away behind the cruiser. And on either side you'll see the bow wake, which when the surface is anything other than flat calm forms a double line of concentrated wave formations which have a roughly pyramidal shape. The currents created by the ship's passage force the water upward into concentrated shapes which tend to explode in foam and then dissipate. Each one of these formations is unique and its size and shape is subject to variables involving wind and weather but collectively they form a very recognisable phenomenon.

The uncropped version of Bright's photograph shows quite clearly that his 'monster' is simply one of these pyramidal wave formations. The notion that a Nessie is lurking inside a wake is wishful thinking. Let the Bright photo represent all the other photographs of recent years, because in my view they don't merit attention. The case for and against these other photographs can generally be found on the two major websites devoted to discussion of new evidence, those of Roland Watson and Dick Raynor, as well as on various other websites.

Since *The Loch Ness Mystery Solved* appeared in 1983 there has not in my view been a single Nessie photograph that either matches the classics or is of any real interest. No one has photographed what Hugh Gray, Lachlan Stuart or Peter O'Connor snapped, up-close and personal. The fact that those images differ so much and that no one else has managed over the past half century to produce anything resembling any of them further underlines their fraudulent nature.

It is of course much, much harder to fake a Nessie picture nowadays than it used to be. A black and white image can conceal far more than a colour one, especially if a model monster is being used. In any case, the age of single shot images of Nessie is surely over. Nowadays both mobile phones and even cheap digital cameras give everyone the opportunity to shoot motion film.

Although I believe the Gray, Stuart and O'Connor photographs are fraudulent, I don't think one should be too hard on the culprits. At the time their actions must have seemed no more than light-hearted pranks, designed to cash in on an appetite for such images.

There is one final point to be made about some of the classics. It is telling, I think, that Peter O'Connor never seems to have returned to Loch Ness or became involved in the great monster hunt inspired by Constance Whyte and Tim Dinsdale. Surely such a sensational close encounter should have triggered a lifetime obsession with the creature? O'Connor could have become an LNI star yet he dropped away into obscurity. In that he resembled H. L. Cockrell, who also claimed a sensational close encounter but then appeared to lose all interest in the monster. This is in stark contrast to George Spicer and others, who kept on going back to Loch Ness, hoping for another encounter with the beast.

Over the past eighty-four years no one has ever managed to take any motion film of a large unknown animal in Loch Ness at the close range enjoyed by stills photographers Hugh Gray, Lachlan Stuart and Peter O'Connor or by eye-witnesses like John McLean, Norah Atkinson and Greta Finlay. Monster footage always involves objects seen at a considerable distance.

Since publication of *The Loch Ness Mystery Solved* in 1983, only two movie films of unidentified phenomena at Loch Ness have appeared which are of any serious interest.

The first was shot on a sunny summer's day in the summer of 1992 when a tourist at Urquhart Castle filmed fellow visitors at the ruins, then panned across the loch, capturing a mysterious commotion on the surface perhaps half a mile away.

A substantial and not easily identifiable black and white object was visible moving at the surface, with an associated wake. It received wide publicity and was shown on 'Scotland Today' on August 17, 1992, and other channels (at the time of writing it can still be viewed on YouTube at https://www.youtube.com/watch?v=MrvmlEOuP78).

Unfortunately the object is too far away and the photographic image too limited to make a convincing identification. Camera-shake adds to the difficulties. It is also problematic that no information is available as to what happened next to the mystery phenomenon or whether more footage is available.

'Scotland Today' interviewed Professor Peter Meadows of Glasgow University, who remarked, 'I'm amazed by what I see. I haven't seen anything like it.' However, I strongly suspect that Professor Meadows had never been to Urquhart Castle and watched boats turning there, leaving wakes which can appear to be living, moving animals. This was sceptic Steuart Campbell's analysis: what appears on film is merely a standing wave. A frame from the film is reproduced in the 1996 revised edition of his book *The Loch Ness Monster: The Evidence,* together with a discussion of misleading wave effects at Loch Ness

Anyone viewing the footage might at first sight regard Campbell's explanation as absurd, since what is filmed appears to be black and to possess body. It produces the impression of being in motion. But a photographic image can mislead just as much as the eye can deceive. It is a telling coincidence that the mystery phenomenon appears mid-loch, precisely in the area where large vessels turning in the loch leave 'monster' wakes.

5. A 'monstrous' boat's wake at Loch Ness, photographed from Urquhart Castle.

Scott II used to steam out from Inverness and turn here; so, too, do the modern boats which bring tourists out from the harbour below The Clansman hotel for a sixty-minute cruise. The object shown may not be the average 'monster' wake, but it is more than likely that this very briefly filmed phenomenon is simply a patch of turbulent water resulting from the passage of one or more boats. The lurid white aspect of this 'Monster' is probably no more than reflected sunlight.

Believers will find it evidence for a Monster; sceptics will regard it as ambiguous, inconclusive and susceptible to a reasonable alternative analysis. The short piece of footage shows the ruins of Urquhart Castle filled with tourists, yet none react to the supposed 'monster' and no one else filmed or photographed it. This underlines the probability that this was merely a wave effect produced by the passage of one or more boats.

On May 26, 2007, monster hunter Gordon Holmes filmed a dark, mysterious shape moving across the surface of the loch. A slim, eel-like head appears to dart forward at the front. Holmes was not using a tripod, so the footage is jumpy.

What is it?

No one knows. It's a very unusual phenomenon.

Dick Raynor, who has probably spent more time on Loch Ness than anyone associated with the Loch Ness story, believes the film shows a disturbance 'caused by localised turbulent air interacting with the water surface'.

Raynor's considered analysis strikes me as infinitely more plausible than the explanations of those who find it evidence of a large unknown animal. Even today localised wind currents remain mysterious and phenomena such as waterspouts are not entirely understood.

That this lake was a zone of disturbance was understood as far back as 1857. William Reeves wrote that 'Owing to the narrowness of Loch Ness, and the great elevation of the hills with which it is walled in on either side, it is subject to squalls and currents of wind, which are both violent and capricious.'

8

The Dinsdale Film Revisited

Here I was, after less than an hour's concentrated watch, close to hallucinating from the intensity of my expectation.

Victor Perera, *The Loch Ness Monster Watchers* (1974)

When Tim Dinsdale wrote his classic book *Loch Ness Monster* he was very much aware that his old comrade in arms, the hitherto pro-Nessie zoologist Maurice Burton, believed his 1960 film showed not a large unknown animal but a local fishing dinghy. Dinsdale went out of his way to describe how, prior to filming the monster, he had calmly examined it through binoculars. At first the animal was motionless on the surface, displaying a huge blotch on one side of its hump. Then it started to move. It was only after he'd verified the object's identity as a huge animal that he began to film it. Dinsdale asserted that he was entirely familiar with the appearance of the local salmon fishing boats and that it was absurd to suggest he'd somehow been misled into filming one.

One of the curiosities of the Dinsdale film (making an event like it unrepeatable in the modern era) is that there was apparently no TV reception at Foyers in 1960. This meant that local people who might have been able to identify individuals or boats crossing the loch from the village at 9am on that particular Saturday morning in April 1960 never saw the BBC 'Panorama' feature broadcast seven weeks later on June 13. The passage of time made any such possible identification more and more remote.

Instead of television, the locals still had to make do with cinema for their entertainment. Aptly, 1960 was the year when a film was released which began with scenes at London Airport (where Tim Dinsdale was then employed) and which involved a man who was convinced that 'gigantic creatures of the long dead Jurassic period' still existed. The movie was a remake of *The Lost World* – a fictional story containing numerous ironic parallels to the Loch Ness story.

In *The Elusive Monster* Burton argued that the object in Dinsdale's film could not be identified for shape, left a propeller wake, followed the exact route commonly used by boats crossing the loch from Foyers and was travelling at a speed of around 7 mph. This speed, he sarcastically observed, was 'the maximum recorded speed for a shrimp and 1 m.p.h. less than the maximum recorded for a minnow'. He also noted the significance of Dinsdale's initial description of the monster as possessing 'a back like an underfed horse'. Burton suggested that since this analogy had been used by at least one previous witness (whom he did not identify), Dinsdale's recall of the episode might have been shaped by it. Furthermore, what did that phrase actually signify? Burton deduced that Dinsdale had misperceived 'a row of sou'-westers worn by several men sitting in a line from stem to stern in a 15-foot dinghy – no uncommon sight on Loch Ness'.

In their books, published almost simultaneously, neither man mentioned that they knew each other. The index to *The Elusive Monster* contains two brusque references to 'Dinsdale, Mr T. K.' and Burton's discussion of the film is so brief as to be almost perfunctory. When the dustjacket blurb refers to 'a faith that borders on religious mania' only the benefit of hindsight and the knowledge of their falling-out allows one to understand precisely who Burton had in mind. For his part, Dinsdale could not even bring himself to mention Burton by name, let alone acknowledge their former friendship or the loan of the camera which had magically transformed his life.

The force of Burton's critique was weakened by two things. Firstly his book's insistence that 'vegetable mats, or masses of peat' explained a great many sightings of the monster was so wildly implausible and unscientific that it discredited him as an expert on Loch Ness by indicating his ignorance of its habitat. Even if the phenomena sometimes occurred it was simply not credible that a gas propelled vegetable mat *always* avoided heading for the shoreline. Deflated monster-sized vegetable mats were in reality every bit as elusive as plesiosaur bones.

Burton's conclusion that there was no monster in the loch but that there might well be one lurking around the shore in the form of a new species of giant otter was simply bizarre. It indicated that Burton was still bewitched by a residue of eye-witness testimony but that once again he had a very limited understanding of the Loch Ness environment. However, his colourful theory conveniently served to further marginalise the Dinsdale film.

Burton noted that Dinsdale's supposed 'monster' crossed the loch from Foyers, made a half-turn to the right, and later turned left, travelling parallel with and close to the opposite shore: 'This is precisely the route frequently taken by local boats in crossing over from Foyers.' However, he produced no evidence to support that claim, nor did he trouble to explain what a boatman's motive might be in taking that particular route. His assertion that the Dinsdale film simply showed a dinghy containing a line of local fishermen dressed in sou-westers on a bright April morning was particularly unconvincing. In all my time at the loch I had never seen such a spectacle. Besides, how many men does it take to form 'a line'? Burton didn't even bother to speculate.

In any case, if Burton was so certain of his case, why didn't he hire some fishermen to cross the loch in a dinghy and film them from the same spot using the same camera which had been loaned to Dinsdale? If what he argued was correct such footage would, at a stroke, have destroyed the credibility of Dinsdale's 'monster'. Nor did it occur to Burton to, at the very least, take a photograph of Hugh Rowand's dinghy, used for the comparison footage. This is another loose ending never discussed in the substantial commentary provoked by the Dinsdale film.

In 1960 Maurice Burton was not simply a solitary, pioneering doubter of the Dinsdale film, he was actually in a very strong position to demonstrate what it was that had been filmed and how meaningless the comparison footage was. He owned the camera and he spent time at Foyers. But neither Burton nor anyone else ever tried to reproduce the Dinsdale film in his lifetime. And as the years passed that experiment at that location would become impossible because of the growth in height of the trees adjacent to the road, obscuring the loch. And now not even a photograph of Hugh Rowand's dinghy survives.

The final blow to the credibility of Burton's critique of Dinsdale was the JARIC report of January 1966. This highly technical analysis, by apparently reputable but unnamed photographic experts from the RAF's Joint Air Reconnaisance Intelligence Centre, concluded that the object which Dinsdale had filmed 'was travelling at or approaching 10 mph' – too fast for a fishing dinghy of the type which Burton had suggested. Moreover, the comparison boat filmed by Dinsdale displayed 'an irregular "broken" shape' which you might expect from a target such as a fishing dinghy. But the mystery object filmed earlier was 'triangular' and had 'a solid look about it, as if in fact it was an object with a continuous surface' (in other words, just like the hump which Dinsdale had sketched in his book). The anonymous JARIC analysts acknowledged that a power boat could easily reach the speed of the mystery object and would also appear to have a continuous surface. However, a power boat would be easily identifiable as such to an observer located where Dinsdale was when he shot his film. 'The assumption is therefore that it is NOT a surface vessel.'

A submarine would also be able to match the object's speed and would appear to have a continuous surface but could reasonably be excluded as an explanation. That left only one conclusion. The mystery object in the film 'is probably an animate object'.

In short, the report's sub-text was obvious, even though never explicitly articulated. Time and time again the report confirmed that *what Tim Dinsdale had filmed was indeed the Loch Ness Monster*. The report contained mouth-watering details: 'If animate, the surface shape of the object will NOT be angular. As expected the apex of the triangle has a rounded shape'. Once again, technical analysis implicitly confirmed Dinsdale's drawings of a massive hump. Moreover, the animal's dimensions were spectacular: 'a cross section through the object would be not less than 6 ft wide and 5 ft high'.

Dazzling stuff and one in the eye for a sceptic like Maurice Burton!

In 1983, the year that *The Loch Ness Mystery Solved* was published, the Dinsdale film remained an iconic piece of 'hard' evidence for the monster. This famous piece of black and white 16mm film was matched in reputation only by the Surgeon's photograph. But whereas R. K. Wilson had always seemed a shadowy figure, whose reputation was secured exclusively by his social status as a senior practitioner of medicine, Tim Dinsdale was a ubiquitous presence on the Loch Ness scene. He was personally known to thousands and his passionate enthusiasm was never in doubt, bolstered by a warm, friendly, generous personality.

Back in the 1980s I could see one outstanding flaw in the JARIC paper. This was its gullible acquiescence in the notion of the objective observer who would have no trouble identifying boats on the loch for what they really were. Like Maurice Burton, personal knowledge of Tim Dinsdale had led me to doubt him. Being present at Loch Ness in the immediate aftermath of his 1971 sighting I had a gut feeling that his account didn't ring true when he returned from Foyers to present it at Achnahannet. Likewise, I did not believe for a moment that Tim was anywhere near as calm, collected and rational as he described himself as being when he rolled down the Upper Foyers road at 9am on April 23, 1960. His account in *Loch Ness Monster*, where he insists that he was 'completely familiar' with the distant appearance of local fishing-boats, was plainly designed to armour-plate his narrative against Burton's critique.

My assault on the Dinsdale film in *The Loch Ness Mystery Solved* was further coloured by a second equally unacknowledged aspect. As a teenager at Loch Ness, I encountered a leading monster investigator who informed me that there was a red motor boat moored at Foyers in April 1960. He believed that was what Dinsdale had filmed. At the height of my youthful passion for Nessie a tiny seed of doubt was planted.

This private knowledge remained unexpressed in my book. Dinsdale's own *Loch Ness Monster* provided quite enough material to question his psychological state at the time he shot his legendary film.

Re-reading *Loch Ness Monster* with a sceptical eye, it was easy to understand that its author had become an extreme victim of 'expectant attention'. After the long, lonely drive to Scotland and night after night of little sleep, Dinsdale was in a state of extreme fatigue and nervous tension. That morning he had been up since 5am, with no breakfast. He was hyped-up by his meetings with Constance Whyte, Hugh Gray, Father Carruth, Colonel Grant and, especially, Alex Campbell. The evidence for the existence of monsters was overwhelming, but frustratingly he'd only had *one* sighting after four long days of surveillance. On that occasion he'd shot film and the circumstances had some uncanny parallels – location, excited rush to the lochside – with his second sighting.

It was sufficient, therefore, to argue that Dinsdale in his excitement had misperceived a motor boat with a planning hull (capable of travelling at JARIC's estimate of 10 mph). His claim that the monster submerged was nonsense; the motor boat merely entered a band of dark shadow. His boat comparison footage was bogus because it was shot later, when both surface and light conditions had changed. The boat used as a comparison was plainly much paler in colour, which made it strikingly different to the reddish brown object which Dinsdale had filmed earlier that morning.

How long a period had elapsed between the 'monster' footage and the boat footage has never been clarified. In *Loch Ness Monster* Dinsdale wrote that he watched the loch from 9.07am until 10am and then 'Filmed supporting sequences of boat' from 10am-12 noon. These timings are contradictory, since by his own account Dinsdale returned to the Foyers Hotel for breakfast, after which he 'spoke to the proprietor about getting a boat to go out on the loch'. When this had been agreed Dinsdale accompanied him down to the loch to help him launch his boat, then 'climbed back up the mountainside to the hotel'. After that he returned to the filming point (presumably either or on foot or by driving the short distance there).

In his introduction to the LNI publication of the report, David James stated that the filming of the boat occurred 'An hour later', but this simply cannot be true if Dinsdale really did linger by the lochside until 10am, hoping to see his 'monster' again (as he almost certainly did). A two hour gap between the two film sequences seems much more probable. During this period of time the surface of the loch had plainly changed, as had the lighting conditions. This transformation radically undermined the credibility of the exercise with the hotel proprietor's boat.

In challenging the Dinsdale film I argued that it was very revealing that, in the final section, a vehicle on the north shore can be seen driving past his 'monster' with no reaction at all from the driver, who simply continued on his or her way. This last argument would later be ignored by everyone except Dinsdale's friend and supporter Henry Bauer, who called it 'ill-founded' and jeered: 'With reasoning like that, one can prove just about anything.' Today, Bauer is Dinsdale's last prominent defender. But it is a fact that sightings by witnesses in moving vehicles have always formed a key component of the Loch Ness story. Believers have had no problems at all accepting the evidence of Mrs Mackay or the Spicers. Yet here is the case of someone driving along a length of road with an unbroken view of the loch and a massive creature approaching them just 100 yards offshore. If the vehicle had skidded to a halt and the driver jumped out to gaze in wonder at the massive back of an animal churning its way across the loch surface, it would have provided sensational verification of Dinsdale's version of events. The fact that the driver just kept going indicates that what was visible on the loch surface was something very ordinary – a boat. Dinsdale, of course, never acknowledged this possibility. The mystery driver faded from view.

I also argued that Dinsdale could not possibly have seen his 'monster' through X 7 binoculars with the detail which he claimed. As JARIC established, it was further away than he believed at the time. It was far more probable that upon sighting the mystery object Dinsdale became hysterical with excitement. If he managed to train his binoculars upon it his hands were surely shaking wildly. His action in stopping filming and driving down into Lower Foyers was another symptom of his over-excitement. Tellingly, I pointed out, *he neither saw the object appear nor disappear on the loch's surface.*

Just as it was for Mrs Mackay, the Spicers and numerous other eye-witnesses, the monster was already present when Dinsdale arrived at the site of his epiphany in a moving motor vehicle.

Three years after *The Loch Ness Mystery Solved* was published, a third sceptic stepped forward to challenge the Dinsdale film. Steuart Campbell was a formidable critic with an approach altogether more technical than my own. In February 1986, he published a detailed critique in the *Photographic Journal*, later summarising his findings in his book of the same year, *The Loch Ness Monster: The Evidence.*

Campbell argued that JARIC's report contained 'many defects'. He had grasped the significance of something which had quite passed me by. The third sentence of paragraph one of the report reads: 'All examination has been by optical enlargement of the film thus obviating losses by photographic processes.' What this jargon indicated was that JARIC had never once seen the film *projected.* All they'd examined were individual frames – frozen moments of time. Their understanding of the film's content was entirely static. They apparently never saw or studied Dinsdale's unidentified object in motion. It was an extraordinary omission in what was supposed to be a sophisticated, highly professional analysis of a length of 16mm movie film.

Because of this major analytical flaw the analysts, Campbell argued, had failed to grasp that the film was not a continuous sequence but must have contained two winding breaks. By erroneously treating the film as a single strip of continuous footage the JARIC analysts had over-estimated the speed of the object.

Campbell identified another 'major error'. JARIC had based their calculations on a filming position assumed to be 91.4m above the loch surface. They had overlooked the fact that Loch Ness is not at sea level and therefore the filming position was only 75.4m above the loch. Campbell's highly technical article made many other criticisms, including the assertion that JARIC had miscalculated the length of the object.

In short, the speed of the object was entirely consistent with it being a powered dinghy, as was its shape and size. With the collapse of the JARIC analysis, Maurice Burton's argument that what Dinsdale had filmed was merely a local fishing boat was reinstated as an entirely valid interpretation. Campbell's reinterpretation made a glancing reference to 'Dinsdale's mental set' – by which he plainly meant *expectant attention* – and argued that it had disabled his ability to see what was in front of him:

> Without binoculars he thought that it was stationary and side on, with a patch that must have been the occupant. In fact the boat must always have been travelling away from him, as he found when he looked at it through binoculars.

Although this is a plausible interpretation, it is inaccurate in so far as Dinsdale's own testimony is concerned. Dinsdale described how with the naked eye all he noticed was something which looked shorter and higher than a fishing dinghy, with 'a curious *reddish brown* hue'. It was only then, when he raised his binoculars, that he was able to see a massive hump, which was stationary, with 'a huge dark blotch' on the left flank.

Campbell was on shaky ground when he cited Maurice Burton's evidence from Loch Ness. This was purely anecdotal. Burton claimed he had seen a dinghy following the same route as Dinsdale's monster, which had then appeared to disappear as a result of shadows along the far shore, and that observers had reported the boat as a monster. What is more, 'Enquiries revealed that, at the time Dinsdale filmed his "Monster," a local farmer was crossing the lake from Foyers in a powered dinghy!'

Claims like these by Burton always need to be taken with a very large pinch of salt, since he supplied not a scrap of evidence to substantiate any of these anecdotes. One might ask why a local farmer would need to cross the loch at this point, using this route, since there was nothing on the far side but barren rock. Besides, if Burton had indeed sensationally identified both the boat and its occupant, why didn't he simply replicate Dinsdale's monster film with one of his own, using the same camera at the same spot to film the same boat and the same occupant?

And what had happened to that line of men in the boat wearing sou'westers?

Others had also come to the conclusion that Dinsdale had simply filmed a fisherman's dinghy. In 1984 Ricky Gardiner, Tony Harmsworth and Adrian Shine were holding a late night discussion of the monster and the Dinsdale film. Harmsworth put on a video of an American documentary which included some of the Dinsdale footage and they made a startling discovery. Harmsworth explained that 'Our television set, for whatever unknown reason, had the contrast turned up too high and, in the sequence showing the object moving parallel to the shore, a man could easily be seen sitting in the back of a light coloured boat.'

When Shine published a belated review of *The Loch Ness Mystery Solved*, some two years after the book first appeared, he made a cryptic, highly oblique allusion to this discovery. However, he chose not to challenge the film publicly. Harmsworth explains that this was for 'various reasons including friendship and respect for the unwell Dinsdale'. This is not particularly convincing reasoning, since Dinsdale was still journeying to Loch Ness to look for the monster right up to 1986. To wait until Dinsdale was dead before publishing the 'helmsman' interpretation was to deny him the right of reply.

When Tim Dinsdale died in December 1987 he had said and published nothing by way of reply to his two prominent new critics, Ronald Binns (May 1983) and Steuart Campbell (February 1986). However, he had at some point composed a rejoinder to Steuart Campbell, which appeared posthumously in *The Photographic Journal* in 1990. It is unclear why it did not appear earlier.

His response was revealing in what he chose to respond to and what he remained silent about. Campbell suggested that the map Dinsdale had supplied to the JARIC investigators 'may be identical' to the inaccurate one used in *Loch Ness Monster*. Dinsdale refuted this suggestion, insisting he had sent a different one (which, however, he did not include with his rejoinder to Campbell, and which even today has never been published). Secondly, Dinsdale argued that there was no confusion involving Spot Heights, claiming that the OS map showed a Spot Height of 291 feet 'marked on the road a little to the East' and downhill of the location used for filming. Dinsdale judged that this location was some '60-70 feet' up the hill, even 'perhaps a little more'. Knock off 52 feet (the height of the loch above sea level) and you arrive at the figure of 299-309 feet, 'roughly the 300 feet above loch level I quoted to JARIC'.

But Dinsdale's account is hard to square with the terrain. The 2007 OS Explorer Map (416) indicates two Spot Heights for this particular stretch of the B852. One, lower down the hill, identifies a height of 86m (282 feet), and another one, beyond Dinsdale's filming point, marks a height of 109m (357 feet). Dinsdale seems to have been more or less equidistant from these two points, indicating that his height above sea level was probably in the order of 320 feet, not the 350-360 feet he claimed. Deducting 52 feet gives an actual height above sea level of 268 feet, not 300.

But of course, all of this is speculative because neither the exact filming point nor its precise height is known. By the late 1980s even Dinsdale seemed uncertain about identifying the precise location from which he'd filmed, explaining that it

> was originally known to me exactly by a dip in the wooden railing by the roadside, and a vast unobstructed panorama of Loch Ness – today the railing has largely fallen down, and a wall of 30ft conifers block the view entirely

The rest of Dinsdale's response to Campbell was a mixture of bluster and defensive anecdotes about prints of individual film frames. He curtly dismissed the suggestion that 'tricks of light and shade' accounted for the supposed submergence of his monster, and insisted that when projected 'full screen' the impact of his footage was 'breathtaking'.

What is most interesting about Dinsdale's rejoinder, I think, is that he entirely evades the issue of camera rewinds. The argument about the speed of the object is central to Campbell's demolition of JARIC's conclusions but Dinsdale offers no insights into the clockwork motor conundrum.

Adrian Shine and Dick Raynor have each published lengthy studies which identify the 'monster' as a fishing dinghy containing a solitary figure, 'the helmsman'. The original Shine analysis was far from persuasive, since it was based on a poor quality video copy, and the white blob which he and his two associates identified as a person was not dissimilar to other white blobs in the area of the boat outline. However, Shine now insists that modern analysis using digital overlayering confirms that analysis, and states that members of the original JARIC team (still unidentified) have confirmed this interpretation. Shine and Raynor have supplied single frame images which do indeed greatly resemble the outline of a dinghy containing a figure towards the stern.

This interpretation has been challenged by Henry Bauer, who argues that Shine's analysis involved an inferior video image and that he possesses a superior version ('an authentic 16 mm copy of the film itself') in which no boat or helmsman can be identified. He reproduces single frame images of the mystery object to prove his case. They do not resemble a boat and there is no putative helmsman visible.

Other defenders of the Dinsdale film insist that the original JARIC report was correct and has been confirmed by later analysis. In the words of Dinsdale's son Angus:

> One of the technical operators noticed something and switched the film over to view it in negative. He then laid a number of the same frames over one another to reveal a shadow underwater. This shadow is unmistakeable in its shape, clearly showing a large diamond-shaped fin, a body, and what appears to be a tail, just under the surface. For someone who's literally had a lifetime of the monster, and viewed my father's film from all angles, it was startling to see.

The problem with digital manipulation of single frames taken from copies of unknown quality of the Dinsdale film is that it can produce results equally pleasing to the eye of the believer or the sceptic.

Personally, I find Dick Raynor's deconstruction of the Dinsdale film the most technically compelling one. His conclusion that Dinsdale filmed through the *closed* window of his vehicle is both plausible and enlightening. This had the effect of making the mystery object less sharp than his comparison boat, which he plainly filmed while standing outside the vehicle, on the road. (He cannot have been inside the vehicle as he was signalling to Hugh Rowand in his boat.)

If you accept the validity of the digital enhancement process that's been used then it makes perfect sense that the bright spot at the front of the 'monster' is actually a fishing dinghy's licence plate reflecting the morning sunlight. Raynor's suggestion that the boat contained a second figure, who was situated near the bow and whose presence helps to explain those rhythmic pulses of foam (interpreted as paddle-strokes by Dinsdale and his supporters) is also persuasive. However, if there *is* a second figure in the boat, close to the bow, it raises the question of why digital overlayering has failed to identify this passenger.

Where interpretation rests on analysis which purports to be factual, scientific and beyond dispute, two caveats must be entered. Firstly, the Loch Ness story now has something of a history of individuals insisting that the truth can be found in objective scientific data which subsequently turns out to be far less substantial and authoritative than it first seemed. The material supplied by Robert Rines (sonar charts annotated with expert explanations and astonishing underwater photographs) seemed impressive at the time. However, it has now been shown to have been based on false assumptions about equipment siting, plus bogus sonar and photographic interpretation, as well as fraud. The anonymous JARIC report has been discredited for its analytical flaws and its complacent assumptions about individual perception. The impressive-sounding scientific paper by LeBlond and Collins appeared authoritative in its identification of the height of the object in the Wilson photograph using 'A Size Determination Based on Physical Principles', but it turned out to be based on false information about the time and date when the image was obtained, which meant the meteorological data involved in the calculation was worthless.

The second caveat is that despite all the high-tech chatter and high-precision data, there are some troubling lacunae in analysis of the Dinsdale film. For example, in *Loch Ness* (2006), Adrian Shine writes that Dinsdale 'took a 4 minute film, of something moving across the loch'. In fact the footage lasts exactly 65 seconds. Shine is hardly alone in his error, which suggests that even as late as 2006 *he had not actually seen the complete footage*, merely a short extract.

Until relatively recently this has been a problem for all analysts of the Dinsdale film. When I wrote *The Loch Ness Mystery Solved* I had seen the film on a number of occasions, including on television. Although I can't be absolutely certain of this, I probably saw its television premiere on June 13, 1960. I have a distinct memory of seeing it broadcast decades ago, with the 'hump' enlarged and moving across the loch to the thrilling throb of bars of Dr-Who-style electronic music. I had also seen the film shown by Tim Dinsdale himself at the Loch Ness Investigation Christmas parties. But when I wrote my book I was relying on memory plus the single frame images which Dinsdale had published in his books. These images, of course, are cropped and enlarged versions and are misleading in so far as a reproduction of any of the original full frames would have demonstrated just how tiny and faraway the unidentified object was.

The advent of the internet has removed the obstacle preventing viewing of the 65 seconds of footage, assisted by the Dinsdale family's willingness to allow it to be screened online, without cuts.

But problems remain. The film was 16mm, shot on a Bolex Cine H-16 running at 24 frames per second. Dinsdale described shooting approximately 50 feet of film, which was correct but a slight over-estimate. Richard Carter states that 50ft of 16mm cine film runs for 83 seconds; Roland Watson calculates it would be only 77 seconds. The Bolex camera which Dinsdale used had a clockwork motor, which required him to rewind it at intervals. Since the 65 seconds of film is not continuous footage this raises the question of when Dinsdale ceased filming to rewind. In *Loch Ness Monster* he describes 'firing long steady bursts of film like a machine gunner, stopping between to wind the clockwork motor'. Roland Watson takes this to mean that 'he only rewound the camera once' but Dinsdale's description is too vague to allow such a confident conclusion, since he does not identify how many 'long steady bursts of film' there were.

Establishing where the breaks occur is crucial in determining how accurate JARIC's assessment of speed was in the first part of the film. It is a reasonable assumption (but not necessarily a reliable one) that the camera was fully wound up at the point when filming began, so the first question is how often a rewind was required. Campbell states that the Bolex Cine H-16 ran for about 20 seconds before the motor ran out, requiring fresh winding which would take 12-13 seconds. This is the figure accepted by later sceptical analysts. Watson disagrees: his research suggests that the camera would have run for 28 seconds before stopping. That would mean the first break occurred around frame 672 (using JARIC's numbering). However, in a film lasting 65 seconds that would still require two breaks to rewind, not one. Watson's way round this difficulty is to suggest that Dinsdale 'managed to run his rewinds longer' and that the first film break occurred a little later, at frame 720. This ingenious calculation breaks down, however, because that still only adds two seconds to the break. A second rewind was still required to shoot 65 seconds of film.

Campbell calculated that from the moment Dinsdale began filming the object took about 90 seconds to arrive at the point where he stopped filming and impulsively drove down to Lower Foyers. Dinsdale, he argues, was filming for only two-thirds of this time: 'There must have been two winding breaks and about 8 seconds were lost in pauses in the initial sequence'. (I assume he means pauses in addition to the two 12 second delays required to rewind, totalling 32 seconds of non-filming during the object's 90-second journey.)

However, Dinsdale described the filming process as taking 'approx. 4 minutes' from 9.00am – 9.04am The only person as yet to address the question of why it took four minutes to film 65 seconds of film is Watson:

> I speculate that the missing three minutes came during the rewinding of the motor... Why would Tim Dinsdale take three minutes to rewind the cine camera when it should only take a tenth of that time? In the excitement and tension of such an event, it is easier to take longer over things. Perhaps he had finger trouble, a temporary mechanical problem arose or he was distracted by something.

Perhaps; perhaps not. However, I am entertained by Watson's logic, which makes assumptions about Dinsdale's fraught emotional state.

Watson's key argument is that even if JARIC missed the first film break it is irrelevant to their analysis that when moving away from the observer it was travelling at 10 m.p.h. because it occurred *after* the first break: 'they analysed frames 1 to 384 to derive a speed of 10mph'.

> The first jump in a 20s run occurs at frame 480, but by then JARIC had already analysed frames 1 to 384 and calculated a speed of 10mph. Furthermore, I would find it incredible that the professionals at JARIC had failed to take pauses to rewind into account. The Bolex H-16 was a well known and popular model and they must have known about this. I doubt they would have made such a schoolboy error in their calculations.

Watson concludes: 'The analysis seems clear to me. The estimated speed of 10mph calculated by JARIC stands and this is a problem if you think the object in the film is a common boat.'

Anyone can now watch the footage online and carry out their own analysis. It's a strangely jerky, lurching, flickering film sequence, with hairs in the film gate. Towards the end of the film the 'monster' almost disappears from view at the vertical edge of the screen, suggesting that Dinsdale was struggling to see it.

My own impression from watching the film repeatedly is that there are *at least* three breaks (possibly more). The first occurs at 8 seconds. The second, when the view shifts from Y (depth of view) to X (field of view) occurs at 28 seconds. There is a third break at 43 seconds. If this interpretation is accurate then it indicates that *the pauses were not determined by the limitations of the camera,* as is conventionally believed. There was no logical reason for Dinsdale to cease filming after 8 seconds, assuming that the camera was fully wound in the first place.

The break at 8 seconds does not in itself invalidate the original JARIC estimate of 10 m.p.h. but it does make it reliant on the question of how far the object had travelled before filming resumed. My impression is that it hadn't gone very far, therefore the speed of the object at the beginning of its filmed journey might hypothetically have exceeded the maximum speed of a dinghy. But accurate measurement is impossible, given the limitations of the currently available data.

Only an objective examination of the original 16 mm film (or a reliable copy) can resolve the arguments surrounding this legendary footage.

If Dinsdale *did* stop filming after 8 seconds, one wonders why.

In retrospect it's clear that Burton was trying his best to make sense of Dinsdale's original description of the monster as having 'a back like an underfed horse'. Burton then made the classic error of accepting the literal truth of an eye-witness description and trying to naturalise it and process it into something exactly equivalent. But at best it is arguably the case that in his condition of extreme excitement Dinsdale perceived in his monster only *irregularity* along the supposed back and *symmetry* in the overall shape. Both aspects are entirely consistent with a boat, irrespective of what kind of boat it might be.

Burton puzzled over what Dinsdale *meant* by 'a back like an underfed horse'. He concluded he had in mind 'a row of protuberances like the neural spines in a horse's backbone'. He also pointed out the difficulties of interpretation which stemmed from Dinsdale's distance from the object and the power of the binoculars he was using. Burton calculated that 'the protuberances must have been 8-10 ins. high and 2-3 feet apart'.

Burton did not bother to explain the basis of his calculations. But flawed though his presentation may have been, Burton had focused attention on an aspect of Dinsdale's sighting experience which would change significantly between his *Daily Mail* interview (June 13, 1960) and his book, published a year later. In *Loch Ness Monster* there is no mention of an underfed horse. Instead the monster now is described as being reminiscent of 'the back of an African buffalo' and accompanied by two sketches of an 'upturned boat' shape with a *smooth* spine-like crest.

As I argued in *The Loch Ness Mystery Solved*, the April 23 episode mimicked Dinsdale's reaction to the sight of waves breaking against rocks, just two days earlier. Having shot film of a bogus 'monster' (a mysterious 'violent disturbance' surrounding 'two long black shadows or shapes, rising and falling in the water!') he then returned the next day and set up posts in the loch to provide 'some finite reference to scale' by which to estimate the creature's dimensions.

Fascinatingly and revealingly, Dinsdale did not conclude it wasn't a monster *until he saw the film projected*. At this point he decided that the April 23 film *was* a genuine monster but the April 21 film *wasn't*. As he breezily confessed regarding the earlier film footage, 'it proved to be a patch of rough water caused by waves breaking over a shoal of rocks, just under the surface. I was not to know that at the time, however…'. Dinsdale is also revealingly vague about how much film he had shot of the disturbance at the river mouth. He describes it when projected as 'running on for several minutes'. It sounds very much like an hysterical over-reaction to what by his own account turned out to be rocks.

Dinsdale's monster had 'a curious *reddish brown* hue about it' – consistent with it being a boat and unlike traditional descriptions of the beast, which is usually perceived as being grey or black. This aspect is easily forgotten because Dinsdale used black and white film. Ironically even David James forgot this when he introduced the JARIC report in a special LNI edition. 'Tim Dinsdale filmed a black object,' he wrote.

The object in the Dinsdale film behaved as one might expect of a vessel from Foyers engaged in salmon fishing. It crossed the loch from the vicinity of Foyers pier, then turned sharp left to hug the shoreline, travelling towards Invermoriston. In due course, no doubt, at some point it crossed the loch and then, hugging the south shore, it returned to Foyers. If Dinsdale had stuck around in Foyers instead of rushing off back to England he might well have met his reddish-brown monster returning home. His 'monster' may even have returned to Foyers while he was eating his lunch at the hotel, prior to his departure. If he had been in Foyers the following Saturday at 9am he might well have seen his 'monster' again, travelling the identical route.

Dinsdale attempted to represent his actions that morning as being those of a calm, detached individual, fully in control of the situation. But his own narrative in *Loch Ness Monster* was capable of an alternative reading which exposed him as a tired, fraught, jumpy individual who lurched into sudden hysteria at sighting a far distant object which, with shaking hands, he was unable to identify. His extreme excitement was underlined by his futile rush to Lower Foyers, which Dinsdale revealingly sketched on a lopsided and inaccurate map. This not only sent him in the opposite direction to the path being travelled by his 'monster', it also meant that with the passage of what he casually alluded to as 'just a very few minutes, two or three at most' he put himself in a position where his loss of elevation and restricted view meant he could no longer see that distant boat, still chugging towards Invermoriston.

In retrospect, what my analysis did not do was point to the curious fact that the film Tim Dinsdale shot in April 1960 *has never once been publicly shown*. By this I mean *the entire film reel*, with Dinsdale's earlier bogus 'monster' by the mouth of the River Foyers, which was filmed on April 21. (I'm assuming Dinsdale had 100 feet of film loaded but it's always possible he used two 50 ft reels. This is just one of many ambiguities surrounding the circumstances of his film.)

Nor, when I wrote the book, was I sufficiently alert to Dinsdale's extraordinary revelation that it was only when he viewed this reel of film for the first time at Kodak that he decided which footage showed a monster and which didn't. The river mouth disturbance he now decided wasn't a monster after all, but the distant blob footage *was*. I can't help thinking that if he hadn't seen a boat on his last morning he would have convinced himself that the river mouth footage was The Real Thing.

As a parting shot, Dinsdale acidly remarked, in his *Photographic Journal* piece, that 'Mr Campbell...has never seen these films, incidentally'. But that simply served to focus attention on the obstacles which Dinsdale himself had deliberately and repeatedly placed in the way of independent analysis of his film. As he explained in 1965, he'd 'withheld this film since 1961 because...I realised that examination by someone not properly trained or equipped for photo interpretation could do more harm than good'. That is desperately defensive and feeble reasoning.

Even when he was obliged to hand over his film to JARIC, he felt it necessary to append a framework of interpretation and explanation, which was clearly designed to influence the organisation's interpretation. Nor did he want the analysts to project the film. Dinsdale in reality was plainly terrified of a truly independent assessment of his footage. Deep down he was surely uneasily aware of what its conclusions might be.

Many years after Tim Dinsdale's death, Adrian Shine published his own critique of this iconic film. In it he suggested that even Dinsdale himself may have doubted what he'd really filmed. Referring to the comparison footage which Dinsdale shot of Hugh Rowand in his boat, Shine writes, 'It might be asked whether his filming of the known boat was in itself an act of personal reassurance that his monster was not one.' That strikes me as offering a brilliantly shrewd insight into Dinsdale's personality.

In his commentary for JARIC Dinsdale attempted to deflect Maurice Burton's repeated insistence that the object was not a monster but a surface vessel. Dinsdale asserted that he was 'entirely familiar' with the appearance and size of local fishing boats. He flaunted his aeronautical qualifications (which would inevitably be regarded with deference by RAF personnel, who may well have known that Dinsdale himself was ex-RAF). He wrote of his experience of whales, seals, crocodiles, etc. He invited the analysts to note the similarity between his monster's back and Lachlan Stuart's famous photograph of three humps. He asserted that the loch surface was 'Flat calm' with 'little or no wind' – a claim which a moment's glance at the footage *in motion* shows to be false.

Revealingly, it was none other than Tim Dinsdale who laid down the extraordinary condition which successfully disabled an accurate interpretation: 'this film is NOT for projection under any circumstances'. Why on earth not? This was a most peculiar condition to insist upon when one's film is about to be analysed by individuals who are supposed to be the nation's supreme experts in photographic analysis and interpretation.

Then, as if even this weren't enough, he demanded that once the analysis was completed it must remain strictly confidential until he had personally decided on 'the best course of action' regarding publication and 'use in furthering the "cause"'. None of this sounds like someone who is confident about what the possible outcome of impartial third-party photographic analysis might be.

Dick Raynor believes that had he lived longer Tim Dinsdale would ruefully have accepted his error and acknowledged that his film shows nothing more than a distant fishing boat. Although Raynor can claim a much more intimate friendship with Dinsdale than me, I regard this belief as implausible and unconvincing. My own view is that had he lived on into old age Dinsdale today would still be just as dogmatically insistent that he had really had filmed a monster as his dwindling band of admirers are. This latter group includes his immediate family, which is not in itself particularly surprising. Ironically, when in 2013 his youngest son Angus published an affectionate memoir of his father, he included some startling information. As a young man Tim Dinsdale had applied for entry to the RAF, wanting to become a pilot, but it 'proved to be a little harder than Tim had originally hoped'. His first try ended in rejection, as a result of failing a practical test involving the identification of targets 'in low-level light and at distance'. Angus cheerily explains this as being 'a bit like taking your driving test on a dull day and having to read a number plate at sixty yards'.

The revelation that Dinsdale had poor eye-sight even as a young man and was unable to identify a distant target is hugely ironic in the context of his controversial film. Angus Dinsdale goes on to describe how his father found a way around this difficult practical test. On his next attempt to apply for admission to the RAF he cheated, getting closer to the target than was permitted.

The Man Who Filmed Nessie helpfully provides some context to Tim Dinsdale's original infatuation with the Loch Ness Monster. Angus Dinsdale describes how his father read a feature about it in *Everybody's* and how his interest was aroused. He ascribes it to 'a curiosity, the engineer's brain wanting to know more'. But this explanation is an unsatisfactory one for an obsession which literally overnight became all-consuming. Reconfiguring your life on nothing more than some sensational journalism in a popular magazine is a very strange thing to do. *Everybody's* was not exactly *New Scientist*. On the spectrum of nineteen-fifties British news publishing *Everybody's* belonged at the trashy end. It was pitched at the kind of readership which enjoyed features on royalty, celebrities and mystery, combined with other delights, such as photographs of attractive full-bodied young women wearing very tight tops and very short shorts.

Dinsdale was plainly in the throes of some kind of early mid-life crisis. His life was transfigured by this article which, ironically, highlighted Alex Campbell's first monster sighting of 1933, subsequently retracted and now reinstated in a revised form. Astonishingly, Dinsdale *immediately* proceeded to produce plans for a grand Loch Ness expedition, sending out letters seeking support from government departments, businesses and philanthropists. He outlined to them this awesome research project 'with timelines, costs, and *expected results*' (my italics).

Remarkably, it was only when these overtures were ignored that he realised he needed to know more about the subject and proceeded to read his first book on the subject: *More Than a Legend*. He then cultivated the friendship of that other top monster expert, Maurice Burton – an episode which Angus Dinsdale revealingly chooses not to mention in a book which is essentially not biography but hagiography.

Barely a year after first reading the piece in *Everybody's*, Dinsdale was at Loch Ness, equipped with Burton's 16 mm camera. Apart from maintaining surveillance of the surface, Dinsdale made a number of calls upon local eye-witnesses and Nessie experts, including Hugh Gray, Constance Whyte, Father Carruth, Colonel Grant and, last of all, Alex Campbell.

Dinsdale's 'Daily Log' records an epic conversation with the water bailiff which lasted from 1.00pm to 6.00pm. However, he also describes how he left Campbell's cottage at 7.30pm, so presumably he was invited to stay for supper.

Campbell's monster sighting as described in *Everybody's* had transformed Dinsdale into a zealot and now finally to be in the water bailiff's presence was obviously intoxicating. It was just *forty minutes* after leaving Campbell's house, arriving 'on the hill behind the bay at Foyers', that Tim Dinsdale 'quite suddenly' saw the Monster – 'two long black shadows, or shapes, rising and falling in the water!'

Two days later (some 37½ hours after leaving Campbell's cottage) he repeated the experience, only this time the Monster was on its way to the far side of the loch.

Expectant attention had worked its magic and produced the inevitable results. But Dinsdale not only deceived himself, he also deceived others. He told the *Daily Mail* that he had viewed the monster's huge humped back using binoculars which were 'powerful German ones used on espionage work'. In recent years it has become clear that Dinsdale was using not field glasses but small, cheap, lightweight binoculars more akin to the sort you can hire in an opera house.

Others have confirmed the conclusions I reached three decades ago: 'the miniature 7x binoculars he used had a much wider field of view than the viewfinder in the Bolex movie camera... [they] would have shown him little more than a speck at 1300 yards distance'. Dinsdale's own illustrations of 'the back of some huge animal' were pure fantasy. As I argued in *The Loch Ness Mystery Solved*, 'he could not possibly have seen it with the size and detail which he portrays in his sketch'. Ironically, the comparison sketches in my book of what Dinsdale claimed to see and what he would *really* have seen erred on the side of over-generosity to Dinsdale.

Tim Dinsdale will always be the man who mistook a boat for his monster. The time and effort he then put into watching the surface of Loch Ness with negligible results simply underlined the reality that the great tradition of sightings and photographs amounted to nothing at all of zoological interest. For the next ten years, after his first trip to Foyers, no one observed Loch Ness with greater dedication or intensity than Dinsdale. But he saw nothing.

Maurice Burton, the Nessie fan closest to Dinsdale in that first year of the aeronautical engineer's obsession with the Monster, realised from the start that his comrade-in-arms had merely filmed a boat. Much the same thing seems to have happened when Dinsdale had his next sighting in August 1970. In 1972 a revised and expanded edition of his *The Leviathans* was published in an American edition, re-titled *Monster Hunt*. Dinsdale used this new edition to describe his 1970 'telegraph pole' sighting. But the book ended on a tetchy note. Dinsdale was convinced that the object was *at least* ten feet high:

> This figure was probably thought to be an exaggeration at the time by the majority of people who had not seen the object. They were too polite to say so, but their very lack of comment made this apparent.

But who those sceptics were (and presumably they were LNI people – either volunteers or staff), their quiet scepticism, and the reason for it, are left unrecorded. In *Project Water Horse* (1975) Dinsdale's treatment of his 1970 sighting is remarkably perfunctory.

His third and final sighting occurred in 1971. In the original published version Dinsdale describes how,

> Standing at the wheel I glanced to starboard and instantly recognised a shape I had seen so often in a photograph – the famous 'Surgeon's Photograph' of 1934 – but it was alive and muscular!

Dinsdale's self-deception and confirmation bias never ceased.

9

The Archive Problem

The technical problems posed by the Monster are as nothing compared with the human problems connected with it.

Tim Dinsdale, *Loch Ness Monster* (1961)

The fact that the Dinsdale film remains unavailable for scrutiny more than half a century after it was taken underlines the extent to which the Loch Ness story is a ragged, threadbare tale full of gaps. Much of it will probably remain forever open-ended and inconclusive. One day, hopefully, this particular film will escape from protective custody but others are probably lost forever. The enigmatic film sequences of a shape-shifting object, shot in colour in 1938 by a South African tourist named G. E. Taylor, was described at length by Maurice Burton in *The Elusive Monster*. But Burton proved obstructive when others sought to view it and returned the film to Natal, where it vanished into obscurity. In 1966 Mrs Margaret Edwards shot some 8mm footage of the monster at the surface near Abriachan, described by the *Daily Express* as 'a colour movie which no one else in the world can boast of'. But this, too, has vanished from sight. And in *The Great Orm of Loch Ness*, Ted Holiday famously introduced a breathtaking discovery: two sensational close-up films of monsters, taken during the 1930s by a retired doctor named MacRae, who had decided to keep them secret. If they really exist, they have yet to surface.

Dinsdale's film remains unavailable for inspection, as is what must be a fairly substantial archive. It would be interesting to examine those binoculars, too. Dinsdale told the *Daily Mail* that they were 'powerful German ones used on espionage work' but it has since been suggested that they were cheap, low-powered ones than the type of high-grade military ones intimated by Dinsdale. Although this archive will, one day, hopefully be made available for independent scrutiny, other archives are lost forever. Rupert Gould must surely have owned a fascinating cache of material from his 1933 and 1934 visits to the loch but it all appears to have been destroyed. It is only by a fluke that his annotated edition of *The Loch Ness Monster and Others* survived, and it was only Gould's interest in Harrison's marine chronometers and the success of the book *Longitude* which created an opening for a biography, which drew attention to Gould's sensational change of mind about the Spicers' land sighting. By such attenuated threads does the true Loch Ness story hang.

The uncovering of the complex human story behind the Surgeon's photograph was a last minute effort, just in time to obtain Christian Spurling's account of how the 'monster' was made, but too late to interview his step-brother, Ian Wetherell, who alone knew the circumstances in which it was photographed.

Constance Whyte's archive presumably remains in the hands of Nicholas Witchell. The whereabouts of Ted Holiday's archive and unpublished manuscript about lake monsters are unknown to me. Maurice Burton's archive likewise remains in private hands, along with the camera loaned to Tim Dinsdale in 1960.

When the Loch Ness Investigation closed down, David James gifted its treasure trove of material, including film and eye-witness reports, to Adrian Shine, who retains ownership. Some of this material, such as LNI log books, appears to be in the possession of Dick Raynor. The Loch Ness Investigation was an organisation based on comradeship and team work and I believe it was a serious misjudgement on the part of David James to transfer ownership of its records and film in the way that he did. This material belongs in a public archive.

It is not a happy situation that so much archival material remains in private hands and not in a public collection. The LNI accumulated a fascinating collection of film shot by members. Some of it was shown at LNI Christmas parties (I vividly remember seeing the long-range footage of a large 'monster' wallowing in the shallows of a south shore beach). Some of it was never shown, presumably having been rejected as evidence. But it must have amounted to a fairly substantial collection.

I find it disappointing that no Scottish institution has ever put Loch Ness studies on a professional basis. It is, after all, a multi-faceted subject, involving folk tradition, media studies, psychology, social history, zoology, environmental studies and sociology. Nessie has become part of Scottish national identity and the association between monsters and Loch Ness has become an important part of the Scottish tourist economy, yet no Scottish academic body has ever shown any inclination to engage with the monster legend as a legitimate study area and there seems to be no inclination on any part of Scottish governance to open a museum at Loch Ness which would match the professionalism of those at Culloden and Urquhart Castle.

Currently, the appropriate interim destination for archival material of the sort mentioned above is surely the Highland Archive Centre, Inverness. At present this Centre's holdings on the monster consist of material related to Frank Searle. This is not a happy state of affairs. When I am finished with the Loch Ness Monster, this Centre will be offered my own modest archive of material, including books, letters and original film and photographs. I would hope that one day others in possession of unique historical material will do the same.

10

What Lies Beneath

'It took me by surprise or I'd have noticed it better.'
Thomas Connelly, interviewed by Ted Holiday.

Thirty-four years after publication of *The Loch Ness Mystery Solved* the 'hard' evidence for large unknown animals in Loch Ness remains conspicuously lacking. There is nothing tangible for a zoologist to analyse – no live specimen, no tissue sample, no dead animal, no bones, no eggs, no spoor. The accumulated photographs, movie film and sonar contacts are either discredited or, at best, ambiguous and inconclusive. None supplies the kind of proof which believers seek. When it comes to *persuasion* the 'soft' evidence – eye-witness testimony – has always been much more compelling.

On his blog *Loch Ness Monster*, Roland Watson supplies a list of 'famous Nessie sightings from decades past' with links to his analysis of each one. These witnesses, he argues, saw 'Nessie up close and personal in such a way that (let's face it) there is not much room for error.' The 'Classic Sightings' list includes such legendary figures as Aldie Mackay, Margaret Munro, John McLean, Marjorie Moir and Greta Finlay.

In discussing the Moir sighting Watson remarks that 'it is easy to lose sight of these classic sightings and the persuasive power of them' and notes that 'none of the books on Nessie which are skeptical of a new, unclassified creature mention the Moir sighting. Perhaps it was a case too hard to crack for them.'

Marjorie Moir was one of five women in a car who, in 1936, were driving between Foyers and Dores when her sister cried out that she could see the Monster. The driver stopped and the women ran to the water's edge, where they

> stood and watched the Monster for 14 minutes. A slight drizzle was falling, the loch looked grey, the sky was grey and the colour of the creature was a very dark grey, very clear and well contrasted against the background of water and sky. The Monster was resting on the surface of the loch, facing towards Inverness, and the length appeared to us to be about 30 feet. It was difficult to judge the exact length or the distance from us, but it was near enough to afford an excellent view. There were three humps, the middle one the largest, the one behind the neck the smallest. The neck was long and slender, the head small and without any discernible features. Quite often the head dipped into the water as if the creature were feeding, or perhaps just amusing itself.

As the women stared in amazement, the Monster

> suddenly turned and shot across the loch towards Urquhart Castle, all the time the top of one humps was just visible above the water or it may have been the head, and a tremendous wash was put up. After travelling a long way across the loch the Monster suddenly turned and came back to the same spot where it had previously been. It came right towards us and at such great speed that we involuntarily all stepped backwards. It came to rest at the same place as before and remained quite still, resting on the water: this time the humps were not so much in evidence, but the head and neck remained well up out of the water.

Mournfully, Mrs Moir reflected on her inability to supply hard evidence of this wondrous event: 'If only we had a camera! What pictures we might have taken! One of the finest opportunities so far offered was lost.'

It is instructive to compare the experience of Mrs Moir and her friends with a similar sighting by a group of women at approximately the same location some 33 years later. It involved someone I shall call

'T.J.' This was someone who lived in Inverness, described in a national newspaper as 'a 47-year-old level-headed housewife, a woman of absolute integrity'. T.J. had two women friends visiting her and decided to take them for a drive along the banks of Loch Ness. It had been raining, then the weather improved and the sun came out. They drove along the south shore and stopped at a lay-by opposite Drumnadrochit to admire the view. Suddenly one of her visitors said: 'There's the monster.' T.J. told a reporter, 'I looked at the loch and saw this peculiar thing. I thought, "*My God – it is*." 'And sure enough, it was.

T.J. explained what happened next:

All I'm saying – and I'd stake my honour and reputation on it – is that I saw something moving in the loch, something not natural, something that could not be explained by a wake or a log. It was something moving down the loch.

That 'something' in the loch was a massive animal, displaying several humps, each some ten feet in length.

T.J.'s friends, – two sisters – were tracked down to their home at Portree on the Isle of Skye and interviewed. They confirmed her story.

Could what they had seen perhaps simply have been the wake of a boat? This idea was 'flatly rejected'. One sister, Phemie, explained why they could be so sure it was what they'd seen was not a boat's wake.

My father and his father and all our family are seafaring people. You might say we have been brought up by the sea. Do you think I do not know the difference between something moving in the water and the wash of a boat? There was something in the water, moving down the loch towards Fort Augustus. What it was I do not know. But it was not the wash from a boat.

The other sister, Joan, a teacher, described what she saw:

It passed right in front of us. At first we were so flabbergasted we could only stand and stare. I could see six humps. I counted them over and over again to be sure I was seeing right. The humps seemed to be about ten feet long. The object was moving down the loch at a bit faster than a quick walking speed. Then it submerged. The humps disappeared from sight and as each one went down it left a little whirl, an eddy on the water. Then that disappeared and the loch as smooth as it had been.

I never thought there was anything in the Loch Ness Monster story before. But now I will say there is definitely something in the loch. What it was I just don't know, but we saw something in the water, something alive, and it was most definitely not the wake from a boat.

The reporter added that all three witnesses 'were emphatic that there was no boat within sight on the loch'. A neighbour paid tribute to the veracity of the sisters, describing them as 'cultured and well-educated people'.

What could a sceptic say in the face of such eye-witness testimony? That these three women saw a boat's wake? Yet they insisted there was no boat in sight on the loch and two of the witnesses were from a seafaring family and were well acquainted with what a boat's wake looks like. Since it wasn't a boat's wake that they saw, what could it possibly have been, if not a large unknown water animal? A family of seals? A line of swimming otters, perhaps? But seals are rarely seen in the loch and when they are present they are usually solitary specimens. Otters do sometimes swim in line but to see six at once would be truly remarkable. Porpoises? Remotely possible but very, very unlikely.

Besides, no known animal found in Loch Ness could possibly be displaying a curving hump ten feet in length. Surely these women had spotted Grandfather Nessie – that giant specimen of the family which Ted Holiday believed reached stupendous proportions. Quite possibly the same outsized monster which surfaced in Peter Macnab's amazing photograph.

What could a sceptic say in response to this eye-witness testimony which would ever convince a believer? At best the sceptic might conclude that they saw a family of otters and, in their excitement, exaggerated the size and number of the animals. The simplest explanation is that these women saw a boat's wake, but the believer will simply retort that all three were adamant that what they'd seen wasn't a wake effect, and moreover two of them were fully conversant with boat's wakes. The sceptic will never convince the believer and the believer will never convince the sceptic.

But in this particular case we are helped by the fact that T.J., unlike Marjorie Moir in 1936, was able to take a photograph of her monster. Sure enough six low, dark, elongated hump-like shapes can be seen on the surface of the loch. Whether or not they are really ten feet in length is debatable but they certainly appear to possess body, and at the rear a pale, spreading wake can plainly be seen.

A classic Nessie photograph? Unfortunately not. Even in the relatively poor-quality monochrome reproduction spread across a full page of the *Sunday Express* (September 7, 1969), a very obvious anomaly can be seen. The wake at the rear of the humps can also be seen *ahead* of them. Another pattern of disturbed water can be seen in the background – a wash which appears to be converging on the wash in front of the six-humped 'monster'.

The photographer, who up until now I have called 'T.J.' was Jessie Tait. Her photograph received wide publicity. It was almost certainly her photograph which was referred to in the *Loch Ness Investigation 1969 Annual Report*, which mentions how 'a national newspaper insisted on publishing a photograph of a known and recorded wake against our most urgent advice'. Indeed, the Tait picture is reproduced later in the Report, with the caption: *The commonest source of error, bow waves from a vessel which has already passed out of sight.*

Ironically this bogus Nessie photograph remained in circulation and the full colour original print appears spread across the front and back cover of a little booklet, *Loch Ness and the Monster: A Handbook for Tourists*, published by J. Arthur Dixon in 1971, with a text edited by Ronald Hastain and written in collaboration with one Nicholas Witchell. This crystal-clear reproduction makes it starkly obvious that Mrs Tait photographed one arm of a boat's wake. And there's the rub. In those rare cases where the eye-witness testimony is supported by photographic evidence the contradiction between the two versions emphatically underlines the fallibility of individual perception.

The outstanding proof of this last assertion is surely supplied by the case of Tim Dinsdale. If we did not have his 65 seconds of 16 mm. ciné film, and if we did not have the text of that very revealing book *Loch Ness Monster*, it would be difficult for a sceptic to challenge his testimony of what occurred on April 23, 1960. Without the film or the book it would be hard to question the eye-witness account, which might well seem irrefutable. Tim Dinsdale was, on the face of it, a cool, objective, impressive witness. His social status was that of a respectable, down-to-earth family man. He was a former RAF pilot and an aeronautical engineer – a sober, professional person. Here was an eye-witness who, on first sighting a strange, unusual object on the loch surface, examined it with cool, objective detachment through powerful binoculars. He observed the back of an enormous aquatic animal – the

Monster. His view of it was so good he was even able to make out a large blotch on one side of the animal's curving back. As he stared at the enormous creature it suddenly moved off, crossed the loch, then turned, displaying the frothing commotion from immense paddle strokes. Finally the animal submerged.

Faced with the sceptic's argument that the object he'd seen was a boat, Dinsdale retorted firmly that he was *completely familiar* with what vessels on Loch Ness looked like. Besides, by hurrying to the lochside, Dinsdale was able to establish that the loch surface had no vessels whatever on it. How, then, could such detailed testimony from an objective witness equipped with binoculars be credibly refuted? In his book Dinsdale is at pains to emphasize how calm and collected he was – 'Unhurried', focusing his binoculars on the mystery object 'carefully'. All a sceptic could possibly say, rather feebly, would be 'I think you were mistaken.' But the believer would reasonably reply that Dinsdale viewed the Monster carefully through binoculars and was able to see not only that it was an animal with an immense curving humped back but was even able to distinguish a marking on its side.

It is only because we have the book and the film that it is possible to arrive at a very different interpretation of this episode. As I argued in *The Loch Ness Mystery Solved*, the book's revelations make it easier to understand that Dinsdale was in such an acute, shuddering condition of 'expectant attention' that when he saw something moving in the distance across the loch he instantly processed the object as the back of a huge, living animal. His examination of the object through binoculars was carried out in a state of extreme anticipation. His hands were probably shaking, his perception blurred. He was a man who was physically exhausted and living on his nerves. He was desperate to see the Monster and this moment on the road above Foyers was quite literally his last chance before he packed up and drove home.

We also have the film and now, over half a century later, there can't really be any doubt that Dinsdale was in a condition of uncontrollable excitement when he saw something on the loch surface and that he *instantly* processed that object as the monster, even though what was actually there and what he filmed was a boat. Most probably it was a perfectly ordinary local fishing boat containing two men. They had just left Foyers and were crossing the loch to fish along the far shore, before presumably crossing back and returning later that day along the south shore to Foyers. Or, just possibly, it was the mysterious red motor boat which I'd been tipped off about.

Tim Dinsdale spent perhaps more time gazing at the surface of Loch Ness, looking for the monster, than anyone who ever lived, yet the results of a lifetime's dedication were paltry. When he sat at a fixed point on the lochside he saw nothing – something which was reciprocated by the Loch Ness Investigation Bureau. But when Dinsdale started watching from a moving object he had better luck. Apart from his 1960 experience, he had two other sightings. A decade later, while drifting in his boat, he spotted a 'telegraph pole' sticking out of the water, which then streaked across the loch and out of sight behind a promontory. It was 'such a brief experience'. Almost one year later he had another head and neck sighting, again from a moving boat and again very brief. But Dinsdale was in no doubt that he had seen the monster, insisting that in 1970 'it had been entirely real' and in 1971 that it was 'real enough'. But in neither case did he have time to take film or photographs, which would have allowed analysis of the mystery objects. If anyone should have seen the Loch Ness Monster it was Tim Dinsdale. Ironically, his lifetime's dedication only serves to underline the reality that the creature is imaginary entity – an invention of the mind, processing explicable phenomena into a giant unknown animal.

Three years before the Tait sighting another Inverness housewife had also seen the monster exhibiting similar behaviour. Mrs Margaret Edwards witnessed something enormous about a quarter of a mile offshore near Abriachan. It was splashing about in a 'thunderous way' and 'making quite a commotion'. She filmed it on her 8mm home movie camera, achieving what the *Express* dramatically described as 'a colour movie which no one else in the world can boast of'.

This episode is recorded, with some variations in detail, in Nicholas Witchell's book *The Loch Ness Story*. According to Witchell the film lasted

> for about one minute. She saw a big hump and what resembled a tail but the 8mm. film, according to the experts who studied it, only revealed a disturbance in the water and suggested the presence of something solid.

The identity of these 'experts' is not supplied. Neither the *Express* nor Witchell give the time or the particular day in June 1966 when she had her sighting. Thereafter Margaret Edwards' sighting and her allegedly unique film drop from view, attracting no interest from students of the mystery. In the 1982 Corgi paperback edition of *The Loch Ness Story*,

Witchell quietly deleted all mention of Margaret Edwards and her encounter with the monster.

By the sound of it, what Mrs Edwards saw was a boat's wake, and the fact that she had film of her 'monster' is what helped finally to discredit it. If she had not filmed the disturbance all we would have is her verbal testimony, and she would probably feature in lists of sightings for 1966, instead of being absent.

What also strikes me about Mrs Edwards' sighting is how much aspects of it resemble that of Donaldina Mackay's in 1933. A commotion just off the north shore, in the vicinity of Abriachan. Of course Mrs Mackay went on to supply details which would militate against the phenomenon being a boat's wake – but only if those details were accurate. If the verbal eye-witness statement is regarded as a photograph in words, then sceptical analysis becomes harder. Dick Raynor, accepting Mackay's account as accurate, asserts that the description plainly involves 'a typical seal mating display'. Steuart Campbell suggested an otter as the source of the disturbance. This is what one might call the literal-minded sceptic's approach to the eye-witness problem. It naturalises the reported monster by translating its behaviour into that of a known animal – or as nearly as possible. But a believer can simply retort that Mrs Mackay confidently identified the size of the 'monster' which she witnessed, and it exceeded that of a seal or an otter. The sceptic retorts that her estimate was mistaken; the believer asserts that the sceptic is desperately trying to reduce the monster's size simply in order to fit a theory which is without merit. The gap in interpretation can never be bridged.

As for Marjorie Moir, if she had taken a photograph I am confident that it would not remotely have resembled the amazing sketch which she drew for Constance Whyte and which is reproduced, slightly altered, in Dinsdale's *Loch Ness Monster*. Her 'monster' sounds very much like a group of birds witnessed in adverse conditions (a grey, drizzly October day). The creature's behaviour ('the head dipped into the water as if the creature were feeding') and the sudden rush across the water is entirely consistent with bird activity. Moir's perspective was also a very limited one: as she herself admitted, 'It was difficult to judge the exact length or the distance from us, but it was near enough to afford an excellent view.'

In a later account given to Tim Dinsdale she estimated that the Monster was one-third of the way across the loch, which, if at all accurate, indicates something 600 yards away. She had no binoculars and was at surface level, which creates a foreshortening effect and makes estimates of distance very difficult. Nor do we have witness statements by her four companions. 'Expectant attention' was also plainly a factor. Moir's sketch is a moment frozen in time – a single remembered image from a sighting which by Nessie standards was a lengthy one. She was unwavering in her recollection that the episode lasted exactly 14 minutes (a strange statistic, since who, on first sighting the Loch Ness Monster, then looks to see what time it is?).

But by the time Moir drew her sketch for Constance Whyte the memory had solidified and the story been told many times ('Dear Mrs Whyte, *As I have often told you* I once saw the Loch Ness Monster' – my italics.) When Tim Dinsdale appeared on 'Panorama' in 1960, one of the enthralled viewers was Marjorie Moir, who promptly wrote to him, re-telling her sighting:

> The creature was quite stationary, and often dipped its head into the water, either feeding or amusing itself. We watched in awe and amazement, for about 5-8 minutes; then suddenly it swung away from the shore and shot across the loch at terrific speed, putting up a wash exactly similar to that I saw in your film... You can now – I hope – understand why your film was of such absorbing interest to me, so much in it was exactly what I saw and remember so vividly. One more thing – the composite picture shown at the end of your film was the same in every detail as the Monster I saw in October, 1936, even to the approximate length. Many people have seen this creature, it does exist.

If nothing else, this reveals how impressionable Moir was. How could the wake in the Dinsdale film be 'exactly' what she saw? Moir was standing on a beach, viewing the Monster at surface level. Dinsdale's film was shot from a road high above Lower Foyers, from a completely different perspective. Dinsdale's monster also leaves a faint propeller wake.

When Mrs Moir wrote of the Dinsdale film that 'so much in it was exactly what I saw and remember so vividly' her comment is baffling, since the object in that film neither resembled the Monster which Moir believed she had seen and subsequently sketched nor did it behave in the same way.

Dinsdale himself was obliged to correct Moir's description of a 'composite picture', with a footnote pointing out that this was 'Actually

[a] half-section model'– namely 'a model of the Monster, made out of clay and carrying the same peculiar mark on its flank I had seen so distinctly. The model was no more than a prototype, based on average statistics, showing the animal with three humps instead of two most commonly reported – or the single hump that appeared in the film.' But of course Dinsdale's model Nessie was based on his analysis of 100 sightings plucked from a larger body of material, with no identification of the eye-witnesses or why their sightings had been selected in preference to hundreds of others. However, it seems highly likely that a detailed sighting like Moir's, given prominence in *More Than a Legend*, was one of Dinsdale's hundred sightings. If indeed it was, then the process becomes self-referential: Moir was exclaiming in wonder at the authenticity of an image which she herself had unknowingly contributed to.

In old age, providing another account of her sighting, Moir added a telling new detail:

> all of a sudden it turned and fled – turned round away from us and went straight across the loch, and it made a terrific wave on the shore, and Ann had to get out of the way of the wave. It came up onto the shore.

A wake that crashes onto the beach is plainly not created by wild birds. But neither is it likely to have been generated by an animal. As Maurice Burton liked to point out, aquatic animals are streamlined. The act of swimming is smooth and does not involve creating great commotion or turbulence at the surface. Such phenomena signify an object encountering resistance – an object, say, like the hull of a power-driven boat pushing its way across a lake surface.

But of course, Mrs Moir's memory may in this instance have been a false one. In her eighties she believed she had been driving the car that day, which contradicts all previous accounts. Her passionate sincerity was never in doubt but her conflicting narratives underline the difficulty presented by sightings which lack other forms of verification.

Oddly, no one ever seems to have connected the Moir sighting with that of Mr G. Jamieson, who on December 27, 1933, had a very close encounter with the Monster. He was driving east along the north shore road between Fort Augustus and Invermoriston when he spotted the animal 'within 100 yards of the shore. The road at this point runs close above the Loch and overlooks it.' The Monster appeared to be some fifteen to twenty feet in length and consisted of a head, neck and two humps. Gould's book reproduces an image, captioned 'Mr Jamieson's Sketch', which is very similar to Moir's. The biggest hump, he said, stood three feet above the water and the smaller, two feet. The Monster was greyish-black in colour, with a skin which seemed 'rough and mottled, or knobbly'. It swam 'rapidly and obliquely across the Loch', heading south. It was eleven in the morning, the weather was clear and the loch surface was 'like glass'. Mr Jamieson saw that there was a boat on the other side of the loch, which the Monster was swimming towards. He sounded his horn to alert the crew. Evidently reacting to the sound, the Monster 'turned its head quickly, and dived below. In a second or two it had completely disappeared, leaving a well-marked wash still showing'.

The Jamieson sighting raises what might be called the problem of *transmission*: who is telling the story and how are they telling it? This particular sighting narrative originated in a letter which Jamieson himself sent to the *Scotsman*, which, after publication, was then rewritten by Rupert Gould, appearing as sighting number 35 in *The Loch Ness Monster and Others*. Gould corresponded with the witness, who supplied a sketch of the monster 'which he made later'. But though the monster drawing in *The Loch Ness Monster* is captioned 'Mr Jamieson's Sketch' it is, in fact, as the author acknowledges, Gould's re-drawing of the original. In the absence of the original, of course, there is no way of knowing if Gould 'improved' it.

One might ask why Gould felt it necessary to re-interpret the original. The answer, implicitly, is for purposes of persuasion. The original sketches of monster sightings would have been amateurish and lacking in the potency of Gould's undoubted skills as a graphic artist. But how far his 'improvement' involved exaggerating body shape and size is something we can now never know. The illustrations in *The Loch Ness Monster and Others* purport to be exact representations of what the witnesses saw; they are equivalent to photographic snapshots of an actual scene. Some, such as the marvellously flexible eight-humped monster witnessed by Mr W. U. Goodbody of Invergarry, have been quietly sidelined, whereas others, such as Arthur Grant's plesiosaur-style monster, became central to the evolving Nessie template. Others are so obvious they simply underline Gould's naïvety, such as Dr. J. Kirton's sighting of what is all too plainly a distant fisherman in a dinghy.

The simple act of soliciting a sketch from a witness helped the process of objectifying a brief sensory experience. To a believer the sketch vindicates that belief and cannot be reduced to anything other than a large unknown animal. But from a sceptical perspective a number of things are evident about Gould's December 1933 witness, Mr Jamieson. The exact location of the sighting is not known. The witness was driving a van at the time of his sighting – another classic instance of an observer in a moving object on the loch side sighting a moving object on the loch surface. The length of time of the sighting is not given but it appears to have been momentary. The witness evidently never got out of the driver's cab during the entire experience. From a sceptical perspective what Mr Jamieson saw was nothing more than a bird or a group of birds swimming across a 'Loch like glass'. The mirrored surface simply made the birds' wake appear large and hump-like. The monster's rough skin ('rough and mottled, or knobbly') was simply the irregularity of a feathered bird or a cluster of birds. When Jamieson sounded his horn the Monster 'turned its head quickly, and dived below' – behaviour perfectly consistent with a diving bird.

But of course what Mr Jamieson saw in the loch on December 27 1933 can never be known. 'G. Jamieson', van driver, is an enigma. We do not know his age or anything about him. He was quite probably a resident of Fort Augustus – a village in the grip of Monster fever. Rupert Gould's correspondence with this eye-witness threw up one new piece of information. Jamieson told Gould he had seen the Monster again, just fourteen days later. This time he had only caught a glimpse of it – 'a portion of the big hump disappearing below the surface'. From a sceptical perspective, two Monster sightings in a fortnight suggests a deeply impressionable individual. But with flawless logic the believer can retort that the Monster was more visible during the winter of 1933, possibly because the disturbances associated with the roadworks brought the animal to the surface more often, or possibly because the loch side had been cleared of vegetation, making its appearances easier to see, or possibly because more people were actively looking for it.

The problem of *transmission* – who is telling the story and how are they telling it? – is raised in an acute form by the case of the Jean Macdonald and Patricia Harvey land sighting, which probably occurred on January 30, 1934, and which was first reported a month later, in the March 3 edition of the *Glasgow Herald*. At a location on the edge of Fort Augustus the two local girls reported seeing 'a weird-looking creature' which crossed the burn and vanished in the direction of the loch. There was a full moon and the animal was only twenty feet away.

It seemed to be from eight to ten feet long.

Roy Mackal concluded that the girls' sighting 'would appear to be misidentification of wild or domestic animals, such as deer or highland cattle'. But deer or cattle are hard to square with the animal the girls described. Steuart Campbell's conclusion that the description 'is very close to that of an otter' seems much more plausible, if you believe that what they saw had a commonplace explanation and did not involve an encounter with an unknown animal. Roland Watson, however, argues that the sighting involved an authentic encounter with the Monster and that claims of exaggeration can be disregarded:

> I think it is clear that it would be a bit of a push to mistake an otter for something ten foot by six, especially since the witnesses had multiple frames of reference, such as the adjacent trees and the burn being crossed. Put yourself in their place, could you mistake such a creature for something smaller? I don't think I would either.

> Perhaps it was indeed a large animal such as a deer or cow? Again, put yourself in the place of the witnesses and ask whether an animal familiar to these rural people could be so easily mistaken for this larger creature with a dramatically sloping back at such a short distance. Again, common sense suggests this is not likely.

These interpretations can never be reconciled. To a believer like Watson an exploration of the location of the sighting adds to its authenticity. But as a sceptic what I find interesting about the sighting is its brevity. It was, it appears, the briefest of sightings: 'impressions…gathered in a few moments'. It's questionable whether a momentary sighting really allows an objective assessment of size and shape. This is a sighting on a par with that of the Spicers – a sudden, out-of-the-blue, very brief perception of something animate.

Besides, how old were these witnesses? They are identified only as 'girls' which might mean anything from five years old to considerably older. Agatha Christie's 1934 story, 'Sing a Song of Sixpence', includes a character described as 'A tall, dark girl of close on thirty'. They were, one suspects, teenagers. In a small village gripped by monster fever it's not hard to understand how a pair of young people might unexpectedly have come across an animal, shrieked in amazement, and run off. Fort Augustus was a place where even the pillars of the community were processing objects on Loch Ness as 'monsters', so it is to be expected that the young people would be influenced by the prevailing atmosphere of extreme *anticipation*.

But what finally renders this sighting worthless as evidence is its source. The *Glasgow Herald* refers to 'a statement made to our Fort Augustus correspondent' and the *Northern Chronicle* (March 7, 1934) states, 'They told our own correspondent...'. The unidentified correspondent in both cases can only have been Alex Campbell, once again actively soliciting evidence for his very personal obsession. But we know from the Mackay sighting that his seminal report was both inaccurate and imbued with his own agenda. Neutral reportage was not Alex Campbell's *métier*. The story appears to be based on a face-to-face interview conducted with both girls simultaneously. But the extent to which Campbell asked leading questions or polished their answers is impossible to ascertain. Did the two girls even see the published versions of their sighting?

These questions are unanswerable now. But it is a reasonable conclusion that even if the girls did see the press reports of their experience, they were in no position to challenge them, should they have wished to do so. But of course we'll never know. No later investigator ever tracked the two women down to find out if the 1934 reports of their sighting were accurate, even though it is likely that both remained in the vicinity of the loch and were available to be interviewed during the 1950s, 1960s and 1970s. All we are left with is a version of an experience mediated at second hand by Alex Campbell, and that in itself makes the episode valueless.

The same point applies to the better-known Margaret Munro land sighting of June 3, 1934, when the Monster was observed through binoculars for 25 minutes, lying on a remote beach overlooking Borlum Bay. Munro, who was probably a teenager, was interviewed by the 'representative' of the *Inverness Courier*, which published a report (June 5) on the sighting:

Miss Munro said that it was the largest living creature she had ever seen, and only a portion lay clear on the water, the giraffe-like neck and absurdly small head being out of all proportion to the size of the body, which was dark-grey in colour... The head and neck, Miss Munro stated, was exactly like those portrayed in the London surgeon's photograph of the Monster.

The report concludes: 'It might be added that Miss Munro, who is a native of Fort-Augustus, firmly refused to believe up till now in the existence of the Monster.'

There really can be no doubt at all that this report was concocted by Alex Campbell (that final sentence is very characteristic of his reportage, both in style and content). *There is no other source at all for this sighting.* Constance Whyte quotes a diary entry by Dom Cyril Dieckhoff, but this is plainly nothing more than a re-hash of Campbell's news report. It is blatantly obvious that the Surgeon's photograph, published just six weeks earlier, cast a giant shadow over this sighting, as it did over others at this time. The previous month Kenneth Cameron was reported to have observed the Monster near Dores, stating that it was identical to the animal in the surgeon's picture (*Inverness Courier*, May 8, 1934). Whether or not that image distorted Margaret Munro's perception and memory of the animal she viewed, or whether Campbell doctored her eye-witness testimony, is something we can never know. By itself this eye-witness report is worthless because it is contaminated by Campbell's involvement. Things might be different if in later years someone had gone in search of Margaret Munro and re-interviewed her. But no one ever did.

When a witness is re-interrogated the sceptic will always look for alterations to the narrative. In such classic cases as Donaldina Mackay, George Spicer and Father Gregory Brusey, the variations are illuminating. This is particularly the case with a classic sighting which ranks high in Nessie lore – the terrifying close-up encounter with a monstrous creature experienced by Greta Finlay and her son Harry on August 20, 1952. Constance Whyte obtained an account from Mrs Finlay just two days after her sighting, supported by a sketch drawn by her 12-year-old son and fellow witness Harry. It was evidently a momentary encounter. Greta Finlay heard a great deal of splashing which, as it continued and grew louder, attracted her interest. She walked round her caravan, which was situated beside the loch in the grounds of Aldourie Castle, and saw 'not 20 yards away' a grotesque creature. What attracted her attention was 'the strange appearance of the head and neck':

What astonished me, apart from the hideous appearance of the head, was that there were two 6-inch-long projections from it, each with a blob on the end. The skin looked black and shiny and reminded me of a snail more than anything.

Mrs Finlay's description of her encounter is a collage of vagueness and extreme precision. She said she was 'so taken up with the strange appearance of the head and neck that I did not examine the rest of the animal at all closely'. Nevertheless, 'There were two or three humps and the total length visible would be about 15 feet.' The sketch by her son shows two humps. 'The head and neck together were 2-2½ feet in length, the head alone being about 6 inches long and of about the same width as the neck.'

Itis extremely doubtful that anyone could possibly be so precise about an animal glimpsed only momentarily. It is also clear that the statement in *More Than a Legend* was not something written by Mrs Finlay but rather Constance Whyte's digest 'of conversation'. In this original version of the sighting, Mrs Whyte ran back into her caravan for her camera. 'As she returned the creature moved off quickly, then disappeared in a great commotion which set waves breaking on the shore.'

Some eight years after her sighting Tim Dinsdale contacted Mrs Finlay and received back a letter which described her experience. In this version the sighting was an unbroken experience, with no running into the caravan for a camera.

> My son and I stood looking at this creature in amazement. Although I was terrified, we stood and watched until it submerged, which it did very quickly causing waves to break on the shore.

It transpired that Harry Finlay had drawn 'several sketches' of the Monster, one of which was sent to Dinsdale. Unfortunately the image as reproduced in *Loch Ness Monster* (Figure 13) appears to have been redrawn by Dinsdale (perplexingly it is captioned 'Mrs Greta Finlay's Sketch'). One suspects the version he was working from was the same one reproduced in *More Than a Legend*, which it resembles. However, the Dinsdale version shows the monster's neck joined to a longer body consisting of a small hump or curve which precedes two large humps of equal size, all of which are visibly connected above the surface. It is a great pity that Harry Finlay's other sketches have never been reproduced, as it is possible they would have shed further light on this legendary sighting.

Maurice Burton shrewdly noted that there was a disparity between Mrs Finlay's testimony and her son's sketch as it appears in *More Than a Legend*. She estimated that the head and neck together rose 2-2½ feet out of the water, with the total length visible about 15 feet. But in the sketch she selected the total length of the monster is less than twice that of the height of the head and neck, which would indicate a length of only four to five feet. Tellingly, Mrs Whyte described the animal as 'a relatively small edition of the Monster'. As far as Burton was concerned Mrs Finlay's monster was nothing more than a deer in shallow water.

He also made the acute observation that the only three eye-witness reports of monsters with antennae all occurred during the month of August: 'The red deer stag, in its second year of life, carries a pair of short unbranched antlers. During July and August these are in velvet.' The term 'velvet' refers to the soft protective tissue around newly forming antlers. It's entirely plausible that Mrs Finlay's perception of a monstrous creature with a head with 'two projections from it, each with a blob on the end' was nothing more than a brocket – a young red deer with simple unbranched antlers in velvet. The term 'red deer' is misleading, as the animals can present a dark appearance.

It was also sensible of Burton to note the brevity of the sighting: 'How long did she spend observing the object? It might have been two seconds or five, probably no more, and she was in a surprised state.' Since there was no time to take a photograph it all happened very quickly and 'there was too much confusion for careful observation'. Two days had passed before the incident was reported to Constance Whyte: 'Her memory of a confused situation had had time to grow dim, the visual impression she had carried away could have become distorted.'

I believe that Burton was fundamentally correct in his analysis of the Finlay sighting. But problems remain. Mrs Finlay claimed in her original account of the incident that she saw the monster submerge and vanish from sight. In the face of this a sceptic like Burton is reduced to the theory of a swimming deer which died from shock and sank below the surface. He also produced a version of Harry Finlay's sketch and set it alongside one of his own of 'how a two-year red stag deer might appear in August, standing or swimming in water and facing the onlooker, with its antlers in velvet and its ears back.'

This is what might be called the problem of the literal-minded sceptic. A believer in Nessie can draw attention to at least two difficulties with the sceptic's case. The first is that of the deer's ears, which Greta Finlay didn't see. Roland Watson argues that 'the ears are a bit of a stick out problem. Ears are important to a deer and are constantly rotating around like radar assessing any potential dangers. This would be especially true when they are in a vulnerable environment like water.' The second is the animal's submergence. Watson asserts: 'Deer do not submerge and disappear under the surface (unless dragged under the surface by the Loch Ness Monster). If this was a deer then it would have remained in sight for a long time or clambered onto the shore.' He reinforces his arguments based on his own unexpected encounter with a deer.

I think Watson is wrong. Since he reinforces his argument with a personal anecdote, let me tell one of my own. A few years ago I was the front seat passenger in a car being driven along a quiet road through an English forest. It was early afternoon, on a sunny day. Suddenly, without warning, an animal rushed out of the trees on my side and hurled itself across the road. The driver had no time at all to react. The animal ran past and vanished into the trees on the far side. I had no problem at all in identifying this animal as a deer. It was big, it was dark, it ran fast. It wasn't the shape of a horse or a cow. It can only have been a deer. It was deer-sized. And that was about it. I couldn't possibly have given exact measurements as to how far it was away (five yards? Ten yards? Fifteen yards? Somewhere in that range). Nor could I have said what the animal's dimensions were. It all happened so quickly. I can't even be *certain* it was a deer. It could in theory have been an unknown animal. It was big and dark in that setting and it all happened so quickly, so unexpectedly.

And this, I think, it was happened to Greta Finlay. She almost certainly didn't have the slightest idea that deer could swim. When she walked round her caravan and saw the animal in the water she immediately processed it as the Loch Ness Monster. She ran back into her caravan for her camera. And when she emerged? Believers, reasonably enough, mock the suggestion that a swimming deer conveniently expired before her eyes and slipped beneath the water. However, when Ted Holiday went to see Greta Finlay in 1964 he reported a different version of the episode: 'Mrs Finlay rushed into the caravan for a camera but, by the time she ran out, it had submerged.' In other words, Mrs Finlay *neither saw the animal appear on the loch surface, nor disappear*. In this version it is entirely plausible that what the two Finlays encountered at very close quarters was a deer in the water. It was making a commotion because it had either just jumped into the loch or had swum across it and was trying to scramble up on to the shore. By the time Mrs Finlay had located her camera and run out again the deer had succeeded in climbing on to land and had galloped silently away into the adjacent trees. The sighting occurred in an area which is full of deer.

But of course, the two interpretations can never be reconciled. Ted Holiday had no problem connecting the Finlays' 'large and most repulsive animal' to his Orm theory, while Maurice Burton observed the striking parallels with a swimming deer. Greta Finlay herself remains an enigma, someone of whom we know almost nothing. Her character and personality are unknown. Like so many of the classic witnesses, she is as much a figure of myth as the Monster she believed she had seen.

Two years after publication of *The Loch Ness Mystery Solved*, Adrian Shine was still in thrall to the power of eye-witness testimony, and used it to justify his own continuing presence at the loch. A quarter of a century earlier Maurice Burton was similarly bewitched, writing that there was still a hard core 'of convincing accounts of a long neck and head seen at close quarters' which meant that he could confidently reject at best '95 per cent of the evidence'. He cited the example of a sighting by Mrs Norah Atkinson, who was idly gazing out across the loch from the roadside somewhere beyond Dores:

Suddenly, there was a terrific upheaval of water and up came a long swan-like neck with a small head. Then the whole body appeared, elephant grey in colour, two humps and very long and powerful... What a terrifying sight it was, and one I shall remember for the rest of my life.

Burton decided that the usual sceptical explanations would not do for this encounter.

An equally baffling sighting occurred at roughly the same location in June 1990, when a married couple witnessed the sudden appearance at very close quarters of an enormous animal 'between 20 and 25 feet long, and about 4 feet out of the water at the highest point... Then suddenly a neck and head rose up out of the water at the right end of the body, the same end as the above mentioned hump... The creature's mouth opened slightly and we both saw what appeared to be sharp but almost greenish, murky teeth. The whole experience was utterly horrible, and nothing less than traumatic. The neck arched about 3 times, the head lowered to the water, and then with hardly any turbulence the entire creature sank vertically and disappeared.'

What can a sceptic say in response to such testimonies? It is hard to rationalise them naturalistically, as Burton conceded in connection with the Atkinson sighting. The first response is to seek more information. But in both these cases there isn't any. The Atkinson sighting was set out in an unsolicited letter which Burton received. He never met the sender and his efforts to seek more information were rebuffed. And in the case of the 1990 sighting, something strange occurred. It appeared on Roland Watson's blog on February 27, 2016, titled 'An Extraordinary Nessie Story from 1990'. It provoked 24 comments, none sceptical, with one person asking for more detail regarding how close the witnesses were to the water. No reply was forthcoming even though a response was promised by the husband.

Watson subsequently deleted this story from his blog. Presumably he'd been hoodwinked by a hoaxer. In its own small way this episode illustrates the ongoing process of revisionism which has always affected the Loch Ness story. For example, no one nowadays sees monsters which create massive turbulence at the surface or which travel at speeds of 30 m.p.h. Those kinds of monster have been quietly shelved.

A more tangible witness is John McLean, who saw the Monster at very close quarters on June 28, 1938, near the Alltsigh Burn, below The Half-Way House. The interviewer, we can be certain, was, as always, Alex Campbell. The dialogue is likely to have been rewritten and polished rather than raw.

'It was the monster's head and neck less than twenty yards from me,' he said, 'and it was, without any doubt, in the act of swallowing food. It opened and closed its mouth several times quite quickly, and then kept tossing its head backwards in exactly the same manner as a cormorant does after it has devoured a fish.' No sooner had the creature finished its meal than it dived below, but before doing so two distinct humps and the entire length of the tail came to the surface.

The monster then vanished head first but came up again a few yards further west, and there it lay for two or three minutes on the top of the water. The tail was again quite clear at the surface, with the head, neck, and two humps showing. In a moment or two it began to dive very slowly and, in doing so, the head was submerged first, followed by the humps, but at this point the foremost hump became very much larger and rose in fact almost twice as high out of the water as it had been at any time during its appearance.

'The monster, I am sure, is eighteen to twenty-two feet long, the tail fully six feet, and the largest hump was about three feet high. The head is small and pointed, the skin very dark brown on the back, and like that of a horse when wet and glistening. The neck is rather thin and several feet long, but I saw no flippers or fins.'

This, it may be added, is the first time that anyone has seen the monster full length above water or out of it, and the entire tail, which was about a foot thick at the root and tapered to a fine point.

For Roland Watson a sighting like this is unanswerable. A man like John McLean could not have made any error. The witness was re-interviewed in 1964 by Ted Holiday, who tape-recorded the session. There were variations in his narrative, which can reasonably be excused by the passage of time, but his story was essentially the same. A gigantic unidentifiable animal had appeared in front of him at very close quarters. There was a 'massive' hump which rose three feet out of the water. He was even close enough to see a strange pulling motion, which dragged the hump abruptly downward 'Just for all the world like a snake'.

From his description, there seems little doubt that McLean's Monster was feeding on fish. Could the animal have been one or more cormorants, seals or otters? McLean insisted that it could not (though from a sceptical perspective it sounds very much as if he what he saw was a pair of otters). The sighting occurred at 9.15pm, when night was approaching and the loch in heavy shadow.

In the 1960s and 1970s it was commonly believed that the Loch Ness Monster's diet consisted of fish, and McLean's sighting was consistent with that belief. Today, however, Loch Ness is regarded as an unsustainable environment for a family of Monsters because its fish stocks are said to be inadequate.

The problem with monster witnesses is that the more you learn about them, the more the questions pile up. A big question is always how *impressionable* they are. McLean's initial response to seeing a head and neck emerge from the water at close range was to be 'alarmed... at what it was' (or as he said back in 1938, 'petrified'). Within three months McLean had seen the Monster again, which, as Watson sardonically concedes, 'always raises a red flag with sceptics (they don't think people should see Nessie more than once)'.

In fact, it was only because Ted Holiday went to visit McLean in

1964 that we discovered that this classic witness saw the Monster a *third* time, the year after his close-up encounter. John McLean was sitting by a window in the Half-Way House with three other men, one of them being John McDonald, a local born in Glenurquhart. They were discussing the Monster and McDonald expressed scepticism, remarking, 'There's not such a thing in the loch!'

> 'And just with those words out of his mouth this head appeared exactly in the same place as before. And I said, "Well, look here, John – there's it now!" And he jumped out of the window right down to the lochside and came up quite excited. "Yes," he said, "I'm quite convinced now."'

In other words, John McLean was both a man prone to seeing monsters and also a great raconteur.

Every sighting tells a narrative and sometimes they have the magic and power of a good short story. But some of the best ones are shunned by believers, who presumably find them inherently absurd and unbelievable, even by the standards of Nessie lore. For example, a month after Margaret Munro's sensational 25-minute land sighting, another resident of Fort Augustus had an equally amazing experience while working on the Glendoe estate, not far from where Munro saw her monster. Ian J. Matheson reported that at 9am on July 4, 1934, he saw 'a curious wave' break the calm surface of the loch about 100 yards offshore. The wave grew bigger as it approached the shore:

> presently there emerged from the shallows a beast like a horse, but with a body in the form of five humps. With the air of flippers it propelled itself right onto the beach, the body moving with the motions of a wriggling worm or eel. While the beast was actually worming its way ashore, twelve distinct humps were in view. The head was smaller and thicker than a horse's and the neck was heavily maned. The beast shook the water from the mane as a horse does on a wet day.

It was, Matheson said, 'the queerest looking thing I ever saw'. The animal was thirty feet long with small eyes. He watched it for an hour, during which time the Monster ate 'weeds and water plants growing at the shore'. Finally, the Monster wriggled back into the loch with a big splash. As it did so, in the distance the clock in the Fort Augustus abbey chimed the hour of ten.

Matheson's thirty-foot-long vegetarian Loch Ness monster which shape-shifted from twelve humps to five humps seems quite unlike the animal which Margaret Munro saw nearby just weeks earlier, or John McLean's monster, which apparently enjoyed tucking into fish. Consequently his remarkable sighting – one of the longest on record – has been marginalised or shunned in Monster literature.

Constance Whyte was aware that the sightings record was riddled with inconsistencies and contradictions, but with engagingly flawless logic she explained that 'Certain discrepancies in the way *an Niseag* is described by different observers can be accounted for by there being males, females, old and young in Loch Ness.'

The sincerity of eye-witnesses is rarely in doubt. Their conviction that they have seen a large unknown animal is unshakeable. For example, in 1962 Mrs Trude Bryant wrote to Tim Dinsdale to describe how a few years earlier she was walking with a friend:

> It was early evening, but the sun was still shining and the light good. We were both looking out [across the water] and to our surprise we saw a moving object, between 20 and 30 feet in length – resembling a string of lights, travelling at a tremendous pace towards the pier. We were amazed, as we had never seen anything like this before; and I noticed a man and a woman beside us watching the same thing. The 'lights' were presumably phosphorescence; slightly submerged, as I do not remember any ripples being visible. In a matter of seconds this object had headed towards a pier and out of sight. I could not estimate the speed of travel, but it moved very quickly…

This sighting occurred not at Loch Ness but on the seafront at the popular Suffolk resort of Southwold. Dinsdale breezily explained how Mrs Bryant had compared her mysterious 'moving object' to 'a drawing which appeared in *Loch Ness Monster*, showing the multi-hump body shape sometimes exhibited by our old chum in Loch Ness'. This was a reference to a page displaying seven monster silhouettes drawn by Dinsdale for his book. Mrs Bryant, who had read it, singled out 'shape No. 6', which she had seen 'travelling at a furious pace. There appeared to be lights on the humps…'

Dinsdale thought the multi-humped object which Mrs Bryant had seen was typical of so many Great Sea-serpent sightings but he was puzzled by the reported phosphorescence, which would not have been visible in daylight. He mused that perhaps it was actually sunlight 'reflecting off a wet skin surface, creating an impression of lights'. Ironically, in reinterpreting Mrs Bryant's sighting, Dinsdale adopted the logic of scepticism, suggesting that 'conditions of poor light, surprise, fright, or the momentary glimpse of something unfamiliar could cause an observer to draw a wrong conclusion'.

But having made this awesome leap into the dizzy realm of doubt, he quickly retracted this dangerous flirtation with rational analysis and returned to a safer, more comfortable place. For Dinsdale the primacy of meaning and interpretation could only ever belong to the eye-witness: 'it is the observer who is best able to judge the conclusions of others – in relation to something they have not actually seen'. The witness says Monster, the sceptic says otter/wake/cormorant, and since the sceptic did not see the animal and the witness did, the observer alone *knows* what they saw.

Ironically, 'shape No. 6' in the Dinsdale illustration exhibits eight humps of identical shape and size – the classic monster sighting involving a boat's wake. Mrs Bryant did not in reality see a large unknown animal swimming near Southwold pier. In an unfamiliar environment she saw an unfamiliar phenomenon: the curling, moving wake of a boat, quite possibly from a trawler, which had passed from sight, having either disappeared behind the pier or entered the nearby harbour.

'Wonders are many and none is more wonderful than man,' wrote Sophocles in *Antigone*. Or to put it another way, the two big questions with Loch Ness Monster eye-witnesses are always, how familiar are they with the loch's environment and what might appear unexpectedly on its surface, and how impressionable/suggestible are they? The problem with almost all the classic eye-witness accounts is that we can never know the answers to these two crucial questions. But the answer to the first question is that virtually no one can be expected to be familiar with the immense variety of surface phenomena which Loch Ness presents. Even a hardened sceptic such as me was impressed by this account of fish behaviour, given by Simon Dawes:

I saw it at Fort Augustus on the jetty. I was looking at the Loch and in my peripheral vision noticed something come straight up out if the water at a fair speed and drop straight back down. So I carried on looking and it happened again and this time I had a clear view of what looked like a pole straight up and down about 3-4 feet long, I called my dad over and he watched it happen several more times. He knew that it was just a pike fishing but if he hadn't been there we both know what I would've thought I was looking at! He reckons it's how they fish. Swim with the prey between them and the surface of the water and then shoot up so fast they come out of the water as they grab the prey. It fits what I saw but I've never seen it before or since.

From a personal perspective I have only once in my life seen a cormorant transform itself unexpectedly into what appeared to be a large, dark pole-shaped object some eight feet high. My memory of that moment is fixed and solid, yet in truth the experience was very brief, very unexpected and very startling. Even though I had a camera with me at the time it happened too fast for me to get a picture. But if I'd had this experience at Loch Ness in the 1960s or 1970s I'm quite sure I'd have become a believer for life.

I have had other experiences when my perceptions have been false. The dog that scampered across a deserted beach and plunged into the sea a couple of hundred yards ahead of me. The two birds fighting on a churchyard path. In both cases these creatures turned out, on closer inspection, to be plastic bags. On another occasion, I idly noticed some driftwood floating close to the shore on a lonely, empty winter beach. As I approached I noticed that the driftwood, which seemed brown and rough in appearance, also had an eye at the front which was very much alive and staring at me. This piece of wood then silently sank vertically from view, vanishing beneath the surface. It was not driftwood but a seal. I had not been expecting to see a seal but floating debris was an occasional phenomenon at this location and so mentally I'd processed a living animal as something inanimate. My perceptions of its colour and appearance was conditioned by my expectations and were surely quite wrong. Yet what I saw could only have been a seal and was entirely explicable as such.

The scampering dog, the two fighting birds and the knobbly driftwood were encountered in conditions of what might be called emotional neutrality. I had no expectations of seeing anything and when I did my perceptions were conditioned by a quiet familiarity with known objects. Beside the dark waters of Loch Ness that kind of emotional neutrality is impossible and perception is inevitably conditioned by knowledge both of the Monster's implicit presence and supposed appearance. And as Lee Child writes in *Make Me*,

Eyewitness testimony was suspect because of preconditions, and cognitive bias, and suggestibility. It was suspect because people see what they expect to see. Reacher was no different. He was human.

The more impressionable and suggestible you are, the more you are likely to see a monster in Loch Ness, especially if you are unfamiliar with the environment and arrive there with the particular desire to see one. States of physical exhaustion, stress and excitement magnify the likelihood of a sighting. The limitations of eye-witness testimony are underlined by the cases of Tim Dinsdale and F. W. Holiday, whose books shed light on matters which are normally concealed by the sightings record. In most instances the certainty of the eye-witness involves both the subjectivity of human perception and aspects of personality, temperament and individual experience which forever elude the historical record.

11

The Dragon Man

My last view of a dragon had been in 1965. 1966 had been a blank and so had 1967.

F. W. Holiday, *The Dragon and the Disc* (1973)

The outstanding example of an impressionable and suggestible eye-witness is surely Ted Holiday. Upon first arriving at Loch Ness in 1962 he sensed that it was a disturbing place. 'After sunset,' he wrote, spine-chillingly, it was 'not a water by which to linger.' It had (as one would have said at that time) *bad vibes*. Holiday had tuned into something sinister and troubling, which was related to 'man's deepest instincts... our subconscious has accumulated many strange impressions and none of these can be gainsaid.'

On his first day at the loch Holiday met an elderly local fisherman, who had seen the Monster less than a year before, in the form of 'A big hump' which 'stayed for a time and then it went down'. The very next day he encountered two students, who told him there'd been a sighting of the Monster a few days earlier, from Urquhart Castle. On his third night at the loch Holiday woke up around midnight, hearing a mysterious sound which turned out to be a sequence of big waves crashing on the shore. If, as seemed likely, they had been generated by the Monster, it indicated that 'the animal must be of enormous size'. The next day, exploring a stretch of lonely shoreline, he encountered an area of crushed bushes, as if a gigantic animal had crawled out of the loch and lain there. The day after that he saw the Monster. Bizarrely but very revealingly, Holiday suggested that the sighting was the result of him having established psychic contact with the beast.

At 4am, on an impulse which was the consequence of him having established 'some form of contact with the quarry', he dressed and drove immediately to Foyers. Stopping on the road above Lower Foyers, close to where Tim Dinsdale shot his famous film, Holiday scrutinised the loch through his binoculars. After a vigil lasting almost two hours his monster watch was rewarded with a sighting. In the water immediately below him something broke the surface. It was 'black and glistening and rounded, and it projected about three feet above the surface'. At once it dived back under the surface, creating a huge wave. But the Monster was still visible just below the surface and it was at least 40 feet long. Then, disturbed by a sudden noise, it abruptly vanished. Holiday watched for two more days, then returned home.

What is striking about Holiday's first trip to Loch Ness is how much it resembles Tim Dinsdale's. He arrived for the first time already firmly convinced of the Monster's existence. Almost at once he had an encounter with a local man who quietly admitted to two sightings of the legendary creature, including one in the past twelve months. He then heard about a new sighting, just days earlier. His conviction that the Monster existed was confirmed by the sight of mysterious waves crashing along the shore at night and by the strange area of flattened vegetation at the lochside. This thudding sequence of reinforcing episodes climaxed with a personal moment of revelation along the identical stretch of road where, as Holiday was all too well aware, Tim Dinsdale had filmed the back of a massive animal just two years earlier. In a state of extreme anticipation and fatigue, Holiday finally saw the legendary animal for himself. It had taken him just five days to achieve his ambition. And, just like Dinsdale, he would never again have such a decisive and satisfying encounter. Also, just like Dinsdale, if he hadn't gone on to write a semi-autobiographical book about the Loch Ness Monster we would never have known about the days leading up to his sighting, which provide a vital context for understanding and interpreting it.

In later years Ted Holiday had four more sightings of the Loch Ness Monster. On June 15, 1965, he observed a 'large, mustard-coloured mass' some 25-30 feet in length. Six days later he saw a jet black hump. In 1967 he reported seeing a 'substantial' V-shaped wake which he was in no doubt was caused by 'a living animal'. In 1968 he saw a three-humped monster: 'even at a mile range it looked enormous'.

But Ted Holiday did not just see monsters. As his books revealed, he had many other strange experiences. As a young man in his early twenties in Egypt he came across evidence that ghosts existed and soon afterwards had an uncanny experience at the place of the haunting. In 1949 he made a pilgrimage to Borley in Essex, the site of a Rectory which to this day remains legendary as 'the most haunted house in England'. His evident fascination with ghosts was rewarded by a number of strange experiences. At Glandovan Manor in Pembrokeshire, parts of which date back to the sixteenth century, Ted Holiday reported a variety of paranormal encounters. He heard 'an indescribable sound' which he nevertheless managed to describe: 'It sounded as if something very large, sprawling and rubbery were trying to paw its way up the vertical brickwork'. Thirty minutes later he was sat in the kitchen: 'Suddenly, a most peculiar quiver ran across the floor, and for a few seconds it seemed to shake like jelly…. Short of postulating a very localized earthquake, I could not account for this experience.' That night his bedroom light mysteriously switched itself on. Before he could reach for the switch to turn it off it 'quite audibly' clicked off. The next day he heard phantom footsteps which followed him to the kitchen doorway then continued down the corridor to the old part of the house. Later, a small hand bell being rung vigorously sounded just the other side of the kitchen door, evidently made by a paranormal agency.

In Scotland, staying with friends at the isolated Old Ferry Inn on Mull (today a chic holiday house available for weekly rental), Holiday woke in the night hearing ghostly footsteps. The ghost came upstairs, passed through the wall and stood by Holiday's bed. In a strong Belfast accent it demanded to know who he was, then seemed to smash a fist against the headboard. After that it disappeared.

But Holiday did not just see lake monsters and ghosts. He also saw UFOs. On January 6, 1966, he saw 'a glowing, spherical mass giving out a white light which pulsated with a periodicity of about two seconds'. It was about a mile away and silently travelled across Carmarthen Bay at 250 mph before vanishing behind a headland. On October 8 of the same year, in the night sky above Tenby Harbour, he saw 'a small, luminous blue-grey cloud' which was moving slowly in a small circle. This continued for ten minutes, when suddenly a dark object appeared from the cloud which beamed an intense ruby light down at the place from which Holiday was watching. The red light object and the blue-grey cloud then moved slowly away and disappeared from view. Exactly one week later, on the A478 road, he saw a strange flying object which was some 20-25 feet long, with the shape of a flattened oval. 'Its colour was yellow-gold and it had the appearance of being constructed from a glowing, translucent substance.'

Holiday's interaction with paranormal phenomena seemed to reach a climax at Loch Ness in June 1973 as a consequence of his involvement with an exorcism ceremony and his plan to visit the location of an alleged recent UFO landing in woodland near Foyers. At the precise moment he decided to abort the Foyers mission (after being warned that he risked being 'whisked away' by aliens), 'there was a tremendous rushing sound like a tornado outside the window, and the garden seemed to be filled with indefinable frantic movement.' Something seemed to crash repeatedly against the outside of the house. Through the window could be seen 'a pyramid-shaped column of blackish smoke about eight feet high revolving in a frenzy.' Next morning when he went outside he encountered a sinister 'man in black' whose face was masked and who mysteriously and inexplicably vanished. Later, back at the house, Holiday heard one evening a strange, inexplicable knocking.

Anyone who purchased the Loch Ness Investigation *Annual Report 1967* (price one shilling) would have seen a list of 23 sightings regarded as valid. Number 6 (May 27) was by 'F. W. Holiday (46), farmer and journalist', who reported seeing a 'substantial' V-shaped wake caused by 'a living animal'. What the ordinary reader of this sighting report could never have known was the character and temperament of the observer. *This is true of all the classic witnesses.*

On the face of it F. W. Holiday was a very sound observer. He was an ex-serviceman who had travelled around the world. He was an expert fisherman, a published author and a journalist. But thanks to his three quasi-autobiographical books we have many insights into his experiences and his beliefs. When it came to monsters, UFOs and ghosts he was highly sensitive to aural, visual and even tactile stimuli, as well as entities which he perceived as invisible but existing. At haunted Glandovan Manor he 'often had an uncanny feeling'. At monster-inhabited Lough Nahooin he experienced 'a feeling of unease'. Holiday was connected in a way that others aren't. He saw things that others don't.

At Lough Fadda he noticed 'a patch of disturbed water about half a mile distant'. Others might have dismissed it as capillary waves (the form popularly known as cat's paws) but Holiday hints at a Monstrous causation: 'Something just below the surface seemed to be trembling or vibrating. After about ten minutes all activity ceased and the water became calm.'

Perhaps his most bizarre sighting at Loch Ness occurred in 1971 when 'patches of yellow earth' on the opposite shore reflected on the surface to form the word 'Dee' – evidently an evocation of the famous Elizabethan magician, Dr John Dee, whose magic was used at nearby Boleskine House by Aleister Crowley.

At times there were dark, malignant forces which seemed to threaten him, at others he had protection. Once, when he was riding his motorbike at night, a voice spoke to him, telling him to beware of cows. He slowed as he approached the oncoming bend and avoided colliding with a herd of bullocks which had escaped from a field. His life and fate was connected to much bigger things (with spectacular insensitivity he even managed to link one of his UFO sightings to the Aberfan disaster). His own home, he explained, was on a ley line, aligning him directly to mysterious symmetries where UFOs and aliens manifested. At Loch Ness he established strange contact with the Monster, a connection which duly rewarded him with his first sighting. There was also contact between Holiday and the Monster of Lough Nahooin, which made men ill and gave Holiday toothache.

The Monster played strange tricks with those who tried to track it down and film it. In 1968, in *The Great Orm of Loch Ness*, he described his remarkable sighting of a 'yellowish' monster on June 15, 1965. It is an impressive episode, with two witnesses on the opposite shore. But in 1973, in his next book *The Dragon and the Disc*, Holiday supplied information which he had withheld five years earlier. In his account of the sighting written for the LNI he had admitted, 'It could have been a boat.' Holiday now attributed this to a psychological reaction which caused witnesses to be in denial. Either they suppressed all discussion of their experience or they sought to downplay it and shrug it off.

From a sceptical perspective it would be easy to debunk all Holiday's monster sightings in the light of what he reveals about his psychology. Some plainly involved expectant attention and the over-eager interpretation of distant objects or phenomena. The totality of Holiday's paranormal experiences also indicates someone who was probably prone to experiencing mild hallucinations. 'Any consuming passion,' wrote Oliver Sachs, 'may lead to hallucinations in which an idea and an interest are embedded.' Sleep deprivation, physical exhaustion and visual monotony – sometimes the monster hunter's lot –

can produce illusions which seem quite tangible and real but which exist only in the mind.

However, what is more interesting than Holiday's impressionability as an observer and his acute receptivity to aberrant phenomena is his own disillusionment with the great monster hunt. This is what distinguishes Holiday from Tim Dinsdale. The latter never acknowledged that there was a problem with the LNI's failure. He remained cheerily optimistic to the end and never gave up on the hunt. Ted Holiday, on the other hand, acknowledged both that failure existed and that it demanded answers. 'The affair of the Loch Ness monster had been getting ragged around the edges for a long time. It didn't make sense.' The large-scale investigations at Loch Ness had involved several hundred people but the effort had proved 'oddly unsatisfactory'. Surprisingly, 'there was no evidence that the phenomena were, in fact, animals and all attempts at proving this had failed'.

Frustrated by continuing failures at Loch Ness, Holiday eagerly embraced a dragon hunt in a remote area of western Ireland, where the lakes were tiny but the sightings record just as good. But 'After labouring for three years with the mystery of Irish monsters', Holiday concluded that 'there is not the slightest ecological trace of their real existence.' Where once he was convinced that lake monsters ate fish, now he concluded that, oddly, they didn't seem to require food at all.

In a strangely ironic way Ted Holiday was the first monster-hunter to become an unequivocal sceptic. In the space of a decade he had arrived at the unthinkable conclusion that flesh and blood monsters *don't exist*. The more effort you put into hunting lake monsters, the less likely you are to be able to film one. But temperamentally he was unable to pursue the inner logic of his shrewd reasoning. His solution to the difficulties encountered by monster-hunting was to take refuge in the idea that mysterious paranormal agencies were at work. His last published book, *The Goblin Universe*, reads like the work of a mind at the end of its tether as Holiday babbles wildly and incoherently about strange electromagnetic fields and mysterious controlling Minds. His final, wacky conclusion was that the Loch Ness Monster was the phantom projection of 'a colossal worm that inhabited the shallow, warm Permian seas of 200 million years ago'.

Where eye-witness testimony is concerned, I made two observations in *The Loch Ness Mystery Solved* which have both stood the test of time. Firstly, 'No single phenomenon can possibly account for the totality of fifty years of widely-differing eye-witness reports from Loch Ness.'

Secondly,

> The case for the Loch Ness monster rests overwhelmingly on eye-witness evidence, and this is just where the difficulty lies. No one has been able to film what eye-witnesses say they see. This paradox lies at the heart of the Loch Ness mystery.

This paradox has magnified with the passing of the years, since nowadays ownership of cameras and mobile phones is commonplace, and such equipment is usually far more sophisticated than was available in the past. On a sunny summer's day at Urquhart Castle there are scores of people carrying cameras and mobile phones, but Nessie never surfaces nearby, where she could be captured on film from numerous perspectives. Time and time again all we get are ambiguous single shot photographs taken at long range by solitary individuals (for example, Joline Lin in 2016 and Hayley Johnson in 2017).

The ease with which a classic close-up photograph of Nessie can be obtained was demonstrated in 1971, when a couple driving away from Invermoriston were amazed to see the Monster cruising past, near to the shore. They had no difficulty in obtaining some sensational pictures. It wasn't long before they discovered that their 'Monster' was in fact a model being used in the making of the film *The Private Life of Sherlock Holmes*. But though this episode ended in anticlimax, it vividly demonstrated how simply the Monster could be captured on film, if it was as big as eye-witnesses claim and behaved in the way that they say.

The years roll on and still no one can reproduce on film the spectacular sightings of the past – those of Margaret Munro, John McLean, Greta Finlay and all the others. Believers continue to treat sightings as verbal photographs, possessing a basic accuracy; sceptics explain sightings as misperceptions of explicable phenomena. There is always a gap which can never be bridged. The eye-witness's evidence is often too wondrous to be reduced to the dimensions of a mundane, known animal or some other natural and understandable origin. But what strengthens the sceptic's case against the believer's is that the classic sightings, just like the classic photographs, have never been repeated.

12

Reconfigurations

'All things are possible to him that believeth'
Adomnán of Iona, *Life of St Columba*

The two Loch Ness Monster books by Henry Bauer and Steuart Campbell published in 1986 marked the end of that great period of Nessie literature instigated by Constance Whyte and Tim Dinsdale. During the first 23 years of the Monster's existence there was only one full-length book on the subject. From 1957 to 1986 a grand total of eighteen appeared (excluding cut-and-paste jobs but including Peter Costello's lake monsters book). After that great surge of activity things went very quiet. Theorising about the monster was an exhausted topic. Only one other Nessie title appeared in the twentieth century from a mainstream publisher, namely Paul Harrison's *Encyclopaedia of the Loch Ness Monster* (1999). It inevitably covered much old ground but included an impressive amount of new material, including previously unpublicised land sightings. The book has since been updated and expanded and is currently available as an e-book. That same year David Martin and Alastair Boyd supplied the full story of their detective work in a self-published monograph, *Nessie – the Surgeon's Photograph*.

This last quarter of the twentieth century also saw the first publication in an English translation of a book which was to prove hugely influential on later cryptozoologists who sought to broaden the scope of debate, away from zoological realism. This was Michel Meurger's *Lake Monster Traditions: A Cross-Cultural Analysis*, published in 1988 by Fortean Tomes. This book plainly influenced the fruitful analyses of what one might call the cultural cryptozoologists, such as Daniel Loxton and Darren Naish. Meurger's lavishly illustrated, wide-ranging study of lake monster culture located the Loch Ness Monster in a global tradition.

In 2006 Adrian Shine published *Loch Ness*, a short glossy booklet summarising the work of his Loch Ness Project. It marked the beginning of a revival of publications about the Monster. Tony Harmsworth's *Loch Ness, Nessie and Me* (2010) supplied an idiosyncratic account of his involvement with the main exhibition at Drumnadrochit, as well as a sceptical take on the Monster which is full of interesting insights. Soon afterwards, blogger Roland Watson published *The Water Horses of Loch Ness* (2011), an attempt to reconstruct a Loch Ness tradition from the ruins of the demolition work performed by myself and others. Unlike Harmsworth's well-made volume, Watson's was deficient in its production values. The various peculiarities of the text include anarchic paragraphing and spacing, plus a font of a size likely to be highly beneficial to those readers with poor eyesight. Quotations are throughout given without page references.

This book was symptomatic of the parochialism of a cryptozoological literalist like Watson, in so far as it displayed no interest in folklore studies or an analysis like Michel Meurger's *Lake Monster Traditions*. Instead it treated Scottish folklore in the narrowest and most simplistic way possible, as a source of obscured zoological verisimilitude. The contents of Watson's book, though naïve and incoherent in presentation, nevertheless raise questions which, at an empirical level, deserve to be answered (see below, Chapters 13 and 14).

In 2013 Angus Dinsdale published *The Man Who Filmed Nessie: Tim Dinsdale and the Enigma of Loch Ness*. Although beautifully produced and not without some morsels of interest, it proved to be a disappointingly anodyne biography. I reviewed it for *Skeptic* magazine, commenting:

Much of *The Man Who Filmed Nessie* simply recycles material from Tim Dinsdale's own books, either verbatim or in rewritten form. For anyone familiar with the original texts this creates a strong sense of déjà vu. Oddly, the author even changes the details of his father's second sighting. In his book *The Leviathans* Tim Dinsdale described how in August 1970 he spotted a tall, pole shaped object sticking up from the water half a mile away. He alerted his two companions (one of them his eldest son, Simon) and dashed to get his binoculars. But in Angus Dinsdale's account it was not his father but his brother who first saw the monster, and his father rushed off to get not binoculars but a Beaulieu camera. Whether or not this is simply carelessness on Angus Dinsdale's part or a conscious but unacknowledged revision is unclear.

That year also saw the publication of *Abominable Science!*, a handsomely produced collaboration from a major publishing house by Daniel Loxton and Donald R. Prothero. It offered an up-to-date debunking of five cryptid superstars (although 'debunking' is not quite the right word for Loxton's elegant, informed and illuminating deconstruction of the sea-serpent legend). The chapter on Nessie reiterated the multi-faceted sceptical case against this particular entity, concluding that 'Today, the creature has been forced into a paradox as magical as its roots: a giant monster that many people see, but that cannot ever be detected by science.'

My next foray into Nessie reviewing came with the publication of Gareth Williams' *A Monstrous Commotion: The Mysteries of Loch Ness* (2015). This was the first big mainstream book on Nessie since the 1970s. *New Humanist* invited me to write a general piece on the Monster, anchoring it to Williams' book. My more detailed appraisal can be found in the *Times Literary Supplement* (April 15, 2016).

My reviews were generous for a book whose author drew substantially on *The Loch Ness Mystery Solved* without even a single whisper of acknowledgement. The space allocated to them only permitted me to make a small number of points. *A Monstrous Commotion* retold a familiar story in a crisp, readable way. Williams wrote with an engagingly dry, sardonic tone. The Peter Scott archive was an invaluable resource which fleshed out the behind-the-scenes clash of gigantic egos. If you have never read a book about the Loch Ness Monster then *A Monstrous Commotion* is a very good place to begin.

And yet.

I did not wish to write a carping review of a book which anyone interested in the Loch Ness Monster should read. But apart from its unacknowledged debts, the book is seamed throughout with minor mistakes, giving it the appearance of a rushed job. This cacophony of error is odd, bearing in mind Williams' lavish praise of 'a group of sharp-eyed and critical friends' who 'cheerfully read numerous drafts of the manuscript' and were 'absolutely brilliant' at spotting even 'one-letter typos', as well as 'The team at Orion' who are 'A top-class publisher...superb', not to mention three named individuals, top Nessie experts, who 'corrected my many errors of fact, chronology and interpretation'. These last advisors were Dick Raynor, Nicholas Witchell and Adrian Shine.

You would have thought that this sharp-eyed assembly would have spotted Williams' inaccurate rendition of the title of Tim Dinsdale's first book (twice, on pp. xvii and p.113) or the garbled claim that 'In November 1896, John Keele spotted a piece about the Loch Ness Monster in the *Atlanta Constitution*'. It is not true that 'Dinsdale was not mentioned by name' in Maurice Burton's *Illustrated London News* monster article, published on February 20, 1960. Likewise Williams makes the puzzling and erroneous claim that *Nature* magazine did not identify Scott and Rines as authors of the notorious *Nessiteras rhombopteryx* piece, asserting that '*Nature* published "Naming the Loch Ness Monster" as an anonymous item in the News section.'

Williams mocks Dinsdale for 'frequent typographical errors' in his first book, which is a bit rich for someone whose own book mentions how scientists 'poured devision' on the notion that plesiosaurs might be found living in Loch Ness, who spells Steuart Campbell's first name as 'Stuart', and who credits Plate 23 to a photographer named 'Dick Rayner'. On page 262 Williams describes how 'Plate 46' shows Tim Dinsdale on board *Water Horse*. That Plate in fact shows the original sub-surface 'monster flipper' imagery.

Williams is very bad on films and titles. David Lean did not direct the first Loch Ness Monster movie but rather edited it. Williams garbles the title of *The Private Life of Sherlock Holmes*, erroneously calling it *The Secret Life of Sherlock Holmes*. Rupert Gould did not in 1925 publish a book entitled *The Sea-Serpent*, but rather *The Case for the Sea-Serpent*, which first appeared in 1930. Williams wrongly asserts that Gould had changed his mind about the Spicer sighting prior to publication of *The Loch Ness Monster and Others*. In fact, the marginal annotation which Williams cites was made not at the proof stage but rather in a published copy. It is misleading of Williams to tell his readers that Gould's confidence in the Arthur Grant land sighting 'was never dented' when Gould was equivocal about endorsing it as evidence for the Monster.

It is untrue that, in *The Elusive Monster*, Maurice Burton identified the object in the Hugh Gray photograph 'as an otter'. On the contrary, he wrote that the most 'reasonable' explanation was a 'tree trunk buoyed by the gases of its own decay'. It is equally untrue that Roy Mackal wrote in his book *The Monsters of Loch Ness* that the monster had been seen on land '178 times'. Mackal in fact listed a grand total of eighteen land sightings, identifying eight of them as either inconclusive or involving probable misperception of known animals.

Williams mocks Mackal for geographical ineptitude (the map of Loch Ness in *The Monsters of Loch Ness* shows the Horseshoe crag on the opposite shore to its true location), to which one might reply that Williams' own grasp of local landscape is rather shakier. Map 3 in *A Monstrous Commotion* gets the locations of the Gray photograph and the Holiday sighting the wrong way round. The 'single small road' beside the western end of Loch Morar serves not Morar but Bracora and Bracorina. Ted Holiday did not see his monster at 'the mouth of the River Foyers' but where the tail leat empties into the loch – a different location. Williams believes that Drumnadrochit and Invermoriston are 'four miles apart'. You wouldn't want the Professor planning your walking holiday in the Great Glen.

He asserts that JARIC's conclusion that the mystery object filmed by Tim Dinsdale was probably animate 'was based on the fact that it moved too fast to be a boat'. On the contrary, JARIC concluded that a power boat with a planing hull could easily match the speed of the object but 'would scarcely be missed by an observer' – a quite different line of reasoning.

A Monstrous Commotion has a very inadequate index. It misses out entries (for example, Peter Davies) and it cites pages which in fact contain no reference to the entry (for example, Peter F. Baker and p. 179, Rupert Gould and p. 145, and Roland Watson and p. 230). It omits pages which should be referenced for an entry (for example, Clem Skelton on pages 125 and 146 and, spectacularly, Peter F. Baker on pages 169, 178, 303, 320 and 323).

The Bibliography is equally slovenly. Bauer's *Enigma of Loch Ness* was published in 1986, not 1968. The co-author's name is not given for *The Loch Ness Mystery Solved*. The 1969 American edition of *The Loch Ness Monster and Others* was a reprint, not a revised edition. The title of Oudemans' sea-serpent book is not italicised. In the Notes, the title of Price and Lambert's 1936 book is not italicised (Chapter 2, note 36). The quotation from Tim Dinsdale is not properly sourced (Chapter 10, note 64 – a specific link is required, bearing in mind that Raynor's website is vast, with numerous sub-sections). A 'personal communication' requires a date (Chapter 10, note 74). The year of publication of Bauer's monster book is wrong (Chapter 14, note 38 – where Williams also misses out any reference to pp. 3-4, which provide Bauer's account of his pursuit of Gerahty). It would not be necessary to labour these points if Williams wasn't so supercilious in his mockery of Dinsdale and Mackal for quite trivial mistakes, or so gushing in his praise of those who he mistakenly believes have spared his own text from the blight of error.

Other errors simply reflect inadequate research or a lack of direct knowledge of the loch's environment. In *The Loch Ness Mystery Solved* I wrote that, after his 1933 visit, Rupert Gould 'seems never to have revisited Loch Ness'. My own half-hesitation is converted into certainty by Williams: 'Gould himself never returned to Loch Ness.' In fact Gould *did* return to the loch, as I later discovered.

Williams refers to the 'extensive roadworks on the A82 in 1932-1933'. As a completist, those road works have always fascinated me, and the story has yet to be told. In fact the roadworks at Loch Ness were not finished until September 1934. They were part of a major transport project which began in March 1930 and which brought a once-famous British politician to the shores of the loch.

Professor Williams' uncritical acceptance of the 'standing wave' theory reveals a lack of knowledge of what actually happens to bow-waves at the loch. The rocky shores of Loch Ness do not form 'a steep barrier' resulting in a 'reflected wave'. That phenomenon can occur in a swimming pool but not along the Loch Ness shoreline, where there are no high, smooth surfaces but only rough, rock-strewn wastes, which waves collide with and then disintegrate. This is not to say that the 'standing wave' effect does not exist on the loch, merely that it results from a vessel which turns and meets its own wake, or from a meeting of the wakes of two or more boats. Likewise, when Williams asserts that 'seals look nothing like the Monster', he indicates a lack of personal experience of the behaviour of these animals. Seals can resemble the Loch Ness Monster in a number of ways. A solitary seal can look like a single jet-black hump, just as a pair of seals can look like two humps. A seal can elevate its head and neck out of the water in a manner that calls to mind some classic monster sightings. Seals crawl on to land, and display flippers. Seals can also sink vertically out of sight, just as the monster sometimes does. Not all seals resemble the chubby, loveable, wide-eyed creatures of picture postcards and calendars.

When it comes to matters of interpretation and judgement, there is much to question in Williams' account of the Loch Ness story. It seems to me ridiculous to identify Aleister Crowley as one of the 'Key players' in the Loch Ness story. Crowley's presence at Loch Ness actually supplies another peripheral piece of negative evidence, because it is plain he had never heard of any stories of huge animals in the loch when he lived at Boleskine House, above the loch. Crowley was both a prolific writer and a skilled self-publicist. He would certainly have turned any such legend to his own advantage had he heard of one.

To put Rupert Gould alongside Marmaduke Wetherell as equally hungry for 'self-promotion and self-aggrandisement' seems to me deeply unfair to Gould. To accept the story that Albert Einstein was amazed by young Robert Rines's ability with a violin requires a somewhat naïve attitude to its source, one Robert Rines. Williams is also too generous by far to Maurice Burton when he ascribes the zoologist's spectacular lurches of opinion regarding Nessie as the consequence of 'weighing up new evidence as it came in'. Burton was just as keen to cherry-pick evidence to suit a theory as everyone else who writes about the beast. His refusal to share the Taylor film with others who might not have shared his analysis was unscientific and petty.

But Williams is less than fair to Burton when he describes Plate 16 of *The Elusive Monster* as 'a rather bad photograph of something thought to be a vegetable mat that popped up in Loch Lochy and promptly sank again'. To my mind it's an extraordinary image of what might well be interpreted as the curved back of a large reptilian creature with a skull-like head with one deep eye socket visible, surrounded by boiling foam. The presence of a cluster of tell-tale bubbles just in front of the head suggests that it probably really is some sort of vegetable matter which has broken surface. It's an astonishing photograph and it is unsurprising that, together with the Taylor film, it deeply influenced Burton and reinforced his fondness for his vegetable mat theory.

Hard on the heels of *A Monstrous Commotion* came four more titles.

In January 2016 Darren Naish's ebook *Hunting Monsters: Cryptozoology and the Reality Behind the Myths* appeared, subsequently appearing in hard copy format as a paperback in April 2017. It's a fluent, elegant, scholarly book which frames an examination of sea and lake monsters, 'cryptohominids' and prehistoric survivors, with a discussion of the history and changing nature of cryptozoology. Naish demonstrates the limitations of the literal-minded approach favoured by a founding father like Bernard Heuvelmans, who believed that sightings of such legendary creatures were rooted in a zoological reality. In the final chapter of *The Loch Ness Mystery Solved* I argued that the monster's origins were both cultural and psychological, and this is the approach preferred by Naish, who sees cryptozoology in general as being 'more to do with sociology, social anthropology or psychology than it is with zoology'. The Loch Ness Monster is, from this angle, not a flesh and blood unknown animal but rather 'an integral part of how people imagine the world'. I find Naish's approach congenial because he seeks to rescue cryptozoology from the naïve literalists. He accepts the possibility of unknown animals based on eye-witness reports but is more rigorous in his filtering ('a place where large unknown animal species might still be found' does not include Scotland).

Seeking the scientific endorsement of *all* cryptids, including the superstars, is, from Naish's perspective, a barren undertaking. He is much more interested in making cryptozoology a legitimate area of scholarly study chiefly rooted in the human rather than the animal. The problem, of course, is that most cryptozoologists are literalists, with belief often becoming so intense as to transform itself into faith in the sacred. When this occurs, scepticism becomes not a discourse requiring engagement and debate but rather heresy, to be abused and shouted down.

In August 2016 Malcolm Robinson published *The Monsters of Loch Ness*. It would have benefited from editing, as there are numerous textual slips, but I do not wish to be too hard on this author. I have a soft spot for Mr Robinson because he sent me a fan letter after the May 1983 publication of *The Loch Ness Mystery Solved*. I still have that letter and though my book plainly had a big impact on him at the time, it now seems that his loss of faith was only momentary. Rather like Maurice Burton in 1961 and Adrian Shine in 1985, he could not quite free himself from the magnetic power of eye-witness testimony. Father Brusey in particular seems to have exerted considerable influence over his attitude to the monster.

Robinson's lengthy book of almost 600 ages combines a general account of the Loch Ness story with a chatty personal account of the author's enduring interest and involvement in the subject. It includes descriptions of personal expeditions to both Loch Ness and Loch Morar and the transcripts of interviews with Alex Campbell, Adrian Shine, Frank Seale, Father Brusey, and encounters with others who played a part in the saga. The book publishes for the first time Frank Searle's little-known flying saucer photograph. By Searle's shoddy standards it's a rather better image than any of his Nessie fakes.

Robinson is sceptical of the land sightings, including the seminal Spicer account, but supportive of Doc Shiels and his photographs. *The Monsters of Loch Ness* is an idiosyncratic compendium of wonders which recycles old press cuttings, material from Wikipedia, chatty reflections concerning matters monstrous, and anecdotes such as the strange tale of 'the Cumbernauld' photograph, showing a monster which greatly resembled the one snapped by Shiels. For completists, it even includes the full text of 'The Author's Letter From Ronald Binns', dated September 5, 1983.

Malcolm Robinson describes himself as a 'UFO and paranormal researcher', and the book contains much material about those who have followed in the footsteps of Ted Holiday, believing the monster to be some kind of projection of mysterious energy or psychic force. For those readers who prefer a more material monster to 'Super Ghosts', the book reproduces the William Jobes photographs of 2011 and 2015.

Another book pursuing a paranormal angle was published in October 2016. *Nessie: Exploring the Supernatural Origins of the Loch Ness Monster* was written by Nick Redfern, Texas-based author of a number of sensational books about UFOs, including *Body Snatchers in the Desert: The Horrible Truth at the Heart of the Roswell Story*.

Redfern's Introduction luridly asserts that

Magical rituals, satanic rites, necromancy, dragon-worshiping cults that engage in bloody sacrifice under a full moon, bizarre synchronicities, UFO sightings, encounters with the dreaded men in Black, and even exorcisms are part and parcel of the phenomenon that has been known as the Loch Ness Monster.

In short, this book offers a slick, journalistic adaptation of Ted Holiday's journey into the realms of paranormal speculation, but without the charm and interest of that earlier author's personal involvement with Nessie-hunting or his intense and wide-ranging theoretical zeal.

Disappointingly, *Nessie: Exploring the Supernatural Origins of the Loch Ness Monster* is a derivative book which says nothing new about the paranormal side of the quest for Nessie. It is known, for example, that Tim Dinsdale was sympathetic to this aspect, but to what extent remains as yet undocumented. Redfern accuses Dinsdale of cowardice, saying that his reticence 'smacks of a man unsure of himself, and lacking the strength of character to say, publicly, what he really thought'. On the contrary, Dinsdale's reluctance to expand publicly upon paranormal matters was surely much more to do with pragmatism. Too much talk about UFOs and spirits would have risked discrediting the effort put into maintaining surveillance of the loch for a creature of flesh and blood which could be captured on film, something in which Dinsdale clearly believed.

Redfern's sensationalism includes the claim that 'incredibly' Saint Columba's boat was towed at Loch Ness by 'one of the creatures'. But this story is a post-1933 invention. Redfern's bibliography lists the 1995 Penguin edition of the *Life of St Columba*, but there is no evidence that he has consulted this very authoritative text. Instead, his version of the famous River Ness episode uses a different, unidentified translation which refers to a 'river monster', not the Penguin edition's more neutral 'river beast'.

'Prior to 1933,' Redfern writes, 'there was only one road that permitted travel around the loch despite the gargantuan size of that famous body of water. It was the General Wade's road, constructed way back in 1715, which went from Inverness to Fort Augustus. That was it. Nothing else. At all.' A fourth book which appeared in 2016 repeats this preposterous and utterly false claim. Karl Shuker's *Here's Nessie! A Monstrous Compendium from Loch Ness* is an idiosyncratic anthology of previously published material by a prolific author of books and articles about cryptids. I must admit that my heart sank when, on the first page of the first chapter, I read Shuker's claim that 1933 'saw the creation of a new motoring road (the A82) overlooking the northern shoreline of this immense but hitherto-secluded lake'. That people still make such claims decades after the myth of the lonely loch and the new road was comprehensively debunked in *The Loch Ness Mystery Solved* indicates the extent to which some believers have retreated to a bunker where faith thrives untroubled by even the most rudimentary historical knowledge.

Shuker remains convinced that the 1972 Rines flipper photographs constitute 'the most important evidence currently obtained in support of the Loch Ness monster's reality as a huge water beast of a still-undiscovered species' and informs his readers that 'while the sonar had been obtaining traces of the body, the underwater camera had been photographing it'. The authoritative debunking of such an interpretation by Dick Raynor is not acknowledged, let alone engaged with.

Shuker hails Henry Bauer's *The Enigma of Loch Ness* as a 'classic scholarly work' and identifies Bauer as a 'major personality' in the Loch Ness saga (in a list which excludes Rupert Gould, Constance Whyte and Dick Raynor). He also admires Roy Mackal, whose *The Monsters of Loch Ness* he believes 'remains the most scientific, rigorously objective study of the LNM in book form'. These are, to put it mildly, idiosyncratic judgements.

Here's Nessie! is strictly for completists, since it amounts to an anarchic assembly of material of questionable relevance, including a chapter which consists of a Nessie poem by the author, a torrent of public domain illustrations, and a chapter listing songs about the monster. Shuker speculates about giant long-necked otters, long-necked seals, water kelpies, evolved plesiosaurs and much else. For sceptics, there is the curious tale of the monster of Loch Watten, described in a book by the popular writer Peter Haining, but apparently unsupported by any other evidence. Here, Shuker's researches usefully underline the importance of critical scrutiny of sources.

My pulse quickened when I read on the cover of *Here's Nessie!* that the book contained 'a hitherto-unpublished LNM sighting from leading Nessie researcher and eyewitness Tim Dinsdale'. I interpreted this to mean a previously unpublicised sighting by the great monster hunter. Not so. It turns out that Dinsdale was in possession of two sketches of a monster sighting recently sent to him by an eye-witness, and in July 1987 he gave Shuker a copy. Dinsdale died five months later, before he had the chance to publish anything about this new evidence. Shuker does not know the name of the eye-witness, or the date of the sighting. This inconclusive anecdote is another reminder that there is a substantial archive of material held by the Dinsdale family which thirty years after the great monster-hunter's death remains unavailable for scrutiny.

As the year came to a close a fifth Nessie paperback appeared. On November 17 the softcover edition of *A Monstrous Commotion* was published by Weidenfeld & Nicolson, with a blurb asserting that the book 'takes a wholly original look at what really happened in Loch Ness'. Although there was nothing to indicate the fact, this paperback was actually a corrected edition. Gareth Williams had now deleted the erroneous reference to David Lean having directed *The Secret of the Loch*, pointed out by me in the TLS, but had missed numerous other errors I had no space to list.

Of the four review extracts cited on the jacket one was by me, taken from my *Times Literary Supplement* piece: 'Brings a dry wit and a scientist's illuminating perspective to the endless spectacle of Loch Ness.' When I read this I felt instinctively that there was something wrong. Consulting my review, I discovered that with extraordinary cynicism Williams' publishers had chosen to omit the final word of my sentence.

That word was 'folly'.

13

Two-Faced Kelpie

To sum up, when we strip this business of fraud, hoax, chicanery, misleading films and photographs, faulty observations and over-estimations, we are left with precisely what the Highlanders started with – the water-kelpie.

Maurice Burton, letter to F. W. Holiday.

The words which introduced the Loch Ness monster to the world were these:

> Loch Ness has for generations been credited with being the home of a fearsome-looking monster, but, somehow or other, the 'water-kelpie,' as this legendary creature is called, has always been regarded as a myth, if not a joke. Now, however, comes the news that the beast has been seen once more…

The most potent word here is 'monster' but 'beast' and 'water kelpie' are also words which are highly-charged in connection with the Loch Ness myth. 'Beast' can be a neutral word, but it often carries connotations of evil and savagery, particularly in popular media coverage of crimes of violence. A 'beast' is a primitive entity: literally an animal, lacking a moral conscience, driven by instinct. A beast is the opposite of that which is civilised, humane and restrained. A beast can be frightening and is often a creature of the night. Ted Holiday's spine-chilling 'Great Orm of Loch Ness' was just such a beast – a hideous primeval entity which had shadowed humanity since ancient times. It was, in George Spicer's lurid words, 'horrible – an abomination'. The theory that the monster is nocturnal is a recurring theme in the literature. 'After dark I felt that Loch Ness was better left alone,' Holiday wrote. He was woken at midnight by 'a curious sound' that went on for several minutes, 'crystalizing and gathering itself, and presently resolved into the crash of water breaking on the beaches'. *Something* had generated a disturbance on the surface of the starlit loch when no boats were present. If it was the monster, it indicated 'that the animal must be of enormous size'. Scary.

The water kelpie is also malevolent. This legendary creature is an ambiguous, shape-shifting entity, usually incarnated in the form of a horse. In Scottish folklore it is a water spirit associated primarily with rivers, but it is often treated as being synonymous with the water horse and its close relative, the water bull. The taxonomy is loose. The water horse and the water bull are conventionally associated with lochs and their environs. In one influential version of the water kelpie legend, W. Grant Stewart describes the creature as 'an amphibious character' who 'generally took up his residence on lochs and pools, bordering on public roads and other situations, most convenient for his professional calling'. The water kelpie was an agent of the devil and his task was to tempt passers-by into mounting the saddle. The kelpie then raced off and plunged into water, drowning the rider before he or she had time to seek absolution for their sins. The devil got the drowned rider's soul and the kelpie's reward was to feast on the flesh.

Rupert Gould acknowledged that there were old local traditions which associated many Highland lochs, including Loch Ness, with water horses and water bulls, but dismissed this aspect as 'more or less beside the point – except in so far as they provide sceptics with excellent ground for contending that the stories of the "Loch Ness monster" are merely a temporary revival of an old and deep-rooted superstition'.

Constance Whyte felt no such qualms as Gould's when she resurrected the monster from its long sleep, devoting an entire chapter to 'Ourselves, the Highlander and the Water Horse (*Each Uisge*)'. As far as she was concerned the legend was rooted in actual sightings of an unknown water creature.

Recently, Roland Watson has devoted an entire book to this Highland folklore tradition. In *The Water Horses of Loch Ness*, he attempts to reinstate the tradition of pre-1933 monster sightings which I exploded in the third chapter of *The Loch Ness Mystery Solved.*

'Excluding the St. Columba account,' Watson asserts, 'we have reports of one or more creatures going back to Cromwell's time or nearly 350 years ago.' However, his treatment of the body of material which I criticised is not one I find at all persuasive. For example, I pointed out that alleged written references to the Loch Ness monster being seen in 1520, 1771 and 1885 all derive from a letter to the *Scotsman* by D. Murray Rose, published on October 20, 1933. Rose supplied no sources for his sensational claims. Watson responds to my hatchet job by identifying David Murray Rose as 'a Highland historian who specialised in that period of Scottish history... I think a man of Mr. Rose's standing and CV deserves better treatment and respect.' Well, maybe – but the fact remains that thirty-four years after my criticism no one has ever been able to locate any of Rose's sources, including that unidentified 'old book dealing with curiosities' which supposedly contained the remarkable sixteenth century statement, 'no one has yet managed to slay the monster of Loch Ness, lately seen'.

The problem here is not simply that Rose failed to give this fabulous book a title. His amazing quotation is wildly unlikely in itself. The idiom of Rose's unverifiable quotation is twentieth-century. Even allowing for an unacknowledged modernisation of the language, the rhythm and vocabulary are implausible for what purports to be sixteenth century prose. What's more, it appears that Rose lacked any facility in Gaelic, surely something of an impediment for a Scottish historian of that period. The conclusions which I reached in *The Loch Ness Mystery Solved* were echoed three decades later by Gareth Williams, who concluded that, before the 1930s, 'if we only accept contemporary reports, there is nothing'. The ancient monster sighting tradition promulgated by the classic monster books still lies in rubble and only special pleading can pretend otherwise.

Some of the evidence of a tradition which was questioned by *The Loch Ness Mystery Solved* has since crumbled to dust. John Keel claimed that he had once, in the *Atlanta Constitution*, come across 'a full-page article on Loch Ness published in November 1896, complete with a woodcut which resembled exactly the modern drawings of Nessie'. I came across this mouth-watering statement in his sensational paperback, *Strange Creatures from Time and Space* (1976). That Keel was a sloppy writer was indicated by his inability even to get the year of Nessie's modern appearance right (he said it was 1934). No one could find this article until Roland Watson finally tracked it down in 2016. It turned out to be in the May 2, 1897 issue, and was not about

Loch Ness but merely a feature on sea-serpents. Keel's claim that the drawings 'resembled exactly' (*sic*) modern images of Nessie was a characteristic exaggeration (unless you happen to believe that Nessie squirts large jets of water, seizes sailors in its jaws from passing ships, and has large whiskers).

Of much greater interest than Watson's stout defence of a baseless 'tradition' is his focus on the Highland folklore tradition of the water horse. Here he contributes new material to the great Loch Ness saga. Watson describes himself as having 'trawled numerous books on Highland folklore' published prior to 1933, from which he concludes that there are in fact only fifty Scottish lochs specifically associated with the water horse. This is a mere fraction of Scotland's total of around 31,000 lochs and lochans. He argues that it is therefore untrue, as many writers lazily claim, that water horses were everywhere in Scottish lochs. Of these fifty lochs, only twelve are mentioned more than once in connection with *Each Uisge*. Of these twelve, Loch Ness receives most mentions. Watson finds this highly significant.

There are methodological problems with this approach, which include the question of how representative his sample is and the broader cultural context of the Victorian recuperation of oral tradition. But let us not quibble. Watson puts forward nine new Loch Ness water-horse references for consideration.

1. *The Popular Superstitions of the Highlanders* by W. Grant Stewart (1823). This describes how James Macgrigor outwitted 'a most mischievous water-kelpie that lived in Lochness (*sic*)'. (Watson truncates the title. The actual title is *The Popular Superstitions and Festive Amusements of the Highlanders of Scotland*.)

2. *Blackwood's Magazine* (1826). A poetic piece of prose by 'Professor Wilson of Edinburgh University' warns 'Water Horses and Kelpies' to stay away from 'the river' or be swept to destruction against Urquhart Castle on Loch Ness.

3. The *Inverness Courier*, 1 July 1852. The newspaper reported 'A Scene at Lochend' in which the inhabitants of this lochside hamlet were 'suddenly thrown into a state of excitement by the appearance of two bodies steadily moving on the loch'. The onlookers thought that this was a sea-serpent, a pair of whales, large seals or swimming deer. But as the animals drew close a 'venerable patriarch' exclaimed, 'God protect us, they are the water horses!' In fact they

were ponies which had entered the loch, perhaps to cool off on a very hot day.

4. *Popular Tales of the West Highlands* by John Campbell (1862). This book, based on interviews with local people, discussed the water bull. This creature is defined as 'like a common bull, though he is amphibious and supernatural, and has the power of assuming other shapes'. Campbell described how 'Bulls are sculptured on ancient Scotch stones; and there is a water-bull in nearly every Scotch loch of any note.' Loch Ness is full of them, 'but they never go up to the Fall of Foyers'.

5. The *Aberdeen Weekly Journal*, 11 June 1879. There is mention of a water kelpie in the form of 'a beautiful black horse' which lured its victims to their doom. Once they were sat in the saddle the horse sped off 'with more than the speed of the hurricane and plunged into the deepest part of Loch Ness'.

6. James Mackinlay, *Folklore of Scottish Lochs and Springs* (1893). This tells how 'A noted demon-steed once inhabited Loch Ness, and was a cause of terror to the inhabitants of the neighbourhood.' The kelpie waited on the roadside and as soon as 'any unwary traveller' mounted the saddle the horse rushed off and 'plunged into deep water'.

7. *Proceedings* of the Society of Antiquaries of Scotland (1896). 'Tradition tells of a noted Inverness-shire water-horse that drowned its victims in Loch Ness.'

8. *The Secret of the Turret* by Ethel Forster Heddle (1905). This is a novel in which a character refers to 'the legend of the water kelpie on Loch Ness, where I was brought up'.

9. *Story and Song from Loch Ness Side* by Alexander MacDonald (1914). Focused on tales from the Glenmoriston area, MacDonald states that 'Stories of the Water Horse (An t-Each-Uisge) were often heard about the fireside.'

As a folklore tradition, this is a distinctly threadbare one. Examples (3) and (9) don't *specifically* connect Loch Ness with a water-horse tradition, and example (1) seems to provide a source which (5), (6), (7) and (8) merely repeat.

Watson's third example is quite revealing because it shows that local people, upon seeing two ponies distantly swimming in the loch, *did not* instantly associate them with water horses but with other animals. The report states that 'Lochness (*sic*) lay in a perfect state of calm, without a ripple on its surface' – a condition identified in the 1960s as perfect monster-spotting weather. The fact that some witnesses believed they were seeing a whale or whales testifies to the magnifying effect which a flat calm loch surface can have on wakes and on the perception/size-scaling of objects. That other witnesses believed they were seeing a sea-serpent also deals a blow to any idea of a monster tradition at Loch Ness. If local people really had witnessed a large, unknown animal in the loch during the nineteenth century, they would surely have interpreted it as a sea-serpent. When passionate sea-serpent advocate Rupert Gould arrived at the loch in 1933, he analysed the testimony and concluded that the monster combined 'the salient features of almost all the best-authenticated reports of "sea-serpents"'. In the mid-nineteenth century the craze for the sea-serpent was then at its height and reports came in from around the Scottish coast, yet there was never the slightest hint of one being spotted in Loch Ness. No mention is made by the *Courier* of any local tradition of unusual animal, and the choice of seals and deer as an interpretation of the phenomenon shows that some locals were well acquainted with the natural wildlife of the loch.

This leaves two components of Watson's water horse tradition. Example (2), which Watson fails to contextualise (is it fiction or non-fiction?), is plainly a flowery, generalised reference to the legend. But it associates the kelpie with a river, not the loch. The river is not identified but if a specific one is intended then by implication it is the River Enrick or the Coiltie. However, there is no real evidence that the author had any connection with the area or knew its topography. The vagueness is telling.

This leaves (4), which directly connects Loch Ness with lots of shape-changing, amphibious water bulls. This is as close as Watson's tradition gets to what we would now call the Loch Ness monster. But Campbell's water bulls are identified as 'supernatural', linking them to the archetypal water horse narrative which appears in *The Popular Superstitions and Festive Amusements of the Highlanders of Scotland*. This is worth examining in more detail.

W. Grant Stewart attributes his water kelpie story to 'the celebrated Mr Wellox'. This is a reference to Gregor Willox MacGregor, who died in 1833. An obituary appeared in the *Inverness Courier* (16 October), describing him as the last of a line of sorcerers. 'Willox the Warlock' was held in 'awe and veneration' across the northern counties. It seems the Warlock dispensed advice (probably in return for payment) on the basis of his occult powers. These derived from two magical objects. The first was 'a piece of yellow metal resembling the bit of a horse's bridle' and the second was 'a piece of pellucid matter, resembling the nob or bottom of a crystal bottle'. According to the Warlock, the yellow item had been seized by his grand-uncle from the water kelpie which 'haunted the banks of Loch Ness and Loch Spynie', while the lump of 'pellucid matter' was of extra-terrestrial origin and had once belonged to a mermaid. She had given it to MacGregor's maternal grandfather. As MacGregor told visitors, 'in my veins two most potent streams of necromantic blood have united themselves'.

The obituary writer was plainly sceptical about the efficacy of these magical objects and equally unimpressed by the gullibility of those who came to seek help from Willox the Warlock:

Strange as it may seem to the enlightened reader, these credentials transmitted from father to son, obtained for many ages implicit faith among the peasantry of Scotland from Perth to John O'Groats.

But it appears that the sorcerer's reputation suffered a decline 'owing to the rapidly progressing intelligence of the Highlanders' (presumably involving literacy, education and urbanisation). When Willox offered to sell a charm which promised to make the purchaser bullet-proof, the prospective purchaser asked to test it out at once on the vendor. Willox, rather like the water kelpie, promptly turned and fled. Although he promoted himself as a fearful necromancer, it seems that at the end of the day this was just self-advertising, and 'there was nothing very reprehensible in his character or conduct'.

Strange as it may seem to the enlightened reader, Willox's tale of how his ancestor James MacGregor outwitted 'a most mischievous water-kelpie that lived in Lochness, and which committed the most atrocious excesses on the defenceless inhabitants of the surrounding districts' is what underlies the Loch Ness kelpie tradition. This yarn was plainly spun to lend credibility to Willox's 'piece of yellow metal'. Willox's ancestor had it from the (water) horse's mouth that the owner could use it to see 'myriads of invisible agents, fairies, witches, and devils, all flying around you, the same as if you had been gifted with the second sight'. This fable may well have impressed 'the peasantry of Scotland from Perth to John O'Groats', but it creates difficulties for anyone seeking to connect it with the Loch Ness monster.

Gregor Willox MacGregor's water kelpie story, as told to W. Grant

Stewart, involves three lochs. The kelpie plunges its doomed victims into 'Lochnadorb, Lochspynie, or Lochness, where he would enjoy his victim at his leisure.' Another version of this story appeared in Thomas Dick Lauder's *Legendary Tales of the Highlands* (1841), but this omits any reference to Loch Ness. MacGregor told Lauder that his relative had met the water kelpie 'on the lonely shore of Loch-an-dorbe' (i.e. Lochindorb). Since grand-uncle Macgregor 'lived on the banks of the river Dulnan [i.e. Dulnain] in Strathspey', this loch was the nearest large one to his home. What is striking about all this is that neither MacGregor had any local connection whatever to Loch Ness. The Warlock himself lived at Gaulrig, a remote hamlet south of Tomintoul.

Plainly there was a market in Victorian Britain for romantic and mysterious tales of the highlands. The kelpie mongers W. Grant Stewart and Thomas Dick Lauder were joined by Sir Walter Scott and others in the anthology *Weird Tales – Scottish,* first published in 1888 in London and Edinburgh in William Patterson's popular *Nuggets for Travellers* Series. Equally plainly, Gregor MacGregor was widely known for his reputation as 'Willox the wizard'. Lauder was keen to meet this legendary figure and see for himself 'the far-famed magical kelpie's bridle and mermaid's stone, for the possession of which he is so celebrated in all the neighbouring districts'. Grant Stewart's *Popular Superstitions and Festive Amusements of the Highlanders of Scotland* was an early example of this new publishing trend, and Lauder's *Legendary Tales of the Highlands* cashed in on an earlier success, being subtitled *A sequel to Highland rambles.* But upon examining the wizard's 'two wonderful engines of his supernatural power' Lauder was distinctly underwhelmed. He described the mermaid's stone as 'somewhat resembling, in shape and appearance, what is called a bull's eye, used for transmitting light through the deck of a vessel into its smaller apartments below' and laconically noted of the water horse trophy, 'It has not the most distant resemblance to any part of a bridle.'

Roland Watson believes that his inventory of water horse references testifies to an underlying reality: 'Loch Ness was the prime and dominant abode of the Water Horse by virtue of the stream of eyewitness and folklore stories that not only sustained the tale but fortified it above its fellows.' But of course, there was no *recorded* eyewitness testimony prior to 1933. As for the Loch Ness water kelpie legend, which was first promoted in *Popular Superstitions*, this tale was invented far from the Great Glen and did not involve a local family. No one else seems to have heard of the Loch Ness kelpie, least of all the people who lived at the lochside.

What is striking about Watson's tradition is how much it depends on non-local sources. When Ethel Forster Heddle has a character in her novel *The Secret of the Turret* refer to 'the legend of the water kelpie on Loch Ness, where I was brought up' it is far more likely that this author drew on a Highland legends book such as the one authored by W. Grant Stewart rather than on any personal knowledge. Heddle was born in 1862 at St Andrews, Fifeshire. At the age of 21 she married William Marshall in Singapore and the couple's first child was born in 1895 in Java. By 1900 she was back at St Andrews, where she gave birth to a second child. She died on 7 May 1942 at St Andrews. Between 1892 and 1934 she published nineteen works of fiction, mostly written for teenage girls. Another two novels were published under the transparent pseudonym 'Ethel F. H. Marshall'. *Ethel Forster Heddle appears to have had no local connections whatever with the Loch Ness area.*

Roland Watson connects his belief in a water horse tradition at Loch Ness with 'over thirty' land sightings of the monster. But none of the alleged pre-1933 sightings were reported or recorded at the time. He singles out two in particular – one from the 1870s near Aldourie Castle, and another from the shore of Inchnacardoch Bay in 1919. The first episode involved 'an enormous and extraordinary animal, bigger than an elephant, but about the same sort of colour'. It waddled down the slope and disappeared into the loch. The second report involved a creature disturbed in some bushes at the water's edge. It had a humped back, four limbs and a head reminiscent of a camel. In both cases the witnesses described how the animal twisted its head from side to side.

Watson believes that the amphibious nature of the Loch Ness monster explains the water horse legend:

one can readily see how land based stories such as this, if transported back to centuries before, could spawn tales of bridled horses quietly waiting for their next victim by the shore side. This would explain why we have this counter intuitive idea of a water monster coming out of its natural abode to hunt its victims.

This kind of approach to folklore tradition comes in for a blistering critique from Michel Meurger in his encyclopaedic study *Lake Monster Traditions: A Cross Cultural Analysis*. He argues that the subject suffers from 'a deep contempt for irrational world views and the specificity of folk-tradition' and his book seeks to reinstate respect for 'a mystical approach to the world'. In short, 'cryptozoologists and sceptics consciously refuse to accept myth as a product of the human mind, as an imaginary story'. Meurger questions the logic of cryptozoologists who accept the sea-serpent as fact – based on innumerable eye-witness sightings – but who then reject the existence of mermaids. He asserts that there is just as much historic testimony for the existence of mermaids as there is for sea-serpents.

The same argument can be levelled at the water horse tradition. The Scottish folklore tradition includes the barnacle goose which grew on trees, the water imp (part woman, part goat), a dragon with three heads, and the boobrie, a giant bird which ate livestock. Why should these fantastic creatures be condemned as imaginary, while the water kelpie is revived as a real animal? What might be called the problem of selectivity applies directly to the water kelpie itself. Gregor 'Willox' MacGregor's talking water kelpie with its saddle and magic bridle seems a world away from Watson's amphibians of Aldourie and Inchnacardoch. In fact, Meurger's thesis seems underscored by Watson's two examples, because the witnesses in both cases were children. Their experiences were literally marvellous. What could be more fabulous than encountering an aquatic camel at one end of the loch, and, at the other, an extraordinary creature bigger than an elephant waddling past a picnic?

There are other sorts of kelpie than the predominant archetype of the male demon which adopts the form a horse. In 2013 it was reported that researchers at the University of Edinburgh had discovered a previously unknown reference to Morag, the monster of Loch Morar. It was found in a manuscript of Alexander Carmichael, a prolific collector of folklore. Dating from around 1902, Carmichael described how, according to local tradition, Morag 'appears in a black heap or ball slowing and deliberately rising in the water and moving along like a boat water-logged'. However, Carmichael's source also informed him:

Like the other water deities, she is half-human, half-fish. The lower portions of her body is in the form of a grilse [salmon] and the upper in the form of a small woman of highly developed breasts with long flowing yellow hair falling down her snow white back and breast.

But it was not only the inhabitants of remote Scottish settlements who conceived of a water monster in the form of a beautiful naked woman. The minor Victorian painter Herbert James Draper produced 'The

Kelpie' (1913), an erotic canvas portraying a voluptuous naked woman exposing her breasts as she sat on rocks beside a tumbling river, a dark forest behind her, waiting to lure any passing man to his doom. Another sensuous nude displaying ample breasts is portrayed in 'The Kelpie' by Thomas Millie Dow (1895), which adds a serpent dimension by including vipers which, in Steven Huebner's words, 'slide lasciviously from her hair down and around her torso'. In this water kelpie tradition, the psychological and sexual aspects of lake monsters are obvious.

It seems no coincidence that Nessie and Morag are traditionally conceived of as female and, moreover, as threatening. Here, the water kelpie overlaps with the water horse. Transformed into an object of fear, the horse survives even in modern language. To suffer a disturbing dream is to encounter a night-mare. In Scandinavian legend the *marra* is a seductive female demon who climbs on to horses after dark and rides them through the night until they are drained of energy and covered in sweat. Often the *marra* plaits the horses' manes and tails into complicated *marra*-locks which cannot be combed out.

The water kelpie as seductive siren is a myth with more than a grain of truth when it comes to the Loch Ness story, since what are monster-spotters other than lonely voyeurs, hoping for a thrilling glimpse of the kelpie herself? Monster hunters are almost always men: passionate, inquisitive, filled with desire, in thrall to the siren. They seek to capture the kelpie on film. They seek to penetrate her mystery with phallic cameras and submarines (and, lately, underwater torpedo-shaped drones). But she always outwits them. Like the *marra*, she is bewitching but ultimately exhausting. The Loch Ness water kelpie drags men to their doom, consuming their lives and sometimes their reputations and careers. As Ted Holiday confessed in a rather revealing letter to the *Inverness Courier* (August 9, 1963), he went back to Loch Ness with his camera 'like a lover returning to his sinister mistress'.

Grimshaw and Lester supply a Freudian reading, suggesting ways in which lake monsters obliquely represent 'the desires that civilisation refuses'. They delicately note 'the resemblance between the head-neck organisation and the human phallus'. The monster is a shape-shifter, sometimes female, sometimes male. It is both desirable and terrifying. It swells in size and then collapses. It briefly and tantalisingly displays its curves, teasing the watcher. In every sense it is a creature of the depths, confronting the lonely watcher with something magical, desirable and fearful.

Meurger's basic argument that water monsters originate in the human imagination is lent support by Roland Watson's helpful reproduction of Charles Mackay's poem, 'The Kelpie of Corryveckan' (1845). There was no tradition of a water kelpie associated with this famous whirlpool, and if there had been we can be quite sure that Mackay would have regarded it as a fiction, since he is best known nowadays for that vast inventory of human folly, *Extraordinary Popular Delusions and the Madness of Crowds* (1841). In this book he included kelpies alongside 'Ghosts, goblins, wraiths… and a whole host of spiritual beings', which to Mackay represented 'dreams of early ignorance' symptomatic of a people who were known for 'their powers of imagination'. A cosmopolitan Scottish rationalist like Mackay, who spent much of his life as a prominent London journalist, found such superstitions understandable among those of his fellow countryman who lived out their lives 'by the misty glens of the Highlands, and the romantic streams of the Lowlands'. The kelpie was an inspirational creature and Mackay was happy to appropriate it for literary purposes in his own mock-traditional romantic ballad.

'The Kelpie of Corryveckan' embodies Mackay's own argument that Scottish folklore appeals to the imagination and is both reproduced and regenerated by literary form. The activities of kelpies, ghosts and other supernatural entities 'were enshrined in song, and took a greater hold upon the imagination because "verse had sanctified them"'. The same holds true for the Loch Ness monster. It is above all a story, endlessly reproducing itself.

But in the case of stories which purport to be true there is always the question of *transmission*. How accurate is one person's retelling of someone else's story? The discovery of Alexander Carmichael's material about a monster in Loch Morar sounds exciting. But as the BBC report acknowledges, 'He is thought to have spent only a couple of days in the area of Morar and did not claim to see Morag for himself. His main source of information about the monster appears to be a local named Ewan MacDougall.' We know nothing about MacDougall, who seems to have been Morar's answer to Alex Campbell. None of the witnesses to the monster are named. The whole story rests on the testimony of a single individual about whom nothing is known at all, other than his name.

One of Roland Watson's sources is John Francis Campbell, author of the four-volume *Popular Tales of the West Highlands* (1860-62). Although an acknowledged pioneer in the collection of folklore material, Campbell once breezily explained that 'I take the story from the Gaelic and tell it in my own words generally where the scribe's language is prosy.'

The two land sightings which Watson cites also involved retold narrative. The Aldourie episode derives from a letter sent to Tim Dinsdale in 1961 from one Edward P. Smith. Dinsdale's correspondent recalled an incident some twenty-two years earlier when he'd stopped for tea at the Foyers Hotel. There he fell into conversation with 'an old Scottish lady' from Aberdeen. She and her chauffeur had seen the monster that very day. She also confided that she'd seen it many years earlier. Smith's letter at this point assumes the point of view of the old lady, recounting her tale in the first person: 'I've seen it once before out of the water. When I was a wee girl...' The old lady then tells the story of the picnic interrupted by the monster 'passing us a few yards to one side'. The story ends with the narrator and her two brothers being whipped by their father, not for telling a fairy story '"but for telling me a fairy story and pretending it is the truth"'. The letter then reverts back to Smith: 'I never learnt my old informant's name, and she must have been dead these many years; but, on my honour, that is what she told me.'

Even if we set scepticism to one side and accept 'Edward P. Smith' as a genuine source and not someone pulling Dinsdale's leg, this is at best just someone remembering twenty-two years after the event someone else's memories of something which probably happened over sixty years earlier 'in the very late 1870's.' The idea that in 1961 Smith had total recall of a conversation held in 1939 is simply not credible. We have no way of knowing how the passage of time coloured the old woman's childhood memory (a woman who, moreover, on revisiting the loch in 1939, promptly saw the monster). Equally we have no way of knowing how her narrative was distorted by Smith's retelling. Yet this episode is regarded by Watson as if it is transparent in its authenticity and accuracy.

The second land sighting, at Inchnacardoch, was first publicised in the *Inverness Courier*, 3 October 1933, by 'A Fort Augustus correspondent' (beyond doubt the ubiquitous Alex Campbell), where it was identified as occurring 'twenty years ago'. William Mcgruer was described as giving 'a strange description of the strange creature very similar to that of Mr Spicer'. But the creature that Mcgruer, his brother and his older sister saw seems quite unlike the one witnessed by Mr Spicer, who at this point in time had identified it only as 'resembling a dragon or pre-historic animal' with 'a long neck which moved up and down in the manner of a scenic railway'. The Mcgruer sighting involved a pale, sandy-coloured animal which was reminiscent of a camel in relation to its head, neck and humped back, but was smaller than one.

Mcgruer's sister contributed her own account, which appears in *More Than a Legend*. But here too the narrative is processed by an intermediary, in the shape of Constance Whyte. She supplies a summary and only at one point does she quote the witness directly, describing how the animal was 'humping its great shoulders and twisting its head from side to side'. This raises the question of why Whyte couldn't just let the witness give her story in her own words. Why did Whyte feel the need to smooth it out? If there was compression, what was lost? In short: *what's missing?*

Watson notices that the Aldourie and Inchnacardoch descriptions share a common feature in their descriptions of the animal turning its head and neck from side to side. To him, this is redolent of authenticity: the second sighting matches the first. But what I notice is that in telling his tale of the old woman and her childhood monster sighting, Edward P. Smith casually mentions his knowledge of 'Mrs Whyte's book'. Smith, in other words, had absorbed monster lore. When he wrote to Dinsdale in 1961 he had read about the Mcgruer 'camel monster' sighting in *More Than a Legend,* a book which appeared in three editions between 1957 and 1961. The other parallel is the way in which the children in both stories run home, only to be chastised for fibbing. These narrative coincidences underline the problematic nature of children's perceptions of unfamiliar animals and events remembered years after they occurred, which are then narrated by third parties, which further narrations in turn risk being shaped by the contents and conventions of the Loch Ness monster tradition.

Where *transmission* is concerned, there is a final irony in connection with the water kelpie. The origins of the word 'kelpie' are obscure and contested, but one plausible derivation is from the Gaelic word 'cailpeach' ('colt'). The first recorded use of 'kaelpie' (as it was then spelled) to refer to a mythical creature is in a poem by the English poet William Collins. It was written just before or after the winter of 1749 and published posthumously under the title 'An Ode on the Popular Superstitions of the Highlands of Scotland, Considered as the Subject of Poetry'. It includes the melodramatic account of a young man who falls victim to the water kelpie and whose ghost piteously calls out to his anxious wife:

> Nor e'er of Me one hapless thought renew,
> While I lie weltring on the Osier'd Shore
> Drown'd by the Kaelpie's wrath

('Weltering' can mean both 'tossed around' and 'to be drenched', while an 'osiered shore' is one lined by willows.)

The manuscript of this poem was lost but in 1967 it was finally located in a surprising place – Aldourie Castle, on the shore of Loch Ness. This is an aspect of the Loch Ness story which has previously gone unnoticed (and now I have pointed it out I dread to think how some future pro-monster authors will misuse this information). But although it is an astonishing coincidence that the first-ever use of the word 'kelpie' to refer to an amphibious water demon should be in a manuscript found at Loch Ness, it is just that: coincidence.

The poem, which existed only in an unfinished draft, was inscribed by its author to the Scottish playwright John Home, who took the manuscript home with him. Collins died without ever publishing it. The manuscript came into the hands of Dr Alexander Carlyle, who passed it on for publication to Alexander Fraser Tytler (1747-1813). It was duly published, in an amended form, in the *Transactions of the Royal Society of Edinburgh* (1788). Tytler kept the manuscript. His home was Woodhouselee in Midlothian but he acquired Aldourie Castle through his marriage in 1776 to the heiress Anne Fraser, daughter of William Fraser of Balnain and Aldourie. When Tytler died, his second son inherited Woodehouselee and his eldest son inherited Aldourie Castle and his father's books and papers, which evidently included the manuscript of Collins' poem. By the time the long-lost manuscript was rediscovered in 1967, Aldourie Castle was owned by Colonel A. E. Cameron, nephew of the late Colonel Neil Fraser-Tytler.

The poem was in fact written in London, and during his lifetime William Collins never visited Scotland. It's no coincidence that this verse was produced in the aftermath of Culloden, when a vengeful English government put the Highlands under military occupation and set about violently suppressing local resistance and extinguishing clan identity. The 'Ode on the Popular Superstitions of the Highlands' was a work of cultural occupation. Scottish identity had to be domesticated and rendered safe. From now on Scotland was sentimentalised and romanticised. The water kelpie became a stage prop in a colonising project. It was a creature of literature, not zoology. It emerged not from an actual Scotland but from an entirely imaginary one.

14

Lineages

In roaring he shall rise and on the surface die.
  Alfred Lord Tennyson, 'The Kraken' (1830)

In the Sherlock Holmes story 'Silver Blaze' (1892) the curious incident of the dog in the night-time famously involved a dog which did not bark when it should have done. Likewise throughout the nineteenth century and during the first third of the twentieth, the Loch Ness Monster remained strangely mute. It has always been a central contradiction of the Nessie myth that no record of the animal exists prior to the 1930s.

A pre-1930s tradition was later constructed but it is as problematic as those cases where individuals claim to have had premonitions of large-scale tragic events but only happen to mention their amazing foresight *after* the events have occurred. In any case, sceptics were just as able to find pre-1933 evidence as believers. Maurice Burton's vegetable mat theory was endorsed by Marjorie Anderson, who in September 1960 revealed that her husband in 'about 1902' had heard from a gamekeeper named Roderick Campbell who told him how 'about 1880' while working for an estate on Loch Ness he'd learned of a strange phenomenon that sometimes occurred there. It involved

a mass of rotting vegetation carried out into the loch from the mouths of the rivers, raised to the surface by marsh gas, and sometimes shooting along the surface with surprising speed, then, when the gas had gone off, sinking suddenly out of sight. These things looked extraordinarily lifelike and... were sometimes mistaken for living creatures.

One can prove almost anything by anecdotes, especially those told at second or third-hand.

Gould was untroubled by ancestry since he believed there was only a solitary monster and it was a newcomer to the loch, making a visit. But Constance Whyte and Tim Dinsdale believed giant unknown animals had lived in Loch Ness for centuries. These last two authors were both English middle-class professionals, who subscribed to very stereotypical notions of Scotland. Constance Whyte portrayed the Great Glen as a misty, isolated region occupied by a noble savage known as 'the Highlander'. Loch Ness, a lonely spot, as remote as an Amazon rain forest, was, she believed, only opened up to the modern world in 1933. What's more the natives of the glen had a 'taboo' which, she confided, even as late as the 1950s, 'still discourages mention of the Monster'. Tim Dinsdale's view of the Highlands was shaped by Whyte's book, which meant he was in for a shock when he first reached Inverness in April 1960. He was stunned to find that it had 'shops and banks'. It was 'so different from the outpost I had imagined'. The natives were so advanced they might almost have been, well, *English*.

Monster hunters, overwhelmingly English and American, have never been very interested in Scottish social history. In reality Loch Ness has always been a major communications route across the Highlands. Mrs Whyte's allusion to 'the changes brought about when regions not even accessible on foot become a motorists' highway (for tracks in the old days passed along high ridges, not by the water's edge)' was wildly misleading nonsense. The motorists' highways of today follow routes which existed long before Henry Ford was born. One of the busiest tourist sites at Loch Ness today is the Clansman Hotel, featuring a hotel, large car park, Nessie gift shop and lifesize model monster, all adjacent to a harbour where Jacobite Cruises run a regular service of boat trips on the loch. This hub of frenzied activity is actually built on the site of an old coaching inn or 'change-house'. Here 'fresh horses were kept to set the coach on its way'. There was a similar establishment on the other side of the loch, in the vicinity of the legendary Spicer land sighting. In fact there were inns all round the loch, including one by Temple Pier. They were built along the shoreline, with spectacular views of the loch, as of course were Urquhart Castle, Aldourie Castle, the military base which gives Fort Augustus its name and the Abbey subsequently built on its site.

Leaving aside the locals, who left no record of ever seeing large unknown animals, metropolitan Englishmen had been arriving at Loch Ness since the seventeenth century. In both the seventeenth and eighteenth centuries English frigates patrolled the loch when it was necessary to intimidate and subdue the local population. You might think that over the course of three centuries someone, somewhere, would jot down in a diary or a letter or a memoir or a newspaper a reference to stories of a large, strange, unidentifiable animal in the loch. But no such reference has ever been found.

These were two of the pioneering arguments of *The Loch Ness Mystery Solved*. Not only was the centuries-old Loch Ness monster tradition entirely bogus but, to turn this tradition upside down, it was curious that for centuries a new species of large unknown animal in Loch Ness had attracted no attention at all, from either local residents or innumerable well-connected English visitors. This, of course, is exactly what you'd expect if no family of monsters lived there and there was no local tradition of sightings.

Today, the advent of the internet has made searching through old newspapers a much, much easier task than it was thirty years ago, as content is put online and search engines swoop on such enticing words as 'Loch Ness' and 'monster'. In *The Water Horses of Loch Ness* (2011) that diligent researcher Roland Watson cites three newspaper reports from the nineteenth century which were unknown and undiscussed when *The Loch Ness Mystery Solved* was published. He suggests all three supply more evidence of a monster tradition.

The first is a report from the *Aberdeen Journal* (January 31, 1849), which is about the devastating consequences of the River Ness breaking its banks. Flood damage included the collapse of the Ness Bridge in Inverness. The report states: 'Several prophecies are recorded concerning it. One asserts it was not to fall till a monster of the whale tribe, bred in Lochness, came down and attacked it.'

The prophet is not named, the prophecy is not sourced, and this report is not from a publication which is local. You would expect Inverness prophecies to be reported in Inverness publications but this one wasn't. Aside from these rather basic difficulties, it should be remembered that a prophecy is only a piece of imaginative writing, like a poem or a short story. The unidentified prophet is *not* saying that

Loch Ness contains a tribe of whales (let alone a tribe of strange and fearsome creatures) but is merely making the whimsical suggestion that a whale raised in Loch Ness will one day come down the river and attack the bridge, causing it to fall. And how might a whale get into Loch Ness? Well, a massive flood of the sort that occurred in 1849 could permit the passage of a large sea creature, and whales have been known to swim surprising distances up British rivers. In other words, this unidentifiable prophecy, in itself a slight piece of whimsy, sounds both suspiciously topical and entertainingly imaginative.

That there was no tradition of strange animals in Loch Ness is rather underlined by Watson's next example, from the *Inverness Courier* (July 1, 1852), which I have already discussed in Chapter 13. The 'Scene at Lochend' involving two ponies swimming in the loch shows that while some locals believed, not unreasonably, that what they were seeing in the distance were either seals or deer, others with more vivid imaginations thought that the animals were a sea-serpent, a pair of whales or two water horses.

This report is actually a very valuable piece of negative evidence. Firstly, it makes no reference at all to any tradition of sea-serpents, water horses or strange animals in the loch. Secondly, it shows that a parochial episode involving an unusual event was reported in the local newspaper. This raises the question as to why there is no record of other strange sightings in the loch, given that they would have been newsworthy.

That odd events were regarded as newsworthy and publishable is illustrated by Watson's third example, published some sixteen years later in the same newspaper (*Inverness Courier*, October 8, 1868). It concerned the carcase of 'a strange fish' some six feet long, which had washed ashore at Loch Ness. The corpse attracted 'large crowds of country people' who came to stare at it, fascinated by this mysterious spectacle. In due course it was authoritatively identified as a small bottlenose whale which had been stripped of its blubber.

This news report is cast as a comic item. The reporter deduces that the whale had been dumped in the loch as a joke by 'some waggish crew' (presumably sailors on a whaling vessel passing through the loch on a passage down the Caledonian Canal, to or from Fort William). The journalist contextualises the prank with a supercilious reference to the comically dull-witted villagers who live by the loch:

Some of the most credulous natives averred that a huge fish, similar in size and shape, had been occasionally seen gambolling in the loch for years back, and with equal determination protested that its being cast dead on the shore boded no good to the inhabitants – that, in fact, its presence presaged dire calamities either in pestilence or famine, or perhaps both.

Could this 'huge fish' have been the monster? Was the whale carcase dumped there to mock a local tradition of something strange in the loch?

We are told that the mysterious 'huge fish' was 'similar in size and shape' to the dead bottlenose whale. Its reported length was about six feet. That is 'huge' compared to a stickleback or a mackerel and substantially larger than the average trout or salmon. It is certainly bigger than any fish which is known to inhabit Loch Ness, but it is not bigger than two types of fish which *might* live there.

It is harder to draw conclusions about the shape, because it is not clear how much of the bottlenose whale was left. It was presumably a specimen of *Hyperoodon ampullatus*, the Northern bottlenose whale. We are told only that 'the blubber had been taken off'. The purpose of this (the process known as 'flensing') would not have been to make the shape of the carcase any different, as the blubber would have been less than two inches thick. It would merely have altered its appearance, stripping off the black outer skin to expose paler flesh and bone beneath. Of course, we don't know if those responsible for this 'waggish' prank also cut off other sections of the whale's body, to shape it into something unidentifiable to the layman.

If we accept that the anecdote of 'a huge fish' seen by local people is accurate, what conclusions can be drawn from it? The first is that the creature was identified by those who saw it as a fish – not as a sea-serpent, a water horse or a creature unknown to conventional classification. Secondly, it was about six feet long – far too small for the Loch Ness Monster. Thirdly, it 'had been occasionally seen gambolling in the loch for years back'. The verb 'to gambol' has many meanings but they are all associated with playful, lively activity – behaviour which is hard to square with most Nessie sightings.

There is a modern sceptical tradition, associated with Adrian Shine, Dick Raynor and Steve Feltham, which argues that the Loch Ness phenomena can be explained with reference to two types of 'huge fish'. The first is the sturgeon. Dick Raynor has commented:

On the matter of 'great fish' seen 'years back', these would be consistent with sturgeon coming in from the sea to spawn in shallow rivermouths. There are many accounts of them being caught in the Moray Firth area.

There are plenty of monster stories to debate but Richard Franck's Memoirs in 1658 and the Courier's 'huge fish' of 1868 are not part of any such mystery.

The other candidate is the European wels catfish, *Silurus glanis*. It has been suggested that 'it is quite possible that *Silurus glanis* is the largest freshwater fish in the world'. The species was introduced to England from Germany in 1880, when the Duke of Bedford stocked 70 of them into the Shoulder of Mutton lake at Woburn Abbey. It is not inconceivable that someone introduced *Silurus glanis* into Loch Ness during the nineteenth century. Karl Shuker cites the case of Lake Myllesjön in Sweden, which supposedly had a monster tradition involving 'an enormous water beast dubbed the whale-fish', which he concludes 'was probably a giant European catfish (wells) *Siluris glanis*'. One specimen caught in Sweden in 1871 was 11.75 feet long. But the 'whale-fish' illustration in Shuker's book bears no resemblance to Nessie sightings and involves a monster with two enormous frog-like eyes.

There are two fundamental objections to these giant fish theories. The first is that there is no record of anyone ever catching either a sturgeon or a catfish in Loch Ness, which during the past century has been a very popular lake with fishermen, both local and visiting. Moreover, large dead sturgeons have a habit of floating to the surface. This has never occurred at Loch Ness. Secondly, neither fish bears any resemblance to the vast majority of monster sightings.

However, it cannot absolutely be ruled out that the episode of the skinned whale involved a practical joke provoked by the ignorance of locals who had seen a large fish in the loch and been baffled and awed by its appearance. The point of view of the *Courier* report is that of the knowledgeable and sophisticated urban commentator amused by the ignorance and backwardness of country folk – a perspective evidently shared by whatever 'waggish' agency was responsible for the prank. But although the journalist is supercilious and smug, there is no reason to doubt that the mocking description of uneducated villagers terrified that a dead fish signalled the imminent arrival of pestilence or famine was not accurate. That superstition matches aspects of water horse mythology.

Although the journalist was plainly self-satisfied and writing for an educated middle class readership with shared values, that did not mean he had no point. Superstitious belief lingered on, along with the Gaelic language, until both were marginalised by the arrival of modernity in all its forms. Amusingly, no less a person than Rupert Gould once contrasted the misleading testimony of 'local fishermen and crofters' with that of the superior understanding of a 'person of education'.

Ultimately this 1868 *Courier* report is far too inconclusive for any firm conclusions to be drawn. But what is telling is that this story of 'a huge fish' in Loch Ness is never repeated. This silence makes no sense if a huge and unidentifiable fish was consistently seen 'gambolling' at the loch surface. After all, there is no reason in principle why Loch Ness should not be home to an entirely new species of fish. Bala Lake (Llyn Tegid) in Wales is unique in containing a very rare species of whitefish, known as the Gwyniad (*Coregonus lavaretus*). This is a rare survivor which has lived in the lake's depths for 10,000 years. But if there were an outsize fish in Loch Ness which was seen from time to time this would have been reported and written about long before 1933.

That is the central difficulty with the Loch Ness Monster: it is not only elusive physically, it was undocumented until 1933. This is strange when you consider that quite parochial stories involving unusual animals or fish and unusual events at Loch Ness quickly reached the wider world. A pike which gobbled up thirteen young ducks near 'the western extremity of Loch Ness' was reported in the Dublin press in January 1857, recycling a story from an Inverness newspaper. The 1906 sighting by two anglers of an adder swimming one-hundred yards off-shore 'near Urquhart Castle', apparently attempting to cross the loch, was reported in the *Scotsman* and recycled in the *Whitby Gazette*. In September 1914 the outbreak of war in Europe was no impediment to reports in both the national and local press of the unexpected presence of a school of porpoises in Loch Ness.

When I went to the archives of the *Inverness Courier* – something no one had ever bothered to do in half a century of monster-hunting – I discovered that the first sceptic was a man who knew the loch better than anyone. If there was something unusual in Loch Ness one person who should have heard about it was steamship captain John Macdonald, who had been sailing up and down the loch since the 1880s. He calculated he had made 20,000 trips along the loch (and those journeys involved calling at all the local piers en route). In all that time no one mentioned to him seeing or hearing about an unusual animal in the loch.

In 2011 Roland Watson reported that he had found an undated *Daily Mail* cutting which revealed that, when asked his opinion six months on from his letter to the *Courier*, the captain replied, ' If so many reputable people say they have seen "the beast" one inclines to the belief that there is something in it.' But though Watson describes this as a 'recantation', it simply indicates the social pressure to conform that a local functionary such as Macdonald was under. Britain was still a class-ridden society in the nineteen thirties, where deference was required from the lower orders. The case for Nessie has always foregrounded the eye-witness testimony of individuals of high social status. When doctors, businessmen, and even *university graduates* stated that they had seen the monster, to dissent was at best to suggest that they were deluded, and at worst that they were exaggerating, lying or had drunk rather too much whisky. Fort Augustus (which may have been where Macdonald lived and worked) was a very small town in a frenzy akin to that of Salem or Loudon. Even GPs and retired naval commanders were caught up in the desire to see the new local prodigy.

In *The Loch Ness Mystery Solved* I argued that the true lineage of the Loch Ness Monster was sociological and that the public fascination with monsters dates back to the nineteenth century, when dinosaurs first gripped the public imagination and when the idea that some might have survived into the modern age became intertwined with fossil discoveries, the hotly contested theory of evolution and the proliferation of sea-serpent sightings. This matrix was reproduced culturally by novelists and poets, and a pioneer in the unveiling of secret worlds containing marvellous creatures was Jules Verne, with *Journey to the Centre of the Earth* (1864) and *Twenty Thousand Leagues under the Sea* (1870) – titles contemporaneous with the craze for both dinosaurs and sea-serpents. The English tradition climaxed with Arthur Conan Doyle's *The Lost World* (1912), which uncannily anticipated many aspects of the Loch Ness story.

As a recent biographer explains, Conan Doyle's novel had among its inspirations a sighting by the writer himself:

Cruising the Aegean on his honeymoon in 1907, he had seen a creature in the sea which he remarked to Jean looked remarkably like a 'young ichthyosaur', an early Jurassic fish lizard, about four feet long, with a long beak and tail and four flippers. It was probably a dolphin, which are common in the Aegean, and which vaguely resemble ichthyosaurus, but Conan Doyle preferred to believe it a dinosaur somehow stranded in the modern world.

The Lost World is narrated by a journalist and dramatises a familiar debate between the eye-witness who has seen living dinosaurs and sceptics who object on grounds of scientific impossibility or who flippantly attribute sightings to 'Trade gin'. The eye-witness finds cultural support for his belief among the natives, who are reluctant to talk about Curupuri, 'the spirit of the woods, something terrible, something malevolent, something to be avoided'. We are at once in Ted Holiday territory. The evidence, initially, turns out to be ambiguous and includes a photograph which has 'deficiencies and abnormalities' and 'There was talk of faking'. But, of course, the narrow-minded sceptics are proved spectacularly wrong: the marvellous, very satisfyingly, turns out to be tangible and all too real.

1933

The thrilling idea that prehistoric monsters lived on in remote parts of the world was further popularised by the advent of moving pictures. *The Lost World* was first turned into a silent movie in 1925 (another adaptation came out in 1960, the year of the Dinsdale film). The special effects man on the 1925 version was Willis O'Brien, who later found identical employment by recycling his skills on the first smash-hit talkie monster film, *King Kong*. This was released in April 1933.

As I pointed out in *The Loch Ness Mystery Solved*, 'It is probably no coincidence that the Loch Ness Monster was discovered at the very moment that *King Kong*, the masterpiece of the genre, was released across Scotland in 1933.' I also drew attention to the curious coincidence of George Spicer's allusion to the film when describing his monster. In fifty years of Loch Ness commentary no one had troubled either to notice or draw any conclusions from those revealing parallels. You will search in vain for the words 'King Kong' in the indexes of *More Than a Legend* (1957), *Loch Ness Monster* (1961), *The Elusive Monster* (1961), *The Great Orm of Loch Ness* (1968) or *The Loch Ness Story* (1974). Daniel Loxton has since examined one moment from the movie in detail, involving 'a *Diplodocus*-like sauropod', arguing that George Spicer's encounter with the monster on land 'almost exactly recreated this scene'.

But the impact of *King Kong* provides only one aspect of the monster fever which was created. That the birth of the Loch Ness Monster embodied and captured a particular cultural and historical moment is underlined by another fabulous fiction which first appeared that year and which has so far escaped scrutiny in connection with Nessie.

Lost Horizon was a rather wooden novel published by a writer whose prolific output of freelance journalism and fiction had as yet failed to make much impression on the wider world. But though the prose of *Lost Horizon* might have been mundane, the imaginative world created by its author James Hilton, captured the mood of the time. The book's success was reinforced by its adaptation as a Hollywood blockbuster. It even contributed a new name to the English language – *Shangri-La*, which became a popular house name in Britain in the following decades. Shangri-La is a name which celebrates retreat from the troubled, threatening wider world into a private space of tranquillity and order.

Loch Ness was certainly Tim Dinsdale's Shangri-La. He left behind a dreary office job and life in a suburban semi-detached house with a wife and four children to find fulfilment in the solitude of monster-hunting:

> I could not ignore the fantastic beauties surrounding me, the mists of early morning and the silence, enveloping and spiritual.
>
> At times I found it hard to believe I was still in the twentieth century, living on the Planet Earth – I seemed to be floating in another-worldly paradise, another dimension, without time, or material content.

Lost Horizon juxtaposed the political instability of the early 1930s (using revolution in Asia as a metaphor for contemporary European politics) with the peacefulness of Shangri-La, a remote hidden monastery set in a green, fertile, unknown secret valley deep in the Himalayas. Here, a small group of westerners stumble upon a refuge from the troubled modern world in a tranquil exotic sphere which offers spiritual self-discovery, intellectual satisfaction and romance, with the added bonus of a strange slowing of the ageing process, resulting in a lifespan extending to some 250 years. The spirituality is underpinned by the agreeable trappings of an affluent middle-class lifestyle, with central heating, modern bathrooms, delicious food sourced from locally grown ingredients, musical instruments and a massive library. Implicitly, this is spirituality, California-style. No wonder Hollywood loved the book.

But then who would not prefer the delights of Shangri-La to an altogether grimmer alternative reality set out in another book published in that memorable year 1933 – *Down and Out in Paris and London*? Escapism and fantasy always trump the cold, hard mirror which realism holds up to the world. James Hilton was 31 and still living at home with his parents when he wrote his fantasy novel in the bedroom of a modest end of terrace house in South Woodford, close to the North Circular Road. Its unexpected and astonishing success allowed him to relocate to California and join the Hollywood set. Eric Blair, meanwhile, was 29 and also living with his parents when *Down and Out in Paris and London* was published. But Blair's book was not what contemporary readers wanted. Even Blair appreciated that its contents would be unpalatable to some readers and so to spare his parents and himself from distress in their claustrophobic Suffolk town he adopted a pseudonym: 'George Orwell'.

The Great Glen offered a pleasant variation on Shangri-La. If Constance Whyte was to be believed it was almost as remote and unknown to civilised man as James Hilton's imaginary Tibetan valley. And in one sense it brought Conan Doyle's fabulous 'lost world', which had comfortingly familiar dimensions ('An area, as large perhaps as Sussex') back to Britain. Here, a bewitching monster existed, challenging modernity and requiring the devotion of its adherents. Loch Ness was a magical place, with similar amenities to Shangri-La. Rupert Gould stayed in Invermoriston (presumably in some comfort at the Glenmoriston Arms Hotel) and a local guide escorted him to the very spot where, two or three decades earlier, he had observed a strange creature 'some 30-40 feet long'.

In this romantic valley Gould was in his element. He was a man who, at times of great stress, was vulnerable to devastating nervous collapses. He was also obsessive, with a quiet rage for order and design. The Loch Ness Monster provided the perfect focus for a man of Gould's temperament. Here in this tranquil place he assembled a rigorous, detailed inventory of material which he found every bit as fascinating as the internal workings of a typewriter or a marine chronometer. *The Loch Ness Monster and Others* is a book of facts. It is crammed with maps, drawings, dates, names and witness statements which accumulate, are shaped, and lead to an affirmative conclusion. The evidence is marshalled and considered, but the verdict is never in doubt. Gould was honest and intelligent enough to acknowledge the possibility that he had 'assisted various honest but self-deluded persons to create a zoological myth', but in the end his romantic commitment to the existence of the weird and the marvellous made the results of his investigation a foregone conclusion. The author of *Oddities: A Book of Unexplained Facts* (1928), *Enigmas: Another Book of Unexplained Facts* (1929) and *The Case for the Sea-Serpent* (1930) was never *not* going to be seduced by Nessie.

Ironically, the Loch Ness Monster was not the only phantom that Rupert Gould was instrumental in putting on the map. He managed this feat quite literally in 1918 when, at his suggestion, Pagoda Rock (60° 11′ S., 4° 43′ E.) was included on the Admiralty charts. But vessels which went in search of this rock were unable to find it. Its supposed existence actually rested on a single eye-witness sighting dating back to 1845. In the face of modern investigation, Gould was forced to conclude that what the witness had actually seen was nothing more than an earth-encrusted iceberg. However, he justified the inclusion of Pagoda Rock on the charts on the grounds that 'The idea was to direct attention to its vicinity, and so get the question of its existence settled.'

The ironic parallels with the Loch Ness saga are entertainingly obvious.

Fringe Theatre

Though Loch Ness provided the opportunity to escape from the contemporary vexations of European political turbulence and domestic austerity and deprivation by offering the thrill of sighting a huge unknown animal, it could not have captured the public mood without first being brought to its attention. The fake news industry amplified one man's obsession. It was also instrumental in seeing off the competition.

What that competition was, of course, is best summed up by the mocking phrase, *lunatic fringe*. This fringe extends far beyond the paranormal or the realms of cryptozoology. It is strangely apt that in his Foreword to *Here's Nessie!* Henry Bauer recommends an interest in the Monster as a means of expanding one's mental horizons:

this quest can still serve as an excellent thing to get hooked on...
Many people also become fascinated by one or other of the

unexplained matters that fascinate various of my colleagues in The Society for Scientific Exploration… even who the actual author was of the plays and poems officially attributed to William Shakespeare.

The problem with this line of reasoning is that 'unexplained matters' are often all too explicable. What purports to be mysterious is often not mysterious at all, though when represented as utterly enigmatic they possess what George Orwell witheringly called 'the charm of useless knowledge'. Perhaps it would be more accurate to say that mysteries often consist of nothing more than what might be called *false knowledge*. The so-called 'Bermuda Triangle' is a good example. As Lawrence David Kusche established, *there is no such thing*. The area delineated as forming a sinister triangle is no more associated with unexplained disappearances than any other comparable expanse of the globe subject to extreme weather and wide expanses of ocean. Kusche comprehensively debunked the notion in 1975. But this non-existent 'mystery' remains embedded in popular writing. In *Open Skies, Closed Minds* (2014), a book about UFOs, Nick Pope writes, 'The Bermuda Triangle, written about in thousands of books and articles, remains the most mysterious swallower of aircraft, ships and people.' To which one can only reply: no, it doesn't.

That someone like Henry Bauer evidently subscribes to the possibility that Shakespeare didn't write the plays and poetry conventionally attributed to him is interesting. The authorship saga involves a classic accumulation of false knowledge by individuals who believed that Shakespeare's plays and sonnets were autobiographical and contained clues to their real, secret author, who could not possibly be an untutored glover's son from a rural market town, but must instead be an aristocrat. In his entertaining and persuasive demolition of the anti-Shakespeareans, James Shapiro observes that their arguments are 'grounded in fantasy, anachronism and projection'. It is a tale of folly, monomania, snobbery and absurdity, replete with hoaxes, passionate rivalries and bizarre investigations, all in pursuit of a chimera (a bit like the Loch Ness story, then).

Among those drawn to this supposed mystery was Ignatius Donnelly, author of *Atlantis: The Antediluvian World* (1882), who spent six years searching for the cipher which would unlock the identity of the secret author hidden inside Shakespeare's writing. Having previously written about a lost world, he now unveiled a lost writer. The fruits of his obsession were published in a book a staggering one-thousand pages long: *The Great Cryptogram: Francis Bacon's Cipher in the So-Called Shakespeare Plays*. Yet the contemporary documentary evidence that Shakespeare existed as a playwright and wrote the plays published under his name is overwhelming. Those who argue otherwise are unable to provide any corroborative evidence to support their flimsy claims.

Sceptic Richard Gordon notes the pleasurable aspects of searching for the Loch Ness Monster: 'You kindle the warmth of companionship in a common cause.' It is 'more fun' than getting involved in a political campaign. 'Best of all, you provide the excitement of scientific research and the stimulus of scientific controversy, without the tedium of scientific discipline or the bother of acquiring a scientific education.'

As the Shakespeare authorship saga shows, false knowledge does sometimes attract the interest of intelligent people, though they are usually distinguished in other spheres. Mark Twain and Henry James were seduced by the Baconians, whereas Sigmund Freud preferred the claims of Edward De Vere, Earl of Oxford. But as Shapiro shows, each man's views were shaped by a highly personal agenda.

In the Loch Ness story Denys Tucker supplies a prime example of intelligence diverted into folly. For him, monster fever proved destructive, annihilating his career as Curator of Fishes at the British Museum (Natural History). Oddly, having sacrificed his vocation for Nessie, Tucker then seems to have eschewed any involvement with the great Nessie hunt of the 1960s. It was only in 1989 that he emerged from obscurity, with his essay 'The Zoologist's Tale'. It is preceded by a dedication 'To the memory of Pierre Denys de Montfort who, because he compiled accounts of the Kraken and the Giant Octopus in his *Histoire naturelle des Mollusques* (1802) was dismissed from the Muséum National d'Histoire naturelle and died destitute in a street in Paris in 1820. He was faithful to Science in his lifetime and has been wholly vindicated by Science since his death.'

The self-identification is obvious. But this dedication is problematic. Far from being 'wholly vindicated', de Montfort's identification of a 'poulpe colossal' has been described by one modern writer on the giant squid as 'a wild mixture of fact and fantasy'. It was de Montfort who first told the story of a sailing ship off the African coast which had been seized by a hideous sea monster with eight arms which reached to the top of the masts. This terrifying anecdote was illustrated with a picture which Henry Lee, author of *The Octopus*, described as 'fitter to decorate the outside of a showman's caravan at a fair than seriously to illustrate a work of natural history'. Others simply called de Montfort a hoaxer. Contrary to Denys Tucker's version, de Montfort was ridiculed and ostracised because his natural history stories became increasingly ridiculous. Neither naval history nor zoology have vindicated de Montfort's tale of a group of ten warships which were attacked and sunk by an enormous cuttlefish. Far from being a persecuted zoological Galileo, it seems de Montfort's miserable end may simply have been the consequence of a conviction for forgery.

Denys Tucker's obsession with the Loch Ness Monster was cemented by his sighting 'a triangle of foaming water following a hump towards the far shore, where it either sank or melted into the twilight under the opposite bank'. This sounds very much like a case of expectant attention rewarded by the sighting of something which was unidentifiable, distant and witnessed in conditions of poor light. Such details as where Tucker was standing, where the object was when he first saw it, and whether or not he viewed it through binoculars, are not given. It is a classically inconclusive sighting, bolstered by the classic witness's absolute conviction that there was no possibility of having been fooled by anything at all commonplace.

Time has not been kind to some of Tucker's certainties. He believed he had found confirmation of his belief that the Monster resembled a Cryptocleidus skeleton in several classic monster images. The Hugh Gray photograph revealed glimpses of two paddles. The head in the Surgeon's photo matched a Cryptocleidus skull in every particular, even down to 'the meeting between the parietal ridge and the converging posterior processes of the squamosal bones'. The Dinsdale film 'shows a regular left-right-left-right splashing up front of the hump', which precisely imitates plesiosaur paddling behaviour. One of the Rines underwater flipper pictures captures the monster 'at an angle which indicates it must be midway through a recovery stroke'. Rines's flipper photos represent 'a striking mutual corroboration' of George Spicer's description of the monster's 'loathsome texture'. Indeed, Spicer's account of the monster jerking its way across the Dores-Foyers road supplied an 'utterly convincing description and corresponds entirely with what we would expect in the Plesiosaur we have been considering'. To Denys Tucker, everything made perfect sense, even 'the more baffling hump-configurations' which simply indicated 'the presence of two or more individuals'.

The Cottingley Fairies

There are three lunatic fringe British mysteries which seem particularly relevant to the Loch Ness story.

The first is the saga of the Cottingley fairies, which were first photographed in 1917 in a quiet Yorkshire beck by a teenage girl, Elsie Wright, and her nine-year-old cousin, Frances. It was a harmless prank involving fairies made from cardboard. What the girls didn't understand until too late was just how many intelligent adults desperately wanted to believe in beings from another dimension, including, notoriously and ironically, Arthur Conan Doyle. When more photographs were requested they duly supplied them.

The clues that the pictures were fakes were always there for those with eyes to see. Elsie was both 'artistic' and someone very knowledgeable about cameras, photography and film processing. The girls insisted that the fairies would appear only to them and would not come if anyone else was present.

It is no coincidence that the Cottingley images were seized on at a time when Britain was in the throes of the mass bereavements of the Great War. Dodgy 'spirit photographs' of loved ones were a commonplace commodity, spiritualism enjoyed a revival, and there was a great craving for proof of other, more benign worlds. But in the modern world interest in fairies as genuine entities has faded. They are too whimsical and lightweight to match the red-blooded appeal of Bigfoot and the Loch Ness Monster.

It wasn't until 1983 that the two principals grudgingly confessed that the Cottingley photographs were fakes. This long-running saga showed how easily a light-hearted joke could spiral out of control in the face of gullible adults with a desperate emotional need to believe in the unbelievable. For the girls it became a nightmare, as their fun photographs were transformed into paranormal classics. A little childish joke became a massive, damaging shadow over the rest of their lives. The Cottingley saga underlined just how long it can take for the truth to be revealed and how reluctant hoaxers are to confess, especially if a fake photograph has become famous. It literally took a lifetime for the two cousins to own up to the obvious.

When Ted Holiday sought a paranormal explanation for the mysteriously elusive Loch Ness Monster, one of the props of his new vision was the evidence from Cottingley. It's just one more example of how *The Dragon and the Disc* is a ramshackle, jerry-built construction which rests on quicksand. Holiday was contemptuous of 'the sterile theories of the archaeologists', but even his understanding of fairy photographs was less than scholarly. He wrote that there were a 'dozen or so' Cottingley pictures, when in fact there were only five. He suggested that one of the images provided 'actual photographic evidence' of the point of transit from another dimension 'into our space time' – but then didn't bother to identify which photograph he had in mind, let alone use it in his book as an illustration. He did, however, use an image of 'an Icelandic Bronze Age figure' which he suggested bore uncanny similarities with one of the Cottingley fairies. But he didn't say in which museum or publication his Icelandic figure might be found. That most rudimentary requirement of serious scholarship – identification of sources and citations – was bypassed.

Like Alex Campbell, Ted Holiday cannot be trusted to convey accurately the testimony of third parties. Referring to Elsie Wright's 1971 television interview, he reported that 'All she could say, in essence, was that the original story was true and the pictures were genuine. What the creatures were she still didn't know.' In fact, Elsie was equivocal and evasive. What she actually said was, 'I've told you that they're photographs of figments of our imagination, and that's what I'm sticking to.' In a literal sense her reply was perfectly truthful: the cardboard models were imaginary fairies made by a teenager with some creative flair. She was the Christian Spurling of fairyland.

'The creatures do not look like solid objects,' Holiday noticed when he scrutinised the photographed fairies. It was an observation which in its own way was as shrewd as his conclusion that the Loch Ness Monster seemed physically elusive in a manner that defied both organised surveillance and conventional biology. But once again, instead of subjecting his accurate perception to rational analysis, he took refuge in spectacularly wrong-headed fantasy involving extra-terrestrial humanoids. Sadly, what Holiday interpreted as a thrilling image of the moment of transition between worlds was most likely merely double-exposure of a cardboard fairy.

Holiday was always a gullible innocent where photographs of strange wonders were concerned. *The Dragon and the Disc* used Frank Searle's floating tree trunk photograph, supposedly taken on July 27, 1972. Holiday identified this inert object as 'the Loch Ness monster in its two-hump aspect' (and wrote that it was taken 'in August 1972'). He states that 'The photographer lived for three years on the shore of the loch before obtaining the picture' [Plate 4b]. This misleadingly creates the impression of a long and disciplined vigil finally rewarded. But by 1972 Searle was already claiming a staggering fifteen sightings, showing visitors a Nessie photograph taken in 1971 from a range of just thirty yards, and alluding to other 'photographs and film' he had taken. The LNI's foolish and uncritical endorsement of the 1972 tree trunk picture simply served to encourage Searle, and within three months he had more amazing photographs. Supposedly taken on October 21, 1972, three Nessie photographs produced by Searle show misshapen objects which, in one instance, is plainly a small, crude model, while the other two involve floating fake Nessie material, doctored images, or a combination of both.

The duplicity of a fraudster like Frank Searle invariably invited a naïve response from those who needed and *wanted* to believe. Ted Holiday, an intelligent and experienced man, completely lost any critical capacity when presented with 'evidence' which endorsed his idiosyncratic belief system.

That something as inherently absurd as the Cottingley fairy photographs attracted the attention they did, and were still being enthusiastically discussed and analysed half a century after they were faked, is revealing about the way in which the human capacity for belief can suppress reason and intelligence. But it also shows the persuasive power of photographs taken by photographers who swear their images are genuine.

Gef the Talking Mongoose

The Loch Ness Monster was not the only mysterious and enigmatic animal to appear in the mass media during the early nineteen-thirties. In what might almost have been a dummy run for Nessie, the *Isle of Man Examiner* reported 'the discovery of a most weird and uncanny species of nature such as has never previously been heard or seen' (February 19, 1932). A hitherto unknown creature had manifested its presence in a remote location on the island. This was an Indian mongoose which, remarkably for an animal, was able to speak English. At first called Jack, then renamed Gef (sometimes spelt Jef), this prodigy had taken up residence in the home of a local family, the Irvings. Gef informed his hosts that he came from Delhi and had been born on June 7, 1852.

Three weeks later the *Examiner* reported that 'quite a lot of people are making the long mountain trek to reach Mr Irving's cottage, only to gaze upon the walls and reflect upon the possible explanation of this mysterious phenomena'. Before long the talking mongoose had attracted the attention of the national newspapers, as well as paranormal investigators. Dr Nandor Fodor, who enjoyed the position of 'Research Officer, International Institute for Psychical Research', thrillingly concluded that 'the case represents the greatest mystery in all England'. Interest in the talking mongoose climaxed with Harry Price and R. S. Lambert's book, *The Haunting of Cashen's Gap* (1936), which was equivocal in its conclusions and not short of material which invited a sceptical interpretation of the mystery. When the Irvings later left their home Gef also departed, vanishing forever into obscurity. The house was later demolished.

The talking mongoose enigma ran roughly parallel to that of the early years of the Loch Ness Monster, although it does not seem to have gripped the national imagination in quite the same way. Partly this was because the site of the mystery was in a relatively inaccessible location on an island remote from the British mainland. It was also because the Loch Ness Monster was a very much more attractive and plausible phenomenon than an expatriate Indian mongoose which spoke English and claimed to be an astonishing eighty years old.

One wonders if the news about Gef ever reached Fort Augustus in 1932. If so, it must have been intolerable for Alex Campbell to discover that this preposterous freak mongoose was getting publicity and attention while the 'fearsome-looking monster' of Loch Ness remained entirely unknown. In turn the Monster, once famous, may also have impacted on Gef. James Irving had been chronicling Gef's activities in a stream of correspondence to an enthralled believer from 'The National Laboratory of Psychical Research', but the letters dried up in February 1933. By this time the marvel of Gef's existence had faded and even Irving seems to have lost interest. But in April 1934, as monster fever reached a climax at Loch Ness, a new lease of life was granted to Gef as James Irving renewed his correspondence with the mysterious mongoose's number one fan.

That Gef the talking mongoose was a fraud was obvious. Only members of the Irving family were ever able to see the animal. Like the Cottingley fairies, it would not appear for strangers. It was also very clear that the source of the voluble Mongoose's conversation was the daughter, Voirrey. The talking mongoose didn't seem to know much about India or mongooses, but it knew Manx slang and enjoyed gifts of biscuits, chocolate and pie. When tangible evidence of the animal's existence was requested, this ended in farce. Four supposed casts turned out not even to be foot tracks and plainly did not originate with a mongoose or any other animal. A specimen of 'fur' turned out to be hair from the family dog. A photograph of Gef showed what might have been a plump, sleepy cat or a soft toy.

Like the Monster, Gef had an ancestry of sorts. The creature manifested in 'a district steeped in tales of folklore (*Peel City Guardian and Chronicle*, February 20, 1932). This folklore included the shape-shifting buggane, the small hairy sprite known as the phynodderee, and the mischievous mooinjer veggey. It was also claimed that a nearby farm had once introduced mongooses to control the rabbit population. Gef was plainly a cultural hybrid.

The biggest mystery of all was not Gef but why the three Irvings colluded in pretending he existed. They were plainly attention seekers and an exceptionally strange family. Very early on, Mrs Irving wrote to the *Daily Mail* attempting to interest the newspaper in the family's newly discovered resident. The daughter Voirrey displayed classic symptoms of Asperger's. The father was a once-successful man who had fallen on very hard times. The family lived a bleak existence in a small house without electricity, scratching a living with a few sheep on a windswept hillside, at the end of a long, steep, narrow path impassable to motor vehicles.

Perhaps Gef was fabricated simply to give three exceptionally marginalised invididuals a sense of importance in a world which had no use for them. It seems symbolically apt that the mystery originated in some DIY work which had the consequence of *amplification*. As visitors noted, the panelling which James Irving had installed to keep out draughts had the effect of transmitting and enlarging sounds within the house, including those made by Gef.

The family's attention-seeking evidently had a pecuniary motive. Irving 'believed a book might sell well enough to help the family out of their dire financial difficulties', but he was discouraged from writing one by investigator Harry Price – who then unscrupulously ripped-off Irving's material and co-authored a book on the subject. *The Times* reviewed it, calling the Gef saga 'a fairytale come to life'.

Scrutinising the mystery from a twenty-first century perspective, it is possible to see a disturbing sexual dimension. The hairy prodigy was first seen when the father and his twelve-year-old daughter were alone together in a bedroom. James Irving insisted on his daughter moving her bed into the parental bedroom in December 1931, where she slept for several months before returning to her own. Gef would sometimes make strange groaning and moaning noises. Gef was jealous of the other women in James Irving's life. The mongoose was furious when Voirrey's sister came to stay. He screamed that Mrs Irving was 'the witch woman, the Zulu woman, the Honolulu woman!' When Voirrey returned to her own bedroom her parents were kept awake by 'blowing, spitting and growling' and numerous other disturbances. But at the same time Gef said, 'I'm a freak', and called James Irving a 'dirty old sleech!' (devious person). On another occasion Gef cried, 'Oh let me go Jim. Let me go.' James Irving was abused as a 'bastard'. The mongoose was occasionally 'very vulgar'. Once Gef sang an obscene parody of 'Home on the Range' – a song the lyrics of which, even in the original, must have seemed like a hideous satire on life at Cashen's Gap.

When Voirrey was tracked down in middle age she said Gef was the reason why she had never married. But she went to her grave without ever revealing what had *really* been going on in that lonely farmhouse. In the spectrum of possibilities issues of mental health, incest and child abuse seem rather more plausible explanations than the existence of a gifted octogenarian mongoose from Delhi which spoke English. But in the end it may have been no more than a desperate craving for attention and a sense of importance on the part of a desperately needy family which was impoverished in all kinds of ways. If so, it worked. In a small niche of cryptozoological culture the Irvings are famous and Gef the talking mongoose will always be with us. Today what little is left of the family's demolished home is a site of pilgrimage.

The Warminster Mystery

In the 1930s the antics of Gef ran parallel to those of Nessie; in the 1960s and early 1970s the golden age of monster hunting was matched in southern England by 'the Warminster mystery'. This began in a small Wiltshire town in December 1964 with reports of loud, inexplicable noises heard by local residents at various locations. These mysterious sonic phenomena continued for some months and were then replaced by sightings of mysterious lights and objects in the sky. Soon crowds of UFO-spotters poured into the town, hoping to see extra-terrestrial spacecraft from three popular local viewing sites around the town – Cradle Hill, Starr Hill and Cley Hill. The mystery lasted for just over a decade, with sightings reported until the end of 1977. After that interest largely faded away. In recent years it has enjoyed a small revival, although, as is now the case with the Loch Ness Monster, the quantity of publications on the subject is greatly in excess of actual search activity at the site.

What is fascinating about the Warminster mystery is the extent to which it parallels the Loch Ness mystery. It all began with a news report in January 1965 in the local newspaper, *The Warminster Journal*. Headlined 'Strange Noise At Warminster', it reported the experience of an unidentified 'housewife' of Bradley Road, Warminster, who on Christmas morning heard 'a crackling noise' which travelled overhead in the night sky, accompanied by 'a faint hum'. This minor news item was to prove as seminal as Alex Campbell's May 1933 'Strange Spectacle on Loch Ness' report. Soon other reports of weird noises occurred, and as the story grew local residents reported seeing objects in the sky which were obviously alien spacecraft in the great tradition of cigar ships and flying saucers. On August 29, 1965, local man Gordon Faulkner stepped out of his house holding a camera when he spotted an object with an unusual shape 'flying fast and low over the south of the town'. He took a photograph, which plainly shows a flying saucer. This grainy image has since become as iconic of the Warminster mystery as the Surgeon's photograph was of the Loch Ness Monster. Two years after the housewife's strange experience the first book on the subject appeared, which now has the status of a classic: *The Warminster Mystery* by Arthur Shuttlewood.

Shuttlewood is a man who is at the heart of the Warminster saga. Like Alex Campbell he was a local journalist and the man who first publicised an eye-witness account of something strange in the locality. Like Alex Campbell, he was already committed to the mystery he was promoting, in so far as he was previously interested in UFOs. And like Alex Campbell, he was a man who changed from being a reporter of strange phenomena into one who frequently saw them himself.

In fact, Shuttlewood greatly resembles a number of key figures in the Loch Ness saga, all rolled into one. Like Campbell, he used his position as a journalist to publicise the mystery. Like Rupert Gould he wrote the first classic information-packed book on the subject. Like Tim Dinsdale he became a leading figure in the great quest to film and understand the phenomenon. Like Dinsdale he had a warm, friendly personality and was liked and admired by all those UFO hunters who met him at Warminster. Like Dinsdale he fluently expressed his convictions: as one fellow UFO-hunter put it, 'He speaks with the smooth assurance of a professional commentator… He is a persuasive, not a dogmatic person.' Dinsdale was just the same: a charming man, who articulated his belief in the monster with serenity and complete conviction. And finally, Arthur Shuttlewood, just like Ted Holiday, embraced the paranormal with a fervour that took him on a personal journey deeper and deeper into ever more bizarre and idiosyncratic explanations of the nature of reality itself. And just as Ted Holiday had an unnerving encounter with a Man in Black, Shuttlewood also had a disturbing face-to-face encounter with an extraterrestrial, whose eyes lacked pupils and who seemed to possess 'powers, that if unleashed, would perhaps frazzle him to a cinder'.

The parallel mysteries also incubated sceptics from within. Just as Ronald Binns and Rod Bell changed from being passionate believers and monster-hunters into laconic sceptics, so Steve Dewey and John Ries lost their youthful enthusiasm for the Warminster mystery and turned against it. Their book *In Alien Heat: The Warminster Mystery Revisited* deconstructs the phenomenon from the perspective of former active participants in the great UFO hunt. Older and wiser, they focus on the personalities involved and the way in which information is recorded and mediated. Their intimate knowledge of the landscape of the mystery allows them to expose the lazy inaccuracies of those writers who approach the subject from afar.

The tale that *In Alien Heat* has to tell offers many striking structural parallels with the Loch Ness story. At one point the two mysteries even overlap. Ted Holiday drew on events at Warminster in his far-fetched attempt to connect lake monsters with extra-terrestrial spacecraft. Holiday linked Gordon Faulkner's sensational Warminster flying saucer photograph, which looked 'like a disc carrying a large eye on its super-structure' with truck driver Terry Pell's terrifying encounter with a low-flying UFO which resembled 'an enormous human eye'. Holiday melodramatically concluded that Mr Pell was 'the only man in Britain to come into physical contact with the god *Odin*'. He illustrated this with a diagram showing how Faulkner's type of flying saucer had inspired (among other things) Bronze Age symbols, barrows, the design of some Romano-British towns, and rose windows in churches. This is a kind of cultural paranoia: everything is connected and everything makes perfect sense to the solitary perceiver of these symmetries.

Dewey and Ries take Holiday apart. The Faulkner photograph is available only in a 'blown-up, grainy version' – like the Surgeon's photograph it is radically cropped, with the full image almost never reproduced. They describe as 'a Rorschach onto which you can project any UFO fantasy'. They also point out that Holiday exaggerates Pell's testimony, which was reported by Arthur Shuttlewood, who was himself keen to draw a link between the sighting and the photograph. Dewey and Ries are sceptical of that connection, pointing out radical differences between the sighting details and Faulkner's image. Elsewhere in their book they observe that Shuttlewood cannot be regarded as an accurate conveyor of eye-witness conversation and, in a final blow to Holiday's grand synthesis, they identify the Faulkner photograph as a hoax involving a model.

Amusingly, Holiday himself, displaying a characteristic unwitting alertness to an alternative possibility, described Faulkner's flying saucer as being 'shaped like two soup-plates glued together by their edges with a sort of cupola in the middle.'

Quite.

As Steve Dewey and John Ries conclude, 'It is unlikely that 4,003 people saw 5,000 alien spaceships around Warminster. But most of those witnesses wanted to believe there was something unusual about what they saw.'

Ancestries

As one mystery fades and fizzles, another takes its place.

In the summer of 1980 the first crop circles began to appear in the fields of Wiltshire. Dewey and Ries suggest the phenomenon may even have been inspired by Arthur Shuttlewood's identification of 'UFO nests'. And just as the first crop circles appeared in Wiltshire there was competition from Suffolk, with reports of a UFO landing in Rendlesham Forest, near Woodbridge. Today that event is proudly commemorated by a forest walk with alien signs. At Loch Ness, meanwhile, there are giant 'lifesize' monsters to entertain visitors.

The true lineage of all these mysteries can be traced back for centuries. The writer known as 'Gervase of Tilbury' was a sophisticated European intellectual who produced a huge work, *Otia imperilia* ('Recreation for an Emperor'), which was presented to Otto IV, King of Germany and Holy Roman Emperor, probably in 1215. Divided into three books it includes a history of the world, a description of the world and an inventory of marvels. The natural history section includes the revelation that the River Ganges in India contains eels three hundred feet long and worms with pincers which are used to seize and drown elephants. Arabia is described as the home of the phoenix and two-headed snakes with eyes which shine like lamps at night. The book of marvels includes giant Egyptian ants as big as puppies which hoard gold, and huge serpents a hundred feet long and as thick as massive columns. In France there was a raven which gambled and could talk to people and men who transformed into wolves. In Tuscany there were winged snakes which looked like dragons. Sirens were reported off the British coast and in Kent there was a tree which gave birth to birds.

Otia imperilia reads like an encyclopaedia. It assembles a huge inventory of information about the world as it was understood at that time by a European intellectual. Fantastic animals of enormous size are regarded as being as inherently credible as known ones and the contemporary reader had no reason to doubt their reality. A century later another encyclopaedic text recast this kind of fascinating material in a much more readable format. *The Travels of Sir John Mandeville* was the first-person account of a journey around the world in the fourteenth century. Sir John, an English knight from St Albans, reported the many wonders he had seen on a tour lasting more than three decades. He travelled as far as Persia, India, Cathay (China) and the lands beyond. These exotic locations turned out to contain such extraordinary creatures as griffons, creatures capable of seizing a man on horseback and carrying both man and horse back to their nests. On his great journey Mandeville learned of men and women with heads like dogs and hideous giants with only one eye, located in their foreheads. In Silha (Sri Lanka) he discovered the existence of a high mountain on top of which lay 'a great loch full of water'. In this lake lived 'horse eels of marvellous size'.

This last species sounds familiar.

The Travels of Sir John Mandeville proved to be a hugely popular text – the medieval equivalent of a contemporary bestseller. It went through numerous editions and translations across Europe. As a detailed travel book it was respected by mariners for two centuries, who regarded it as providing valuable guidance to anyone sailing into remote, unknown waters. Its reputation nosedived only in the late sixteenth century when pioneering navigators discovered it was a work of fantasy, not fact. Later still it turned out that 'Sir John Mandeville' did not appear ever to have existed. Whoever wrote *The Travels* may never have travelled anywhere at all. The narrative turns out to have involved brilliantly creative plagiarism, its exotic tales derived from a vast array of printed sources. What purported to be an authentic travel diary was perhaps nothing more than a dazzling work of fiction by a very well-read individual of uncertain identity. But though probably a hoax, *The Travels* hit a nerve. Its success showed how much readers crave narratives of the marvellous and the fantastic. *The Travels* remains in print today, a classic of the imagination.

Human psychology delights in the idea of bizarre creatures and species of monstrous size. It feeds creativity itself. In art, the fabulous has always existed alongside realism. Every modern bookstore contains science fiction and novels of fantasy alongside novels of modern life. The parallels can be pushed back centuries. Karl Shuker's compendium includes a chapter on 'the Pictish beast', the famously enigmatic 'swimming elephant' design which appears on a number of Class I and Class II Pictish symbol stones. This image has inevitably been appropriated by a certain type of Nessie enthusiast as an early representation of a Scottish lake monster, even, excitingly, 'an evolved, surviving species of short-necked plesiosaur'. Henry Bauer calls it 'a riddle that cries out for a compelling explanation'. But it seems most unlikely that any authoritative identification will ever be made. In the words of Stuart McHardy, 'the beast does not look like it ever existed. While the head and possibly the appendage to it certainly have echoes both of dolphins and even the blowhole of cetaceans, it is portrayed with legs.' McHardy suggests that, since it is a composite of animal forms from both land and sea, its duality may represent a sacred image related to other, older imagery which has been interpreted as shamanic.

Whatever precise cultural significance it may have had will probably never be retrieved. But in its broadest sense it surely represents the human need for imaginary animals. In any case, the 'swimming elephant' design is not located at sites associated with Scottish lake monsters, and other Pictish symbols are equally enigmatic. The double disc, the crescent, the V-rod, the Z-rod and the notched rectangle are all open to speculative interpretation. Interestingly, Daniel Loxton, in his pioneering deconstruction of the legendary sea-serpent, suggests that the Pictish 'swimming elephant' is simply a variation on the much older horse-headed hippocamp motif. This entirely imaginary creature originated as a pictorial design in ancient Greece and was later adopted by the Romans, who brought it to Britain. Loxton argues that the sea-serpent began life as the imaginary hippocamp, which later fused with Scandinavian folklore and first influentially surfaced as an accredited animal in Erich Pontoppidan's two-volume *Natural History of Norway* (1755). Folklore, Loxton suggests, did not confirm sighting reports but rather generated them.

In itself the Loch Ness Monster was initially just another novelty in a long tradition of marvels unique to twentieth-century Britain. But Nessie outlived them all. The Cottingley fairies declined to appear to anyone but the two girls who had photographed them and interest in the mystery faded. The fortunes of Gef the talking mongoose were tied up with those of the Irving family and likewise lacked longevity. Unidentified lights in the sky around Warminster were so frequent they lost their novelty value and the enigma, finally, was simply a parochial instance of the global UFO phenomena.

Mysteries of this sort require a suitable habitat and suitable witnesses to lend them credibility. The Warminster viewing points were conveniently located near a major military training ground. Here, flares were regularly fired into the night sky. Helicopters blazing with light and sometimes projecting beams cruised at a distance far enough to be seen but not heard. The mysterious 'beep-beeping' sound which was regularly heard at Cradle Hill turned out to be the sound of startled peewits. There was much else to ensure that expectant attention bore its fruits, including car headlights on distant hills. But in the end this kind of experience becomes, even for enthusiasts, repetitious and boring.

This was where the Loch Ness Monster had the edge over all the competition. Victor Perera wrote: 'No one prepared me for the wild natural beauty of Loch Ness.' The lake was a magical place, big enough and rich enough in phenomena to ensure that new witnesses would continue seeing 'monsters' in the decades that followed. Other anomalous phenomena could not compete with the riches which Loch Ness offered up. It also enjoyed a much higher media profile and attracted writers of much higher calibre than, say, an exclamation-mark-spattering sensationalist like Arthur Shuttlewood of Warminster.

Rupert Gould, Constance Whyte, Tim Dinsdale and Ted Holiday were fluent and persuasive. They gave delusion the gloss of intelligence and a fine style. Like novelists, they created a persuasively credible world, with its own logic. Perera describes the effect of shutting himself away with the two first monster books by Dinsdale and Holiday, writing that 'they made engrossing reading. I spent those three days in a trance of suspended disbelief, wholly removed from time and place. When I'd finished, I'd become a believer.'

Who would not?

Since 1980
PLEASE DO NOT THROW
STONES AT NESSIE
SHE IS VERY FRAGILE
THANK YOU

Notes

Preface

'My book': Ronald Binns with R. J. Bell, *The Loch Ness Mystery Solved* (Open Books, 1983).

'Books have continued to be written': Steuart Campbell, *The Loch Ness Monster: The Evidence* (1986; 1996); David Martin and Alastair Boyd, *Nessie: The Surgeon's Photograph Exposed* (1999); Gareth Williams, *A Monstrous Commotion* (2015); Roland Watson, *The Water Horses of Loch Ness* (2011).

1. The Never Ending Story

Josh Bazell: http://news.nationalpost.com/afterword/josh-bazell-the-loch-ness-hoax. (I would not myself call the Nessie legend a hoax, although its survival depended on some foundational fake photographs in 1933, 1934 and 1951. I prefer the term 'myth'); Benjamin Radford and Joe Nickell, *Op. Cit.*, p. 13.

Ted Holiday: F. W. Holiday, *The Great Orm of Loch Ness* (1968), p. 47; Maurice Burton, *The Elusive Monster* (1961), p. 100.

'Burton wrote that "there could be no doubt the photograph was genuine"': *Op. Cit.*, p. 75.

'No single phenomenon can possibly account for the totality of fifty years of widely differing eye-witness reports from Loch Ness': *The Loch Ness Mystery Solved*, p. 183.

'The case for the Loch Ness Monster…': *Ibid.*, p. 165.

'His re-sketched versions of the Alex Campbell and Greta Finlay sightings…': *Ibid*, pp. 167 and 194.

'his commitment to "'the Truth" (with a capital T)': Tim Dinsdale, *The Leviathans* (1966), p. 198.

'there do seem to be rather fewer of them these days': Nicholas Witchell, *The Loch Ness Story* (1989), p. 19.

'biased towards the plesiosaur theory as that seemed to be the general consensus', 'it became important to try to introduce a healthy scepticism into the presentation of the exhibits': Tony Harmsworth. *Loch Ness, Nessie & Me* (2010), pp. 85 and 156.

'blogger and author Roland Watson': lochnessmystery.blogspot.co.uk and *The Water Horses of Loch Ness* (2011).

Tony Harmsworth: http://www.loch-ness.org/personalities.html#binns.

Rupert Gould: *The Loch Ness Monster and Others* (1934), pp. 142-148.

'the pioneering detective work of David Martin and Alastair Boyd': *Nessie: The Surgeon's Photograph Exposed* (1999).

'the belated revelation that Rupert Gould had long ago privately disavowed the Spicer land sighting': Jonathan Betts, *Time Restored* (2011), p. 259.

'When I last visited it': May 11, 2016.

'Roland Watson's blog': http://lochnessmystery.blogspot.co.uk.

'jackboot fascists': http://lochnessmystery.blogspot.co.uk/2016/02/is-hugh-gray-photograph-swan.html?showComment=1456068604009#c8166297474533999380.

'As Daniel Loxton remarked': http://www.skepticblog.org/2013/09/12/breaking-down-a-criticism-of-abominable-science/.

'Naish's assertion…a measured response': see reviews and comments about *Hunting Monsters* on the Amazon.co.uk website.

2. Brief Encounters

'She described the experience': Clive Limpkin, 'The Birth of the Loch Ness Monster': *Daily Mail*, March 25, 1983. Gould interviewed Mrs Mackay and identified Friday April 14 as the date of the sighting (*Op. Cit*, p. 39). Paul Harrison believes it was Tuesday March 14 but notes the many inconsistencies in the versions of this episode: *The Encyclopaedia of the Loch Ness Monster* (1999), pp. 126-7.

'But when Tony Harmsworth and Nicholas Witchell': Harmsworth, *Loch Ness, Nessie & Me*, p. 92.

'In a televised interview': https://www.facebook.com/TheGreatLochNessMonsterDebate/videos/vb.567474829969382/10151443898826260/?type=2&theater.

'Rupert Gould brilliantly defined': *Op. Cit.*, pp. 32-33.

'Kenneth Mackay': Gould, *The Loch Ness Monster and Others*, p. 31.

'something large', *Ibid.*, p. 39.

'suddenly remembered James Cameron's experience': *Ibid.*, p. 32.

'her sighting of humps': *Ibid.*, p. 40.

'The 1914 report of "Porpoises in Loch Ness"': *Fortean Times*, 341, June 2016, p. 33.

'sank suddenly with considerable commotion': Gould, *Op. Cit.*, p. 40.

'She described it': Gould, *Op. Cit.*, p. 39.

Scott II: Steuart Campbell, *The Loch Ness Monster: The Evidence*, p. 20.

'Daniel Loxton has argued': Daniel Loxton and Donald R. Prothero, *Abominable Science!* (2013), pp. 131-2.

'She reported the "annoyance" of the couple': Constance Whyte, *More Than a Legend* (1957), p. 79.

'it was conceded by Rupert Gould': *The Loch Ness Monster and Others*, p. 44.

'the incident originally found its way into print in a rather incorrect form': *Ibid.*, p. 43.

'might have been the end of a long tail swung round to the far side of the body': *Ibid.*, p. 44.

'appeared to be carrying a small lamb or animal of some kind': *Inverness Courier*, August 4, 1933.

'Gould gnomically explained': *Op. Cit.*, p. 46.

'Whyte's sketch is a travesty of Gould's': *More Than a Legend*, p. 78.

'as far as possible, in Mr and Mrs Spicer's own words': *Ibid.*, footnote 2, p. 77.

'Dinsdale smoothes out the twisting neck': *Loch Ness Monster* (1961), p. 41.

'Holiday exaggerated the bulk': *The Great Orm of Loch Ness* (1968), pp. 32 and 141.

'Holiday's version of what the Gray picture shows': *Ibid.*, p. 32.

'resembled "a huge snail with a long neck"': Gould, *Op. Cit.*, p. 44.

'about 30 feet long': *Ibid.*, p. 46.

'I got out of the car': *The Great Orm of Loch Ness*, pp. 30-31.

'They did not stop': Gould, *Op. Cit.*, p. 46.

'Apparently, it could not move fast': Holiday, *Op. Cit.*, p. 31.

'he had disappeared into the loch': *The Leviathans*, p. 58.

'In each instance Holiday replaced': *Op. Cit.*, p. 30.

'given to a reporter shortly after the incident took place': *Ibid.*, p. 31.

'been to the spot many times since': *The Leviathans*, p. 58.

'not succeeded in determining the exact spot': Gould, *Op. Cit.*, p. 46.

'never been fortunate enough to see him again': *The Leviathans*, p. 58.

'rather perplexed': Betts, *Op. Cit.*, p. 259.

'that it was entirely *bona fide*': Gould, *Op. Cit.*, p. 44.

'a lasting and rather unpleasant impression': *Ibid.*

'she saw something which she took to be the head and neck of some smaller animal': *Ibid.*, pp. 45-6.

3. The Sea-Serpent Man

Rupert Gould: *The Loch Ness Monster and Others* (1934), p. 2.
'played a crucial role in directly influencing Stalker's own views': *The Loch Ness Mystery Solved*, p. 24.
'sceptics, such as Captain John Macdonald': *Ibid*, p. 16.
'sporting salmon in lively mood': *Ibid*, p. 16.
'A simple explanation – the product, apparently, of a simple mind': Gould, *Op. Cit.*, p. 115.
'Monsters which moved at "some 13 knots", had eight humps and created "a very violent commotion in the water"': *Ibid.*, pp. 152, 87, 145.
'incidents which have not, at present, been satisfactorily explained': *Oddities: A Book of Unexplained Facts*, p. 5.
'the same charm as one finds in R. Austin Freeman's detective stories or Lieutenant-Commander Gould's collections of curiosities': George Orwell, *The Collected Essays, Journalism and Letters of George Orwell*, Vol. 2 (1970), p. 50.
'Statements by fifty-eight witnesses': Gould, *Op. Cit.*, p. 149.
'I used its illustrations': *Ibid.*, p. 160.
'My change of opinion was a gradual process': *Ibid.*, p. 17.
'The witnesses, almost without exception': *Ibid.*, p. 14.
'to create a zoological myth': *Ibid.*, p. 150.
'a very singular spectacle': *Ibid.*
'the location of "April 1" at the end of the line': *Ibid.*, p. 24.
'a discussion of technical errors': Rupert Gould, 'Mistakes and Misprints' (December 29, 1936), *The Stargazer Talks* (1943), pp. 71-79.
'undoubtedly genuine': *Op. Cit.*, p. 23.
'a great share of good fortune': *Ibid.*, p. 24.

4. Campbell Soup

'Tim Dinsdale opened his book': *Op. Cit.,* p. 4.
'He told Victor Perera': *The Loch Ness Monster Watchers* (1974), p. 38.
'stepped forward to defend his cherished beast': A.M. Campbell, 'No, Dr Burton!', *The Scots Magazine* (May 1962), pp. 95-100.
'had imperiously crushed the fantasies of the local journalist': *The Loch Ness Mystery Solved*, pp. 15-17.

'was quoted by Rupert Gould': *Op. Cit.*, p. 29.

'the believers simply recycled Campbell's information on the second occasion without ever noticing the glaring contradictions involved': Henry H. Bauer supplies the references in *The Enigma of Loch Ness* (1986), p. 171.

'the best PR conceals its own hand': Nick Davies, *Flat Earth News: An Award-winning Reporter Exposes Falsehood, Distortion and Propaganda in the Global Media* (2008), p. 167.

'came rolling on to the shore after X had sunk': Gould, *Op. Cit.*, p. 40.

'it then circulates around the whole body of global communication': Davies, *Op. Cit.*, p. 51.

'the monster sighting, reported by Philip Stalker in the *Scotsman*': *The Loch Ness Mystery Solved*, pp. 76-77.

'a cormorant standing in the water and flapping its wings, as they often do': Gould, *Op. Cit.*, pp. 110-111.

'As I wrote': *The Loch Ness Mystery Solved*, p. 77.

'the satire at his expense which appeared in that newspaper': *Ibid.*, pp. 22-23.

'Henry Bauer states': http://henryhbauer.homestead.com/_Nessie Chapter.pdf.

'The light was very uncertain, there being a fairly thick haze on the water': Gould, *Op. Cit.*, p. 110.

'rose from the water like a monster of pre-historic times': Dinsdale, *Loch Ness Monster*, p. 4.

'Constance Whyte mentioned him directly only twice': *More Than a Legend*, pp. 86 and 97.

'covered with some entangling substance, from which the creature had to shake itself free': *Ibid.*, p. 195.

'another sighting attributed to "A.C"': *Ibid.*, p. 203.

'the treatment, amounting almost to persecution': *Ibid.*, p. 75.

'May, if I remember aright': Dinsdale, *Op. Cit.*, p. 126.

'When shown a picture of one, Campbell confirmed the resemblance': *The Loch Ness Mystery Solved*, pp. 76-77.

'He had "'a very clear view of it which lasted several minutes"'': Dinsdale, *Op. Cit.*, pp. 126-127.

'Campbell was visited at home by Victor Perera': *The Loch Ness Monster Watchers*, p. 39.

'a straw man which he then proceeds to knock down': http://www.scotsman.com/news/a_letter_from_loch_ness_1_663384; http://loch nessmystery.blogspot.co.uk/2017/03.

'implies there were at least two other accompanying Nessie sketches': the date of publication coincides with Rupert Gould's arrival in Scotland, which may or may not be significant.

'a third, somewhat intemperate article': http://lochnessmystery.blogspot. co.uk/2017/04/poor-old-alex-campbell-part-iii.html.

'the element of "expectant attention" was, in my opinion, certainly present': Gould, *Op. Cit.*, pp. 112-113.

'In June 1981 Raynor witnessed "a family group of mergansers" behaving just like the "monster" in his film': http://www. lochnessinvestigation.com/Mergansers.html.

'Looking at the various renditions of the sighting, it is generally stated that the creature was 400 yards away in Borlum Bay': http://loch nessmystery.blogspot.co.uk/2017/03/poor-old-alex-campbell-part-ii.html

5. Pictures of Nessie

Hugh Gray

'Maurice Burton supplied the best description': *The Elusive Monster*, p. 78.

'Gray told a reporter': *The Great Orm of Loch Ness*, pp. 26-7.

'Tim Dinsdale, who interviewed Gray some 27 years later': *Loch Ness Monster* (1961), p. 43.

'Constance Whyte had interviewed Gray in May 1955': *More Than a Legend*, p. 3.

'described in graphic terms the extraordinary bow wave building up': Loch Ness Monster, p. 88.

'undoubtedly genuine': Gould, *Op. Cit.*, p. 23.

'a tree trunk buoyed by the gases of its own decay': *The Elusive Monster*, p. 80.

'Later he changed his mind and decided that it showed an otter': *New Scientist*, January 23, 1969.

'Steuart Campbell suggested that Gray was not truthful': *The Loch Ness Monster: The Evidence*, p. 38.

'a Labrador dog swimming towards the camera with a stick in its mouth': *Ibid*.

'Darren Naish': *Hunting Monsters* (2017), pp. 95-97.

'at the right end of the object an eye and an open mouth can be identified': http://lochnessmystery.blogspot.co.uk/2011/06/hugh-gray-photograph-revisited_26.html.

'bowled over by his obvious sincerity': p. 88.

'some huge animal thrashing about': p. 43.

'Dinsdale's tone is noticeably cooler': *The Story of the Loch Ness Monster* (1973), p. 75.

'lateral organs of the Orm': *The Great Orm of Loch Ness*, pp. 32 and 34.

'I think it helps to tip the photograph on its side': amusingly, the photograph is mistakenly reproduced upside down in Ellen Rabinowich's children's book *The Loch Ness Monster* (1979). It hardly seems to matter.

'looked very much like hard-hatted divers helmets!': *Op. Cit.*, p. 199.

'he was interviewed at Foyers': Whyte, *More Than a Legend*, p. 3.

'appeared to be fairly smooth': *Ibid.*

The Surgeon's Photograph

'In discussing the Surgeon's photograph in *The Loch Ness Mystery Solved*': p. 97.

'the sincerity and integrity of the photographer could not be questioned': *Loch Ness Monster*, p. 46.

'from a purely technical point of view': *Ibid.*, p. 68.

'only because I had held the photo away from me at arm's length': *Ibid.*, p. 69.

'the subtleties involved in the picture proved beyond doubt that it was genuine': *Ibid.*

'there is also a part of the animal underwater, considerably behind it': *Ibid.*, p. 73.

'concluded that the Surgeon's photograph was probably a hoax': *The Loch Ness Mystery Solved* , p. 97.

'The Wilson Nessie Photo: A Size Determination Based on Physical Principles': the text is available online at https://archive.org/stream/scottishnaturali1002scot/scottishnaturali1002scot_djvu.txt.

'David Martin and Alastair Boyd': David Martin and Alastair Boyd, *Nessie: The Surgeon's Photograph Exposed* (1999).

'It took him "about eight days" to create his miniature monster': *Ibid.*, p. 43.

'The life of a deliberate hoax is usually short': *The Loch Ness Monster and Others*, p. 98.

'he felt it should look "like a sea-serpent"': *Nessie: The Surgeon's Photograph Exposed*, p. 44.

'changed the prints from 50mm to quarter-plate': *Ibid.*, p. 92.

'only subsequently to reinvent it later as an authentic monster sighting':
The Loch Ness Mystery Solved, pp. 76-78, 81-82.

'has simply been lifted from one text to the next without any true
research': *Nessie: The Surgeon's Photograph Exposed*, p. 26.

'The contradictions extend to eleven different aspects of Wilson's
supposed sighting': *Ibid.*, pp. 54-55.

'the ease with which the photograph could be replicated at Loch Ness,
using a model twelve inches high': Alastair Boyd and Adrian Shine
demonstrated this for a TV documentary, which at the time of
writing is available for viewing on YouTube. See: https://www.
youtube.com/watch?v=_JU5tngLyUc.

'seeking revenge upon Nessie for their father's humiliation': Karl P. N.
Shuker, *Here's Nessie!* (2016), p. 29 (Shuker further argues that
'The "head and neck" looks to be rather more than 1 ft tall' and then
cites LeBlond and Collins to prove his case.)

'in serious danger of overbalancing': *Ibid.*, p. 28.

'This size is consistent with it being the tail of an otter. The shape is
also consistent with this explanation': Steuart Campbell, *Op. Cit.*, p.
40.

'Boyd declined to discuss the case with me or provide additional
information': *Op. Cit.*, p. 41.

'One may suspect that the story of a model is itself a hoax': *Ibid.*

'Denys Tucker noted how the final proof that this was a living animal':
Nicholas Witchell, *The Loch Ness Story* (1989), p. 226.

Lachlan Stuart

'James Carney's contemporary tourist booklet': *The Loch Ness Monster*
(New Edition, 2014), p. 16.

'Roland Watson has made a very convincing case': http://lochness
mystery.blogspot.co.uk/2012/07/the-lachlan-stuart-photograph-part-
1.html;   http://lochnessmystery.blogspot.co.uk/2012/08/the-lachlan-
stuart-photograph-part-2.html;   http://lochnessmystery.blogspot.co.
uk/2015/03/lachlan-stuarts-daughter-speaks.html.

'his account of the St Columba water beast encounter': Richard Frere,
Loch Ness (1988), p. 35.

'he wrote, with an implicit note of scepticism': *The Loch Ness Monster:
The Evidence* (1986), p. 21.

'a dead pangolin held very close to the camera lens': Karl P. N. Shuker,
Mirabilis: A Carnival of Cryptozoology and Unnatural History
(2013), p. 162.

'There are absolutely no rocks showing above the water between Dores and Foyers': David Cooke and Yvonne Cook, *The Great Monster Hunt: The Story of the Loch Ness Investigation* (1969), p. 108.

'Mr Morrison's six humped monster and Mr Goodbody's remarkable eight humped beast': *The Loch Ness Monster and Others*, pp. 66 and 87.

'the objections to the Stuart photograph are threefold': *Op. Cit.*, p. 100.

'Roland Watson is over-hasty': in a contentious summary of *The Loch Ness Mystery Solved* he writes, 'Even inert rocks get a look in (are people that stupid?)' A few monster sightings almost certainly are of rocks but only those which involve very brief glimpses from moving motor vehicles by witnesses who don't return to the spot. My use of the rock photo at Whitefield was intended to show both how shallow the loch is here and how easy it is to make something relatively close to the shore appear a much greater distance away than it really is. For Watson's summary see: http://lochnessmystery.blogspot.co.uk/2012/03/books-on-loch-ness-monster_13.html.

'He was interrogated by Maurice Burton': *The Elusive Monster*, p. 76.

'a mixture of boredom at the constant intrusions and incredulity that the matter could be of so much interest': *More Than a Legend,* p. 13.

The Cockrell Photograph

'a tremendous psychological bias of belief and expectation': Mackal, *The Monsters of Loch Ness*, p. 104.

'it is even possible to see *through* the curving "hump"': *The Loch Ness Mystery Solved*, p. 101.

'In a detailed analysis, Watson makes the case for Cockrell': http://lochnessmystery.blogspot.co.uk/2016/08/the-hugh-cockrell-photograph.html.

'What I actually wrote': *The Loch Ness Mystery Solved*, pp. 100-101. My belief that Cockrell photographed part of a floating tree trunk (p.182) did not insinuate fraud on his part.

'reminiscent of the time Adrian Shine was rowing on Loch Morar': Tony Harmsworth, *Loch Ness, Nessie & Me* (2010), pp. 216-217.

Macnab

'Roy Mackal...cast doubts on Peter Macnab's probity': *The Monsters of Loch Ness*, pp. 273-276.

'Gareth Williams identifies other problematic aspects': *A Monstrous Commotion*, p. 232.

'Roland Watson': http://lochnessmystery.blogspot.co.uk/2012/02/
analysis-of-peter-macnab-photograph.html.

Peter O'Connor
'Dinsdale's assertion that the back of O'Connor's monster': *Loch Ness
Monster* (1961), p. 156.
'Dick Raynor has argued that O'Connor used a canoe for his monster's
body': http://www.academia.edu/19844058/A_Study_of_the_Peter_
OConnor_photograph_of_the_Loch_Ness_Monster.

6. Seals at Loch Ness

'in all likelihood, a large grey seal': Rupert Gould, *The Loch Ness
Monster and Others*. See his discussion of the seal theory, pp. 142-
147.
'Even Maurice Burton': *The Elusive Monster*, p. 129.
'giving birth in the water': Peter Costello, *In Search of Lake Monsters*
(1974), p. 290.
'the once-influential populist Belgian zoologist': see the critiques in
Daniel Loxton and Donald R. Prothero, *Abominable Science!* (2013);
and Darren Naish, *Hunting Monsters: Cryptozoology and the
Reality Behind the Myths* (2017).
'Gordon R. Williamson subsequently wrote a paper about the episode':
Dick Raynor has helpfully made Williamson's report available on
his website, along with his own photographic evidence and
commentary. See: http://www.lochnessinvestigation.com/Seals.html;
http://lochnessinvestigation.com/SILN.html.
'Daniel Loxton brings the record up to date': *Abominable Science!*, pp.
161-164.
'inevitably reproduces the traditional dissension between scepticism
and belief regarding perceptions of size and shape': http://loch
nessmystery.blogspot.co.uk/2013/10/nessie-on-land-margaret-
munro-case.html.
'The classic sighting by Miss J. S. Fraser and three companions':
Rupert Gould, *The Loch Ness Monster and Others*, pp. 62-65.
'Maurice Burton': *The Elusive Monster*, pp. 119-122.

7. Not So Classical

F. C. Adams
'Roland Watson published a substantial article': 'Some Fin of Interest?',
Fortean Times, 341, pp. 28-33.
'Gareth Williams': *Op. Cit,*, Plate 43.

Jennifer Bruce
'an update to his book': http://www.steuartcampbell.com/loch-ness-
monster.html.
'Roland Watson': http://lochnessmystery.blogspot.co.uk/2013/06/the-
jennifer-bruce-photograph.html.
'In 2016 Joline Lin': https://www.sundaypost.com/news/student-takes-
photo-snake-like-head-sticking-loch-ness/.

William Jobes
'Malcolm Robinson's recent book': *The Monsters of Loch Ness (The
History and the Mystery)*, pp. 505-514, 521-526.

Jonathan Bright
'Bright explained': 'Meeting the Genius Lochi', *Fortean Times*, 308,
pp. 54-55.
'all the other photographs of recent years': http://www.lochness
sightings.com/index.asp?pageid=498361.
'Dick Raynor, who has probably spent more time on Loch Ness than
anyone associated with the Loch Ness story': http://www.lochness
investigation.com/gordonholmes2007video.htm.
'William Reeves wrote': *Life of St Columba* (1857), footnote, p. 150.

8. The Dinsdale Film Revisited

'the maximum recorded speed for a shrimp': *The Elusive Monster*, p.
127.
'a row of sou'-westers worn by several men': *Ibid.*, p. 74.
'vegetable mats, or masses of peat': *Ibid.*, p. 172.
'This is precisely the route frequently taken by local boats': *Ibid.*, p. 74.
'the JARIC report of January 1966': A tantalising glimpse of tiny
extracts from the original report can be seen in Tim Dinsdale's final
book, *Project Water Horse: The True Story of the Monster Quest at*

Loch Ness (1975), p. 12. The LNI published a slightly edited text (report on a Film taken by Tim Dinsdale, with an Introduction by David James [n.d.]). This can be read online at http://www. lochnessinvestigation.com/dinsdale%20paper%202003%20V2.pdf.

'Henry Bauer, who called it "ill-founded"': http://henryhbauer. homestead.com/_NessieChapter.pdf; http://henryhbauer.homestead. com/DinsdaleFilm.html.

'published a detailed critique in the Photographic Journal': February 1986, pp. 54-58.

'Ricky Gardiner, Tony Harmsworth and Adrian Shine were holding a late night discussion of the monster': Harmsworth, Loch Ness, Nessie & Me, pp. 130-138 and http://lochnessunderstood.com/ ch11m24474757.html.

'various reasons including friendship and respect for the unwell Dinsdale': Loch Ness, Nessie & Me, p. 134.

'appeared posthumously in The Photographic Journal': January 1990, pp. 40-43.

'Adrian Shine and Dick Raynor have each published lengthy studies': for Shine, see http://www.lochnessinvestigation.com/dinsdale%20 paper%202003%20V2.pdf; a digitally enhanced frame showing the 'helmsman' is reproduced in Shine's booklet, Loch Ness (2006), p. 12. for Raynor, see http://www.lochnessinvestigation.com/ Remembered.html.

'In the words of Dinsdale's son Angus': Angus Dinsdale, The Man Who Filmed Nessie: Tim Dinsdale and the Enigma of Loch Ness (2013), p. 16.

'took a 4 minute film, of something moving across the loch': Shine, Loch Ness, p. 12.

'the Dinsdale family's willingness to allow the footage to be screened online': http://www.themanwhofilmednessie.com/tims-nessie-film. html.

'Richard Carter states… Roland Watson calculates': http://lochness mystery.blogspot.co.uk/2011/02/dinsdale-jaric-and-carter.html.

'firing long steady bursts of film like a machine gunner, stopping between to wind the clockwork motor': Loch Ness Monster (1961), p. 100.

'about 8 seconds were lost in pauses in the initial sequence': Steuart Campbell, The Loch Ness Monster: The Evidence, p. 59.

'the protuberances must have been 8-10 ins. High and 2-3 feet apart': The Elusive Monster, p. 74.

'the back of an African buffalo': *Loch Ness Monster*, p. 100.

'two long black shadows or shapes, rising and falling in the water!': *Ibid.*, pp. 95-96.

'I was not to know that at the time, however...': *The Story of the Loch Ness Monster*, p. 53.

'running on for several minutes': *Loch Ness Monster*, p. 110.

'just a very few minutes, two or three at most': *Ibid.*, p. 102.

'As he explained in 1965': letter to David James, reproduced in *The Photographic Journal*', January 1990, p. 40.

'Shine writes "It might be asked"': http://www.lochnessinvestigation. com/dinsdale%20paper%202003%20V2.pdf,

'and which even today has never been published': Oddly, in his memoir Angus Dinsdale chooses to recycle the inaccurate map from *Loch Ness Monster* rather than the allegedly superior one submitted to JARIC.

'the miniature 7x binoculars he used had a much wider field of view than the viewfinder in the Bolex movie camera... [they]would have shown him little more than a speck at 1300 yards distance': http:/ /cryptomundo.com/cryptotourism/what-did-tim-dinsdale-see-at-loch -ness/.

9. The Archive Problem

'Burton proved obstructive': Roy Mackal, *The Monsters of Loch Ness*, p. 118.

10. What Lies Beneath

'Roland Watson supplies a list': http://lochnessmystery.blogspot. co.uk/2011/08/classic-sightings.html.

'In discussing the Moir sighting Watson remarks': http://lochness mystery.blogspot.co.uk/2011/01/classic-sightings-marjory-moir. html .

'If only we had a camera! What pictures we might have taken!': Constance Whyte, *More Than a Legend,* pp. 62-63.

'such a brief experience': Dinsdale, *The Leviathans* (Revised Edition, 1976), p. 198.

'real enough': *Loch Ness Monster* (Fourth Edition, 1982), p. 146.

'According to Witchell': *The Loch Ness Story* (1974), p. 164.

'Dick Raynor, accepting Mackay's account as accurate': http://www.lochnessinvestigation.com/history.html.

'Steuart Campbell suggested an otter': *The Loch Ness Monster: The Evidence*, p. 29. Campbell has since changed his mind and believes (as I do) that Mackay saw a wake. See http://www.steuartcampbell.com/loch-ness-monster.html.

'Dear Mrs Whyte, *As I have often told you* I once saw the Loch Ness Monster': *More Than a Legend*, p. 62.

'with a footnote pointing out that this was "Actually [a] half-section model"': *Loch Ness Monster* (1961), p. 122.

'or the single hump that appeared in the film': *Ibid.*, p. 116.

'Moir added a telling new detail': http://lochnessmystery.blogspot.co.uk/2014/02/the-marjory-moir-story-revisited.html.

'The road at this point runs close above the Loch and overlooks it': Gould, *The Loch Ness Monster and Others*, p. 83.

'In a second or two it had completely disappeared, leaving a well-marked wash still showing': *Ibid.*, p. 84.

'Mr W.U. Goodbody of Invergarry…Arthur Grant's plesiosaur-style monster…Dr. J. Kirton's sighting': *Ibid.*, pp. 87, 89, 79.

'a portion of the big hump disappearing below the surface': *Ibid.*, p. 84.

'Roy Mackal concluded': *The Monsters of Loch Ness*, p. 264.

'Steuart Campbell's conclusion': *The Loch Ness Monster: The Evidence*, p. 112.

'Roland Watson, however, argues that the sighting involved an authentic encounter with the Monster': http://lochnessmystery.blogspot.co.uk/2012/09/nessie-on-land-harvey-macdonald-case.html.

'the statement in *More Than a Legend* was not something written by Mrs Finlay': *Op. Cit.*, p. 69.

'then disappeared in a great commotion which set waves breaking on the shore': *Ibid.*, p. 70.

'In this version the sighting was an unbroken experience': *Loch Ness Monster*, p. 124.

'a relatively small edition of the Monster': Whyte, *Op. Cit.*, p. 69.

'During July and August these are in velvet': *The Elusive Monster*, p. 135.

'the visual impression she had carried away could have become distorted': *Ibid.*, p. 132.

'how a two-year red stag deer might appear in August': *Ibid.*, p. 131.

'Roland Watson argues that "the ears are a bit of a stick out problem"':

http://lochnessmystery.blogspot.co.uk/2011/03/classic-sightings-greta-finlay.html.

'He reinforces his arguments based on his own unexpected encounter with a deer': http://lochnessmystery.blogspot.co.uk/2011/04/more-on-greta-finlay.html.

'Mrs Finlay rushed into the caravan for a camera but, by the time she ran out, it had submerged': *The Great Orm of Loch Ness*, p. 52.

'95 per cent of the evidence': *The Elusive Monster*, p. 157.

'What a terrifying sight it was , and one I shall remember for the rest of my life': *Ibid.*, p. 158.

'Watson had deleted it from his blog': It can still be read online at this digital archive: https://web.archive.org/web/20160413144833/; http://lochnessmystery.blogspot.co.uk/2016/02/an-extraordinary-nessie-story-from-1990.html.

'For Roland Watson a sighting like this is unanswerable': http://loch nessmystery.blogspot.co.uk/2015/01/the-john-mclean-sighting.html.

'from a sceptical perspective it sounds very much as if he what he saw was a pair of otters': Steuart Campbell believes only one otter was involved. See *The Loch Ness Monster: The Evidence*, p. 29.

'alarmed… at what it was': *The Great Orm of Loch Ness*, p. 83.

'petrified': Paul Harrison, *The Encyclopaedia of the Loch Ness Monster* (1999) p. 130.

'I'm quite convinced now': Holiday, *Op. Cit.*, p. 190.

'in the distance the clock in the Fort Augustus abbey chimed the hour of ten': Paul Harrison, *Op. Cit.,* p. 141.

''Certain discrepancies in the way *an Niseag* is described by different observers': *More Than a Legend*, p. 179.

'There appeared to be lights on the humps…': *The Leviathans*, p. 164.

'it is the observer who is best able to judge the conclusions of others': *Ibid.*

'the Dinsdale illustration exhibits eight humps of identical shape and size': *Loch Ness Monster*, p. 22.

'It fits what I saw but I've never seen it before or since': http://lochness mystery.blogspot.co.uk/2015/06/the-pole-like-nessie-sightings.html.

11. The Dragon Man

'not a water by which to linger': *The Great Orm of Loch Ness*, p. 8.
'our subconscious has accumulated many strange impressions and none

of these can be gainsaid': *Ibid.*

'stayed for a time and then it went down': *Ibid.*, p. 9.

'the animal must be of enormous size': *Ibid.*, p. 10.

'some form of contact with the quarry': *Ibid.*, pp. 11-12.

'Ted Holiday had four more sightings of the Loch Ness Monster': *Ibid.*, pp. 104-113 and p. 165; F. W. Holiday, *The Dragon and the Disc* (1973), pp. 24-27.

'He heard "'an indescribable sound"'': F. W. Holiday, *The Goblin Universe* (1986), p. 54.

'He also saw UFOs': *The Dragon and the Disc*, p. 109.

'the garden seemed to be filled with indefinable frantic movement': *The Goblin Universe*, p. 182.

'often had an uncanny feeling': *Ibid.*, p. 55.

'At monster-inhabited Lough Nahooin': *The Dragon and the Disc*, p. 59.

'After about ten minutes all activity ceased and the water became calm': *Ibid.*, p. 51.

'It didn't make sense': *The Goblin Universe*, p. 171.

'oddly unsatisfactory': *The Dragon and the Disc,* p. 44.

'there was no evidence that the phenomena were, in fact, animals and all attempts at proving this had failed': *Ibid.*, p. 31.

'there is not the slightest ecological trace of their real existence': *The Goblin Universe*, p. 171.

'Oliver Sachs': *Hallucinations* (2012), p. 231.

'a colossal worm that inhabited the shallow, warm Permian seas of 200 million years ago': *The Goblin Universe*, p. 193.

'No single phenomenon can possibly account for the totality of fifty years of widely-differing eye-witness reports from Loch Ness': *Op. Cit.*, p. 183.

'this episode ended in anticlimax': http://lochnessmystery.blogspot.co.uk/2012/02/interesting-photograph.html.

12. Reconfigurations

'Henry Bauer': *The Enigma of Loch Ness: Making Sense of a Mystery*.

'Steuart Campbell': *The Loch Ness Monster: The Evidence*.

'I reviewed it for *Skeptic* magazine': Vol. 19, No. 2 (2014), pp. 54-57.

'a giant monster that many people see, but that cannot ever be detected by science': *Abominable Science!: Origins of the Yeti, Nessie and other Famous Cryptids*, p. 174.

'*New Humanist*': Spring 2016, pp. 62-64.

'Redfern accuses Dinsdale of cowardice': *Op. Cit.*, p. 139.

'the saint's boat was towed at Loch Ness': *Ibid.*, p. 10.

'river beast': *Life of St Columba* (Penguin Books, 1995), p. 175.

'there was only one road that permitted travel around the loch': *Op. Cit.*, pp. 55-56.

'tourist guides recommended it as a route for motorists from the beginning of the twentieth century': *The Loch Ness Mystery Solved*, p. 63.

'the most important evidence currently obtained in support of the Loch Ness monster's reality as a huge water beast of a still-undiscovered species': *Op. Cit..* p. 32.

'the underwater camera had been photographing it': *Ibid*, p. 33.

'The authoritative debunking of such an interpretation by Dick Raynor': http://www.lochnessinvestigation.com/flipper.html.

'identifies Bauer…admires Roy Mackal': Shuker, *Op. Cit*, pp. 7 and 111.

13. Two-Faced Kelpie

'The words which introduced the Loch Ness monster': 'Strange Spectacle on Loch Ness', *Inverness Courier*, May 2, 1933.

'that the animal must be of enormous size': *The Great Orm of Loch Ness*, p. 10.

'In one influential version of the water kelpie legend': W. Grant Stewart, *The Popular Superstitions and Festive Amusements of the Highlanders of Scotland* (1823), p. 147.

'merely a temporary revival of an old and deep-rooted superstition': *The Loch Ness Monster and Others*, p. 27.

'we have reports of one or more creatures going back to Cromwell's time or nearly 350 years ago': Roland Watson, *The Water Horses of Loch Ness* (2011), p. 205.

'I think a man of Mr. Rose's standing and CV deserves better treatment and respect': *Ibid.*, pp. 68-69.

'if we only accept contemporary reports, there is nothing': Gareth Williams, *A Monstrous Commotion*, p. 289.

'John Keel': http://lochnessmystery.blogspot.co.uk/2016/08/john-keel-and-victorian-loch-ness.html.

'Watson puts forward nine new Loch Ness water-horse references for consideration': I exclude from this list two nineteenth-century newspaper reports, which are not directly concerned with water kelpies. I discuss these in Chapter 14.

'he analysed the testimony': *The Loch Ness Monster and Others*, p. 164.

'in my veins two most potent streams of necromantic blood have united themselves': Thomas Dick Lauder, *Legendary Tales of the Highlands* (1841), p. 18.

'on the lonely shore of Loch-an-dorbe': *Ibid.*, p. 14.

'Willox the wizard': *Ibid.*, p. 5.

'the possession of which he is so celebrated in all the neighbouring districts': *Ibid.*, p. 9.

'It has not the most distant resemblance to any part of a bridle': *Ibid.*, pp. 11-12.

'Loch Ness was the prime and dominant abode of the Water Horse': Watson, *Op. Cit.,* p. 100.

'"over thirty"' land sightings of the monster': *Ibid.*, p. 137.

'It waddled down the slope and disappeared into the loch': *Ibid.*, p. 105.

'this counter intuitive idea of a water monster coming out of its natural abode to hunt its victims': *Ibid.*, p. 137.

'a deep contempt for irrational world views and the specificity of folk-tradition': Michel Meurger with Claude Gagnon, *Lake Monster Traditions: A Cross Cultural Analysis* (1988), p. 11.

'a mystical approach to the world': *Ibid.*, p. 12.

'cryptozoologists and sceptics consciously refuse to accept myth as a product of the human mind, as an imaginary story': *Ibid.*

'Like the other water deities, she is half-human, half-fish': 'Loch Morar monster Morag sightings uncovered', BBC news website, February 25, 2013, http://www.bbc.co.uk/news/uk-scotland-highlands-islands -21574832.

'slide lasciviously from her hair down and around her torso': Steven Huebner, *French Opera at the Fin de Siècle: Wagnerism, Nationalism and Style* (1999), p. 365.

'complicated *marra*-locks which cannot be combed out': F. W. Holiday, *The Goblin Universe*, p. 121.

'Grimshaw and Lester supply a Freudian reading': Roger Grimshaw and Paul Lester, *The Meaning of the Loch Ness Monster* (1976), pp. 32-33.

'by the misty glens of the Highlands, and the romantic streams of the Lowlands': *Op. Cit.*, p. 492.

'I take the story from the Gaelic and tell it in my own words generally where the scribe's language is prosy': http://www.sacred-texts.com/neu/celt/cdm/cdm02.htm#page_xi.

'a letter sent to Tim Dinsdale in 1961': *The Leviathans*, pp. 56-57.

'a strange description of the strange creature very similar to that of Mr Spicer': *The Water Horses of Loch Ness*, p. 135.

'a long neck which moved up and down in the manner of a scenic railway': *The Loch Ness Mystery Solved*, p. 19.

'humping its great shoulders and twisting its head from side to side': *More Than a Legend*, p. 80.

14. Lineages

'vegetable mat theory was endorsed by Marjorie Anderson': Maurice Burton, *The Elusive Monster*, p. 103.

'which, she confided, even as late as the 1950s': *More Than a Legend*, p. xv.

'so different from the outpost I had imagined': *Loch Ness Monster*, p. 79.

'tracks in the old days passed along high ridges, not by the water's edge': Whyte, *Op. Cit.*, p. xv.

'fresh horses were kept to set the coach on its way': Katharine Stewart, *The Story of Loch Ness* (2007), p. 53.

'Dick Raynor has commented': http://lochnessmystery.blogspot.co.uk/2013/01/review-of-recent-nessie-article.html?showComment=1358952407529#c7794250644488100858.

'*Silurus glanis* is the largest freshwater fish in the world': http://www.farnhamanglingsociety.com/species/catfish.php.

'Karl Shuker cites the case of Lake Myllesjön in Sweden': Karl Shuker, *Mirabilis* (2013), pp. 55-56.

'large dead sturgeons have a habit of floating to the surface': http://blogs.seattletimes.com/today/2013/08/eight-foot-sturgeon-found-belly-up-in-lake-washington/.

'no less a person than Rupert Gould': *The Loch Ness Mystery Solved*, p. 204.

'quite parochial stories involving unusual animals or fish and unusual events at Loch Ness': http://lochnessmystery.blogspot.co.uk/2016/02/animal-behaviour-at-loch-ness.html; http://lochnessmystery.blogspot.co.uk/2013/05/dolphins-or-porpoises-in-loch-ness.html.

'In 2011 Roland Watson reported that he had found an undated *Daily Mail* cutting': http://lochnessmystery.blogspot.co.uk/2011/12/recantation-of-john-macdonald.html.

'Conan Doyle's novel had among its inspirations a sighting by the writer himself': Russell Miller, *The Adventures of Conan Doyle* (2008), p. 302.

'Trade gin': Sir Arthur Conan Doyle, *The Lost World and Other Stories* (2010), p. 26.

'something malevolent, something to be avoided': *Ibid.*

'There was talk of faking': *Ibid.*, p. 27.

'As I pointed out in *The Loch Ness Mystery Solved*': p. 208.

'Daniel Loxton has since examined one moment from the movie in detail': *Abominable Science!*, pp. 129-133.

'another dimension, without time, or material content': Tim Dinsdale, *Project Water Horse*, p. 71.

'An area, as large perhaps as Sussex': Conan Doyle, *Op. Cit.*, p. 29.

'some 30-40 feet long': *The Loch Monster and Others*, p. 31.

'assisted various honest but self-deluded persons to create a zoological myth': *Ibid.*, p. 150.

'The idea was to direct attention to its vicinity, and so get the question of its existence settled': Rupert T. Gould, *Oddities: A Book of Unexplained Facts* (1945), p. 147.

'Henry Bauer recommends an interest in the Monster as a means of expanding one's mental horizons': Foreword to Karl P. N. Shuker, *Here's Nessie!* (2016).

'remains the most mysterious swallower of aircraft, ships and people': Pope, *Op. Cit.*, p. 223.

'grounded in fantasy, anachronism and projection': James Shapiro, *Contested Will: Who Wrote Shakespeare?* (2010), p. 28.

'Sceptic Richard Gordon': *Great Medical Mysteries* (2001), p. 105.

'described by one modern writer on the giant squid': Richard Ellis, *The Search for the Giant Squid* (1999), p. 67.

'Henry Lee': *Ibid.*, p. 197.

'may simply have been the result of a conviction for forgery': *Ibid.*, p. 198.

'a triangle of foaming water following a hump towards the far shore, where it either sank or melted into the twilight under the opposite bank': Witchell, *The Loch Ness Story* (1989), p. 211.

'some of Tucker's certainties': *Ibid.*, pp. 219, 222, 224.

'the sterile theories of the archaeologists': *The Dragon and the Disc*, p.

134.

'What the creatures were she still didn't know': *Ibid.*, p. 224.

'The creatures do not look like solid objects': *Ibid.*, p. 223.

'by 1972 Searle was already claiming a staggering fifteen sightings': Victor Perera, *The Loch Ness Monster Watchers*, p. 25.

'three Nessie photographs produced by Searle': reproduced in Barrie Robertson, *Loch Ness and the Great Glen* (n.d.).

'believed a book might sell well enough to help the family out of their dire financial difficulties': Richard Morris, *Harry Price: The Psychic Detective* (2006), p. 180.

'a fairytale come to life': *Ibid.*, p. 229.

'He is a persuasive, not a dogmatic person': Steve Dewey and John Ries, *In Alien Heat* (2006), p. 124.

'powers, that if unleashed, would perhaps frazzle him to a cinder': *Ibid.*, p. 90.

'Holiday linked Gordon Faulkner's sensational Warminster flying saucer': *The Dragon and the Disc*, pp. 135-6.

'Dewey and Ries take Holiday apart': *Op. Cit.*, p. 300.

'shaped like two soup-plates glued together by their edges with a sort of cupola in the middle': *The Dragon and the Disc*, p. 135.

'may even have been inspired by Arthur Shuttlewood's identification': Dewey and Ries, *Op. Cit.*, p. 283.

'an evolved, surviving species of short-necked plesiosaur': Shuker, *Op. Cit.*, p. 225.

'a riddle that cries out for a compelling explanation': *Ibid.*, p. 14.

'In the words of Stuart McHardy': *Pagan Symbols of the Picts* (2016), pp. 99-100.

'Daniel Loxton, in his pioneering deconstruction of the legendary sea-serpent': *Abominable Science!*, chapter 5.

'No one prepared me for the wild natural beauty of Loch Ness': Perera, *Op. Cit.*, p. 12.

'When I'd finished, I'd become a believer': *Ibid.*, p. 19.